(Continued)

SO MUCH TO SAY

Adolescents, Bilingualism, and ESL in the Secondary School

CHRISTIAN J. FALTIS
PAULA M. WOLFE

Editors

TEACHERS
COLLEGE
PRESS

Teachers College, Columbia University
New York and London

Published by Teachers College Press, 1234 Amsterdam Avenue, New York, NY 10027

Copyright © 1999 by Teachers College, Columbia University

Library of Congress Cataloging-in-Publication Data
So much to say : adolescents, bilingualism, and ESL in the secondary school / Christian J. Faltis, Paula Wolfe, editors.
    p.   cm. — (Language and literacy series)
    Includes bibliographical references and index.
    ISBN 0-8077-3797-6 (cloth). — ISBN 0-8077-3796-8 (pbk.)
    1. English language—Study and teaching (Secondary)—Foreign speakers.   2. English language—Study and teaching (Secondary)—United States.   3. Education, Bilingual—United States.   4. Bilingualism—United States.   I. Faltis, Christian, 1950–   .   II. Wolfe, Paula.   III. Series: Language and literacy series (New York, N.Y.)
PE1128.A2S599   1999
428'.007—dc21   98-38225

ISBN 0-8077-3796-8 (paper)
ISBN 0-8077-3797-6 (cloth)

Printed on acid-free paper

Manufactured in the United States of America

06 05 04 03 02 01 00 99   8 7 6 5 4 3 2 1

CONTENTS

FOREWORD

Readers of this volume will come away with three very strong impressions: (1) that so-called language minority students are present in this country's secondary schools in significant and increasing numbers; (2) that there is nowhere near enough understanding of how these students experience school and how schools and teachers respond to their presence; and (3) that secondary education in the United States is in need of far-reaching structural change if it is to adequately meet its mandate to educate these students, and all students, on an equal basis. These are important messages, especially at this time when bilingual education is under direct threat by anti-immigrant, English-only initiatives at local, state, and U.S. Congressional levels.

The numbers are compelling, with increases in foreign-born and LOTE (languages other than English)-speaking populations in the U.S. continuing to outstrip total population growth rates. Currently, for example, about half of secondary-school-aged youth in the U.S. are Hispanic and can no longer be considered a minority in the numerical sense.

However, *So Much to Say* is not only about compelling numbers, but also about compelling insights into how these students fare in school and what we can do about it. This book has a strong research base; yet the overwhelming message with regard to research is that there is a need for far more of it. I would argue further that there is a need to continually develop and refine coherent conceptual frameworks in which to situate and make sense of the research.

To illustrate, let me use the continua of biliteracy framework which I have proposed as an organizing rubric for research and practice in the education of language minority students, a framework which emphasizes the need to create learning contexts that allow students to draw on all their language and literacy resources in developing new ones, because all are on a continuum of interrelatedness. The framework characterizes this continuity in terms of the development, content, media, and contexts of biliteracy (cf. Hornberger, 1989; Hornberger and Skilton-Sylvester, 1998).

A number of insights in this volume illustrate the importance of continuity in biliterate development: For example, spoken language and interaction in ESL classrooms are shown to provide a basis for language minority students' more successful negotiation of written communication in mainstream classrooms. Similarly, students' increasing writing fluency is shown to be related to their increasing oral fluency. Other insights illustrate the importance of continuity of biliterate content: in one case, two Dominican students' regular use of writing at home (in vernacular literacies such as letters and poems) contrasts with their halting participation in literacy activities in school which do not draw on those skills. Likewise, the quality and depth of these students' discussions based on readings of authentic Spanish language literature in Spanish literacy class are in stark contrast to the often mechanical and meaningless use of language and literacy in their ESL, science, and math classes.

There are also insights relating to the importance of recognizing continuity across a range of language structures and literate forms (in other words, across biliterate media). For example, features of students' writing in school may diverge from academic literacy conventions in ways that reflect the oral and written varieties they have acquired outside school (such as writing which reflects oral pronunciation, word agglutination, lack of attention to capitalization and punctuation), but, depending on the degree to which the teacher is tolerant and committed to valuing content and not form, bilingual students' writing will flourish and develop beyond these formal limitations. Finally, there are illustrations of the continuity of biliterate contexts, and in particular the importance of microlevel, oral, and multilingual contexts of interaction for biliterate learners. When the teacher positions the student as a legitimate participant in the community of practice and works together with the student to establish new, mutually constructed understanding, the role and goal of the high school as the student's guide into academic English discourse can be achieved.

Despite the unquestionable importance of the research and theoretical development that provide insights such as the aforementioned, it is also undeniable that teachers and schools cannot wait for definitive research results or fully elaborated theoretical frameworks before beginning to implement change. This volume takes a clear stand in favor of improving education for immigrant and bilingual secondary students through immediate, informed, and situation-based action as well.

No "one size fits all" answer is offered, though, nor should it be. There are examples which might even be seen as contradictory if taken out of context: ESL classes are found in one case to be a relative haven for language minority students (when compared to mainstream classes), while in another case ESL teachers are seen as less than understanding of language minority students (when compared to bilingual teachers). Sheltered instruction is hailed as an alternative which allows students to move ahead on academic content while still developing their English language proficiency, but a warning is also sounded about sheltered classes observed to be rather sparse on subject area coverage.

There are no easy answers then, but plenty of possibilities. Sheltered instruction, and its newer variant, the "push-in" model, is suggested for use in a range of programs including ESL, transitional, maintenance and developmental bilingual education, two-way immersion, maintenance and developmental bilingual education, newcomer programs, and alternative high schools; and assessment approaches and innovations such as classroom-embedded assessment, the graduation portfolio, and graduation by exhibition are described. Yet it cannot be overemphasized that these are no more than potential alternatives, which must be implemented and adapted on a case-by-case basis.

A particular strength of this volume is that the kinds of change envisioned go beyond simply adding on to existing secondary schooling practices, to structuring whole new ways of educating that incorporate language minority perspectives in schooling for minority and majority alike. Among the proposals offered are alternative high school programs incorporating some of the features presently available in GED programs (such as flexible and compact schedules, noncompartmentalized and nondepartmentalized instruction, competency-based credit, and literacy for authentic purposes); administrative support for recognizing and including language minority students' perspectives in coordinated mainstream-ESL education; and "untracking" that goes beyond mixing ability groups to include fundamental shifts in curriculum, philosophy, and goals of instruction. Hopeful initiatives in this regard include the Mellon-funded Program in Immigrant Education and California's CLAD and BCLAD ([Bilingual] Cross Cultural Language and Academic Development) credentials, initiatives which receive substantial attention in this volume.

Beyond recognition of the compelling presence and experience of language minority students in our secondary schools, and of the pressing need for structural change to meet their needs, lies a deeper challenge about changing the very ways in which we conceptualize education for language minority students in the U.S. The present volume suggests that *water* as the pervasive underlying metaphor in language minority education implies not only that it is the language minority learners who must adapt to the mainstream, but also, paradoxically, that the means we have devised for their doing so (e.g., *bridges* and *shelters* and *pull-outs*) in fact keep them out of that mainstream. Similarly, Santa Ana (1997) has shown the pernicious connotations of the water metaphor in reference to immigrants and immigration more generally: immigration as dangerous waters. *So Much to Say* proposes a new metaphor for language minority education: specifically, the metaphor of the *club*. If learning is viewed as joining a club or a community of practice rather than adapting to some preexisting flow of knowledge, it implies that the burden of change and adaptation is no longer on the shoulders of the new members only, but on all members of the club. Such a metaphor suggests open doors at a time when too many are closed. The metaphor evokes a welcome image of a community of learning, constantly changing and evolving as it welcomes new members, making way for its new members and, importantly, for *what they have to say.*

REFERENCES

Hornberger, N. H. (1989). Continua of biliteracy. *Review of Educational Research* *59*(3), 271–296.

Hornberger, N. H., & Skilton-Sylvester, E. (1998). Revisiting the continua of biliteracy: International and critical perspectives. Paper presented at the annual meeting of the American Educational Research Association, San Diego.

Santa Ana, O. (1997). Print media metaphors of immigration in California political discourse. Paper presented at the annual meeting of the American Association for Applied Linguistics, Orlando, FL.

INTRODUCTION

CREATING A NEW HISTORY

Christian J. Faltis

ARIZONA STATE UNIVERSITY

Bilingual and English as a second language (ESL) education at the secondary level is one of the most unexamined and overlooked areas of education in the United States. This predicament can no longer continue, especially in light of the increasing number of secondary (middle and high school) students who either primarily speak a language other than English, were born outside the United States, or both. At least one in six adolescents attending secondary school come from homes and communities in which a non-English language (most likely, Spanish) is the dominant language (see Chapter 1). Of this group of adolescents, almost half reported having difficulty using English for daily purposes, including school. Moreover, significant numbers of these and other immigrant students have had limited or sporadic schooling experiences in their native countries (Minicucci & Olsen, 1992; see Chapter 3). While some immigrant students who enter secondary schools in the United States have smooth transitions from their native countries and from elementary school, most experience difficulty in understanding how school works for them (Phelen, Cao, & Davidson, 1992).

Regardless of their experiences prior to arriving at secondary school, however, immigrant and bilingual teenagers have many of the same social and emotional needs as their English-speaking counterparts: They want to belong to groups; they want to succeed in their daily lives; they want to please their families; and they want to feel confident as young people. How these students fare in formal schooling contexts impacts all of their needs. Students who perform poorly in school are less likely to fulfill their social and emotional needs than those who perform well. Why some immigrant and bilingual secondary students do well or poorly in school is a complex issue, but the most convincing evidence suggests to us that the answer lies chiefly in how the school organizes and supports its students regardless of their native language and prior schooling experiences (Faltis, 1994; Lucas, Henze, & Donato, 1990; Marsh, 1995; Minicucci & Olsen, 1992).

PURPOSE OF THE BOOK

The purpose of this volume is twofold: first, to initiate a research-based dialogue specifically about secondary bilingual and ESL education; and second, to cast a wide net over three major areas of secondary schooling that we believe have an important impact on how students who are either newcomers (i.e., non-English speaking recent immigrants) or becoming bilingual, or both, connect with and benefit from school. It is imperative that the concerns of immigrant and bilingual adolescents be presented as distinct from those of elementary school students. To this end, this book represents a first attempt to develop a new history for secondary bilingual and ESL education.

The three areas of interest are the students, the curricula, and the programs. Educators and teachers need to (1) know who their students are; (2) understand the dimensions of curricula that can and should be adjusted to the needs of students; and (3) be aware of the political, structural, and pedagogical issues as these interact with contextual considerations at secondary school sites across the nation.

The book includes 10 chapters written by researchers and educators who have dedicated the lion's share of their professional lives to understanding and improving education for language-minority children and adolescents. Chapters within each of the three main sections draw mainly from what actually happens in secondary classrooms, programs, and school sites. Although this volume is, first and foremost, research-based, all authors discuss the implications of their work for improving the conditions of schooling for secondary newcomer and bilingual students. Additionally, we have included at the end of the book a unique glossary that not only seeks to define commonly used words in secondary ESL/bilingual education, but also critiques these terms based on their implications for the field.

BUILDING A FOUNDATION

As we present one of the first efforts to bring together new research on adolescents, bilingualism, and ESL in the secondary school, we hope to construct a foundation from which future studies can draw, compare, contrast, and revise. While we find it interesting that there was virtually no research conducted on secondary bilingual students, schools, or programs prior to 1990, the lack of existing information provides fertile ground for future study. Lucas, Henze, and Donato's now-classic study of six high schools primarily serving Latino bilingual students (Lucas, Henze, & Donato, 1990) represents the first major effort to understand effective bilingual secondary schools. Since this study, only a handful of other research studies have been conducted and reported in the literature. Minicucci and Olsen (1992) published a report on *Programs for Secondary Limited English Proficient Students: A California Study* in which they present findings on types of curricula and programs used with immigrant students. Faltis (1993) edited a volume of research studies entitled "Trends in Bilingual Education at the Secondary Level" for the *Peabody Journal of Education*. The studies in that volume examined newcomer centers, effective classrooms, sheltered content teaching, and the role of foreign language teachers in working with Spanish-speaking bilingual students. Harklau (1994a, 1994b) studied the effects of tracking on Chinese ESL students at a large urban high school. Wolfe (1996) presented an analysis of a high school ESL classroom in contrast with a sheltered English literature classroom to show differences in participation and benefit. Faltis (1996) conducted a case study of two bilingual teachers in a middle school who were learning how to teach in two languages without relying on translation from English into the students' dominant language.

WHY SO FEW STUDIES, WITH SO MUCH TO SAY?

With so much to say about secondary immigrant and bilingual students, curricula, and programs, it is difficult to know why so few studies have been carried out, but allow us to speculate. We think the main reason is that the original purpose of the bilingual and ESL education was to equalize educational opportunities for public school students, most often young Spanish-speaking children, who, because they could not understand the language of the classroom, were not progressing academically. When the federal government began funding bilingual education programs in the late 1960s, the Spanish-speaking population was the largest non-English-speaking minority group in the U.S. Bilingual education was viewed as a means of assisting the young children of Spanish-speaking families to prepare for schooling in English. Moreover, since the majority of these children were in the primary grades and native language instruction was considered a bridge to English, few schools saw any need to continue the primary language into the middle or high school grades. The assumption was that by the time bilingually educated children reached middle or high school, they should have acquired enough English to participate effectively in an all-English classroom environment.

The legal history on bilingual education also supports the implicit bias toward elementary schools. To the best of our knowledge, all of the legal battles over the need for some form of bilingual or ESL teaching have involved class action suits brought by concerned parents in which the plaintiffs were elementary school children. With the exception of Harklau's studies (1994a, 1994b) on tracking issues (no legal action was taken) and Arias's work (Arias, 1992) on desegregation (though not specific to bilingual education), no significant legal cases concerning the civil or educational rights of middle or high school immigrant or bilingual students have been litigated.

Given the focus on the elementary school, it is understandable that this has been the venue of nearly all research in bilingual education. A content analysis of major journals featuring articles on bilingual education shows that the overwhelming majority of article topics address issues of children becoming bilingual and biliterate, classroom learning, and school programs. From 1980 to 1996 fewer than 10 articles dealing directly with concerns of secondary-level immigrant and bilingual students appear in the pages of *NABE Journal* (as of Winter/Spring, 1992, known as the *Bilingual Research Journal*), *TESOL Journal, TESOL Quarterly, Linguistics and Education,* and *The Bilingual Review.* It was not until 1997 that books about bilingual education in schools dedicated separate chapters or major sections to secondary students and programs (see Brisk, 1997; Faltis & Hudelson, 1997). Also, in 1997, Teachers of English to Speakers of Other Languages (TESOL) published the ESL Standards for pre-K–12 students and included a section specifically for students in grades 9–12.

A TIME TO REFOCUS

There *is* much to say about adolescents, bilingualism, and ESL in the secondary school. When we do not discuss what is happening in secondary schools where there are immigrant and bilingual students, the school benefits by our silence. High schools can ignore the language and literacy needs of immigrant students. They do not need to pay attention to their developmental and human relations needs when no one is asking questions about them. Schools can get away with placing under- and poorly prepared teachers with immigrant and bilingual students (Sánchez &

Walker de Félix, 1986) and with segregating immigrant students from English-speaking peers. Minicucci and Olsen (1992) reported that a majority of the 19 high schools they studied segregated immigrant students from mainstream students. Moreover, immigrant students had fewer and inferior academic offerings than mainstream students. Most of the schools offered only English as a second language classes, and had substantial gaps in sheltered subject matter coverage within and across grades (see Glossary for definitions).

ORGANIZATION OF THE BOOK

In this book, we focus attention on secondary students, the curricula, and programs, three crucial areas that make a difference in the quality of education students receive.

Part I: The Students. contains four chapters about students—who they are, where they come from, and what happens to them in school under different contexts. Dorothy Waggoner offers a first-time-ever look at who secondary school newcomer and language minority students are, what languages they are likely to speak, where they come from, and the types of schooling experiences they had before arriving at secondary school. Until Waggoner's chapter, there was no way of knowing the numbers of newcomer and bilingual adolescents because the U.S. Census provides figures only for individuals between the ages of 5 and 18 years. Moreover, individuals with limited proficiency in English are not disaggregated from fluent English speakers within the various ethnic populations for whom information is reported. Using the 1990 U.S. Census as well as more recent information, Waggoner calculated a plethora of precise information about adolescent students across the United States. This chapter is invaluable because it clearly shows how large and diverse the adolescent immigrant and bilingual population truly is.

Linda Harklau's chapter on the ESL learning environment in secondary school sends a strong message about how crucial it is for educators and teachers to be vigilant about the issues of tracking and scheduling in high school settings. Harklau correctly points out the difficulties immigrant and bilingual students face once they are placed into ESL and other tracks. Her research reminds us that master schedulers in high schools wield a great deal of power over the lives of immigrant and bilingual adolescents.

Ofelia García's chapter speaks to one of the most difficult issues for secondary schools and teachers: how to educate students with little schooling experience. According to Olsen (1988), most immigrant students enrolling in secondary schools are 2 to 3 academic years behind mainstream students in preparation. Waggoner (see Chapter 1) reports that in 1990, a large number of newcomer and linguistically diverse adolescents who entered high school had completed fewer than 5 years of schooling. Some 3800 of these were foreign-born speakers of non-English languages. García presents a case study of several students who entered a high school program in New York City, and chronicles the efforts made to educate these adolescents, including which curricula strategies were effective within this context.

Paula Wolfe and Christian Faltis use discourse analysis to show the interaction among participation structures, ideology, and gender across ESL, bilingual, and sheltered content classroom environments. They found that participation between girls and boys changed as the nature of the interaction changed: girls were willing to participate in class whereas boys tended to withdraw and resist activities they considered less demanding. This finding was not surprising, as it has been reported in the literature on mainstream regular classrooms. What was intriguing is that the teacher's ideology about the nature of learning and the role of classroom interaction appeared to greatly influence the quality of interaction in the classrooms they analyzed.

Part II: The Curricula. has three chapters pertaining to the kinds of curricula that are used with immigrant and bilingual students. The chapter by Deborah Short uses actual classroom vignettes to show how teachers in a sheltered instruction program integrated language acquisition principles into content teaching to ensure that students participated in and benefited from instruction.

Guadalupe Valdés examines some of the problems three Latino middle school students faced as they struggled to acquire academic writing skills in English. Valdés chronicles how the three students, all of whom were incipient bilinguals, developed into writers in English and how their writing abilities reflected the kinds of teaching they received. This important study points to the complexity of teaching academic writing to bilingual adolescents and raises myriad questions for further research.

Margo Gottlieb takes a hard look at assessment issues. All secondary schools use tests for measuring student learning, for graduation, and for accountability purposes. Very little is known about how schools with large numbers of immigrant and bilingual students address issues of assessment. Gottlieb offers a way to assess adolescent immigrant and bilingual students based on a framework that uses multiple sources of information for making decisions about students' learning. She also discusses issues surrounding the use of standardized tests of content knowledge and literacy for students who are in the process of becoming bilingual.

Part III: Program Considerations. includes three chapters about making schools more responsive to immigrant and bilingual students. Carolyn Temple Adger and Joy Kreeft Peyton begin the section with a chapter that describes approaches being tried at high schools across the nation to enhance the schools' capacity to work successfully with immigrant students and improve their academic achievement. Adger and Peyton stress the importance of teacher planning and implementation teams, and partnerships with parents and other institutions.

Barbara Merino writes about the preparation of secondary-level teachers of immigrant and bilingual students. Merino's chapter describes the context and nature of teacher preparation of secondary teachers who teach students in their second language. What is it that secondary teachers who work with immigrant and bilingual students need to know to be considered "prepared to teach"? To address this question, Merino examines research from various traditions, and focuses on California's approach to preparing teachers of immigrant and bilingual students.

Paula Wolfe's provocative examination of the power of metaphors in bilingual and ESL education serves as Chapter 10. Wolfe writes an intriguing essay on the impact metaphors can have on educators' perceptions of children and how children fit into school. She offers a new set of metaphors for secondary ESL and bilingual education, and asks readers to consider these metaphors as new problems and solutions arise.

CONCLUDING REMARKS

This introduction ends as a beginning, if that makes sense. It is, of course, the beginning of this book, but in a much more profound sense, we hope that this book serves as the impetus to begin additional research and action. Given the immensity and complexity of secondary education, it is obvious that while this book addresses many important areas of concern, many more await deeper and further examination. For example, more thought and investigation are needed in the areas of academic and personal counseling, community involvement, health education, newcomer schools, and vocational education, to mention a few. We need to know more about academic language, sheltered content teaching, and college preparation courses. We need to find out more about working with immigrant students with little previous experience in school. There is much work to be started, and so much more to say.

REFERENCES

Arias, M. B. (1992). Mexican American student segregation and desegregation in California. In R. Padilla & A. Benavides (Eds.), *Critical perspectives in bilingual education research* (pp. 401–422). Tempe, AZ: Bilingual Review Press.

Brisk, M. E. (1997). *Bilingual education: From compensatory to quality education.* Mahwah, NJ: Lawrence Erlbaum.

Faltis, C. (Ed.) (1993). Trends in bilingual education at the secondary school level. *Peabody Journal of Education, 69*(1), 136–151.

Faltis, C. (1994). Doing the right thing: Developing a program for immigrant and bilingual secondary students. In R. Rodríguez, N. Ramos, & J. A. Ruíz-Escalante (Eds.), *Compendium of readings in bilingual education: Issues and Practices* (pp. 39–47). San Antonio, TX: Texas Association for Bilingual Education.

Faltis, C. (1996). Learning to teach bilingually in a middle school bilingual classroom. *Bilingual Research Journal, 20*(1), 29–44.

Faltis, C., & Hudelson, S. (1997). *Bilingual education in elementary and secondary school communities: Toward understanding and caring.* Needham Heights, MA: Allyn & Bacon.

Harklau, L. (1994a). Jumping tracks: How language-minority students negotiate evaluations of ability. *Anthropology and Education Quarterly, 25*(3), 347–363.

Harklau, L. (1994b). Tracking and linguistic minority students: Consequences of ability grouping for second language learners. *Linguistics and Education, 6,* 221–248.

Lucas, T., Henze, R., & Donato, R. (1990). Promoting the success of Latino language minority students: An exploratory study of six high schools. *Harvard Educational Review, 60*(3), 315–340.

Marsh, L. (1995). A Spanish dual literacy program: Teaching to the whole student. *The Bilingual Research Journal, 19,* 409–428.

Minicucci, C., & Olsen, L. (1992). *Programs for secondary limited English proficient students: A California study.* Washington, D.C.: National Clearinghouse for Bilingual Education.

Olsen, L. (1988). *Crossing the schoolhouse border: Immigrant students and the California public schools.* San Francisco: California Tomorrow.

Phelen, P., Cao, H. T., & Davidson, A. L. (1992). *Navigating the psycho/social pressures of adolescence: The voices and experiences of high school youth.* Paper presented at the Stanford University Center for Research on the Context of Secondary School Teaching, April.

Sánchez, K., & Walker de Félix, J. (1986). Second language teachers' abilities:

Some equity concerns. *Journal of Educational Equity and Leadership,* 6(4), 313–321.

Teachers of English to Speakers of Other Languages. (1997). *ESL standards for pre-K–12 students.* Alexandria, VA: Author.

Wolfe, P. (1996). Literacy bargains: Toward critical literacy in a multilingual classroom. *TESOL Journal,* 5(4), 22–27.

PART I

The Students

CHAPTER I

WHO ARE SECONDARY NEWCOMER AND LINGUISTICALLY DIFFERENT YOUTH?

Dorothy Waggoner

NUMBERS AND NEEDS

The 1990 census revealed a phenomenal growth ("Undercount or over-count?" 1991) in the numbers of linguistic minority and foreign-born people in the United States during the 1980s. Because many of these populations are comparatively young, the growth is especially notable among school-age children and youth, and the increase will continue into the next century, regardless of immigration. These youngsters bring to U.S. classrooms languages and cultures previously underrepresented. They have much to offer to the country, but only if they have educational opportunities designed to enable them to meet their full potential.

This chapter examines the numbers and proportions of newcomer and linguistically different youth between the ages of 14 and 19 as re-vealed by the 1990 census and other sources. It compares their character-istics by racial/ethnic group, language spoken at home, nativity (place of birth), and distribution in the various states. It explores the relationships of nativity and home language usage to high school graduation rates, school enrollment numbers and levels, dropout rates, years of schooling completed by dropouts, and poverty.

Study of census information shows that educational and economic characteristics vary by linguistic and national background. These differ-ences affect the planning of educational programs and the preparation of teachers and support personnel to meet the needs of newcomer and linguistically different youth.

BACKGROUND

The United States became much more culturally and linguistically diverse in the 1980s than in previous decades. The foreign-born population grew from 14.1 million in 1980 to 19.8 million, and the population of people who speak languages other than English at home grew from 23.1 million to 31.8 million. While the total population increased by 10% between 1980 and 1990, the foreign-born population increased by 40% and the population speaking languages other than English at home by 38% (U.S. Bureau of the Census, 1984, 1993a, 1993b).

Spanish continues to be the predominant non-English language spoken in the United States. The youth and vitality of the U.S. Hispanic population, as well as the numbers of Spanish-speaking immigrants who arrived between 1980 and 1990, fueled the growth in the number of home speakers of Spanish from 11.1 million to 17.3 million. At the beginning of the decade, the Spanish-speaking population constituted less than half of all home speakers of non-English languages; by 1990, it had increased to 54% of that population (U.S. Bureau of the Census, 1984, 1993b). However, it was the influx of newcomers speaking Asian languages that contributed to the increase in cultural and linguistic diversity.

Spanish-speaking and Asian countries replaced English-speaking countries and countries in which European languages other than English and Spanish are spoken as the principal origins of the foreign-born during the 1980s, as depicted in Figure 1.1.

Mexican- and Asian-born school-age children constituted three out of five foreign-born school-agers, but adults born in Mexico and Asian countries, were less than half of foreign-born adults, who include many long-time residents with European origins.

Recent immigrants from Asia brought languages previously almost unknown in this country. They added to the numbers of speakers of certain languages at the expense of others that were previously among the most widely spoken, as illustrated in Figure 1.2. Between 1980 and 1990, the numbers of speakers of Asian Indian languages and of Vietnamese and Korean, made the most substantial increases. The number of speakers of Chinese languages, which have always been important among Asian languages spoken in the U.S., also more than doubled (U.S. Bureau of the Census, 1984, 1993b).

Chinese has joined Spanish, French, German, and Italian among languages spoken in U.S. homes by at least a million people and now surpasses Italian in number of speakers. Table 1.1 shows the estimated numbers of speakers of various languages in 1980 and 1990 and the percentage change over the decade.

FIGURE 1.1. Percentage Distribution of Foreign-Born People by Language of Country of Birth, 1980 and 1990.

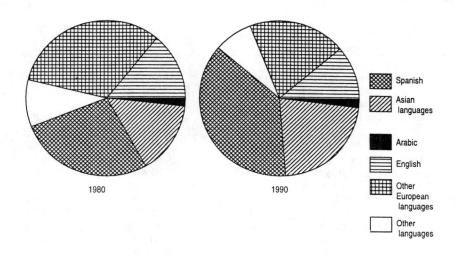

FIGURE 1.2. Percentage Increase in Numbers of Home Speakers of Non-English Languages, 1980 to 1990.

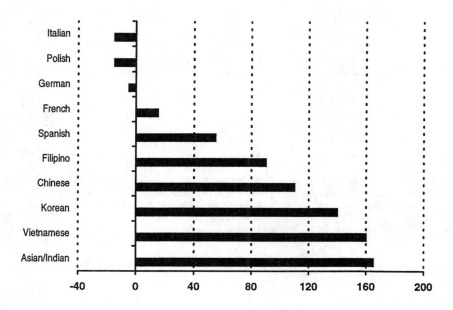

TABLE 1.1. Estimated Numbers of Home Speakers of Non-English Languages, Age 5+, in 1980 and 1990 and Percentage Change by Selected Language or Group of Languages: United States.

Language(s)	1980	1990	Percentage Change
Total (all languages)	23,060,000	31,845,000	+38.1
American Indian/ Alaska Native languages	333,000	332,000	-0.4
Arabic	218,000	355,000	+63.3
Armenian	101,000	150,000	+48.8
Asian Indian languages	243,000	644,000	+164.8
Chinese languages	631,000	1,319,000	+109.2
Czech	122,000	92,000	-24.4
Dutch and Afrikaans	148,000	148,000	+0.1
Farsi	107,000	202,000	+88.7
Filipino languages	474,000	899,000	+89.5
French	1,551,000	1,702,000	+9.8
German	1,587,000	1,547,000	-2.4
Greek	401,000	388,000	-3.3
Hungarian	179,000	148,000	-17.4
Italian	1,618,000	1,309,000	-19.1
Japanese	336,000	428,000	+27.2
Korean	266,000	626,000	+135.3
Norwegian	112,000	81,000	-28.2
Polish	821,000	723,000	-11.8
Portuguese	352,000	430,000	+22.4
Russian	173,000	243,000	+39.6
Serbo-Croatian	150,000	142,000	-5.4
Spanish	11,116,000	17,340,000	+56.0
Swedish	100,000	78,000	-22.5
Thai and Laotian	85,000	206,000	+142.8
Ukrainian	121,000	97,000	-20.4
Vietnamese	195,000	507,000	+160.6
Yiddish	316,000	213,000	-32.6

SOURCES: U.S. Bureau of the Census, *1980 Census Population, Detailed Population Characteristics, United States Summary* (Washington, DC: Government Printing Office, 1984) and *Language Spoken at Home and Ability to Speak English for the United States, Regions and States: 1990* (CPH-L-133) (Washington, DC: Author, 1993).
NOTE: Percentages calculated on unrounded numbers.

STUDY DATA AND DEFINITIONS

This chapter presents the results of a special study of newcomer and linguistically different youth, age 14 to 19, living in the 50 states and the District of Columbia in 1990. These are youth who speak languages other than English in their homes, who were born in foreign countries, or both. The data are from the 5% public use microdata sample (PUMS) of the 1990 census, supplemented by published information on foreign-born and linguistically different populations from the 1980 and 1990 censuses.

Linguistically different youth, as defined in this chapter, are a part of a larger population of youth living in language-minority families who have educational needs related to their language backgrounds and proficiency in English. Many language-minority youth speak only English at home. Others who speak their mother tongues at home also speak English, and some are fully English-proficient. Home language usage and nativity, as proxies for English proficiency, are related to educational attainment and social and economic well-being in American society, as revealed in this study.

Native-born youth include youth born in the U.S., including Puerto Rico and other U.S. territories, as well as those born outside the U.S. who have U.S. parents. Newcomers are all youth born in foreign countries, except the children of U.S. parents. Foreign-born families are those headed by a foreign-born individual.

Home speakers of non-English languages who have difficulty speaking English are those who responded to the census question on English-speaking ability by saying that they did not speak English "very well." People who reported that they speak only English at home were not asked this question. An unknown number of them have difficulty speaking English or otherwise lack proficiency in the language. Some native-born youth who live in language-minority families but speak only English at home are included in the English monolingual comparison group for the study, although they, too, may lack English proficiency.

Speakers of certain languages and immigrants from certain countries report more difficulty speaking English than others. However, English proficiency, including reading and writing ability, is much more closely related than English-speaking ability alone to success in this country. Bilingualism and biliteracy—proficiency in the home language as well as in English—may also be closely related, especially to educational success and, in some fields, to economic success. Unfortunately, data to study these factors are not available from the census.

The census questions on language, nativity, educational attainment, poverty, and other socioeconomic characteristics were asked on the long

TABLE 1.2. Estimated Numbers of Youth, Age 14 to 19, by Nativity, Language Spoken at Home, and Racial/Ethnic Group: United States, 1990.

Group	Total	NB, English only	Newcomer and linguistically different			
			Total	NB, non-English	FB, English only	FB, non-English
Total	20,876,000	17,455,000	3,421,000	2,102,000	174,000	1,146,000
African American	3,056,000	2,818,000	238,000	149,000	60,000	29,000
American Indian/ Alaska Native	199,000	156,000	42,000	40,000	1,000	1,000
Asian/Pacific Islander	676,000	194,000	481,000	102,000	42,000	338,000
Hispanic	2,341,000	598,000	1,744,000	1,077,000	23,000	644,000
Non-Hispanic white	14,576,000	13,672,000	905,000	728,000	47,000	129,000
Other	28,000	16,000	12,000	7,000	1,000	4,000

Source: 1990 census of population.

Note: Numbers may not add to totals because of rounding.

NB = native born; FB = foreign born.

form of the census, which was completed by a sample of about 17.7 million, or 17%, of U.S. household units in 1990. The five percent PUMS contains the data for every twentieth household unit sampled.

The published numbers and percentages based on the entire 17% sample of household units, as well as the numbers and percentages from the study of the PUMS, are estimates. They are subject to sampling error and are subject to other sources of error that affect both the 100 percent and the sample counts. Among the latter is the census undercount which differentially affected minorities (see "Undercount and Overcount?" 1991) and the difficulties of accurately enumerating the foreign-born. For these reasons, the estimates of the numbers of newcomer and linguistically different youth should be considered minimums.

NEWCOMER AND LINGUISTICALLY DIFFERENT YOUTH IN THE UNITED STATES

One in six of all youths age 14 to 19 in the United States either speaks a language other than English at home, was born in a foreign country, or both. There were more than 3.4 million of them in 1990, as shown in Table 1.2.

TABLE 1.3. Percentage Distribution of Youth, Age 14 to 19, in the Various Nativity and Language Categories, by Racial/Ethnic Group: United States, 1990.

		NB, English only	*Newcomer and linguistically different*			
				NB, non-	FB, Eng-	FB, non-
Group	*Total*		*Total*	*English*	*lish only*	*English*
Total	100.0	100.0	100.0	100.0	100.0	100.0
African American	14.6	16.1	6.9	7.1	34.7	2.5
American Indian/ Alaska Native	1.0	0.9	1.2	1.9	0.6	0.1
Asian/Pacific Islander	3.2	1.1	14.1	4.8	23.9	29.5
Hispanic	11.2	3.4	51.0	51.2	13.0	56.2
Non-Hispanic white	69.8	78.3	26.4	34.6	27.3	11.3
Other	0.1	0.1	0.3	0.3	0.4	0.4

Source: 1990 census of population.

Note: Percentages may not total 100.0 because of rounding.

NB = native born; FB = foreign born.

The majority of newcomer and linguistically different youth are native-born. They speak languages other than English in language-minority homes. In 1990, three in five newcomer and linguistically different youth were native-born and a third were foreign-born home speakers of non-English languages. The remainder, about 5%, were born in foreign countries but speak only English at home.

Numbering 1.7 million in 1990, Hispanics, ages 14–19, constitute about half all youth who are linguistically different, foreign-born, or both. They are most likely of all the racial/ethnic groups to speak their mother tongue at home, and a substantial majority of those who speak Spanish are native-born, as shown in Table 1.3. They predominate among native-born and foreign-born home speakers of non-English languages, as depicted in Figure 1.3.

The Census Bureau projects that Hispanics will become the dominant minority in U.S. schools by 2000 and will constitute 30% of the school-age population by the mid-century. The Bureau assumes that one in three of all births will be to Hispanics by 2050 (compared with 2 in 5 to non-Hispanic whites and 1 in 5 to African Americans) and that every year 4 of every 10 immigrants will be Hispanic (compared with 3 in 10 Asians and Pacific Islanders and 2 in 10 non-Hispanic whites) (Census, 1996). If these assumptions hold true, then the Hispanic school-age population will continue to increase.

FIGURE 1.3. Racial/Ethnic Affiliation of Youth in the Total Population and in the Linguistically Different and Newcomer Groups, 1990.

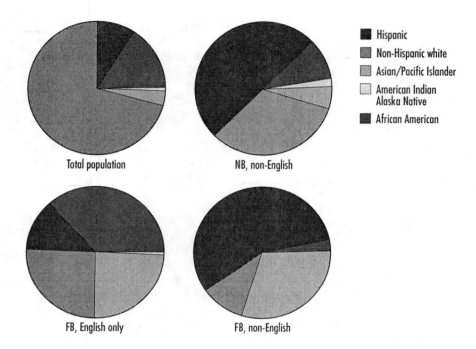

    Mexico is the country of birth of the majority of Hispanic newcomers. There were about 381,000 Mexican-born young people age 15 to 19 in the United States in 1990, as shown in Table 1.4.[1] They constituted a third of all foreign-born youth in that age group. There were six other Spanish-speaking countries, headed by El Salvador and the Dominican Republic, which were the birthplaces of at least 10,000 young people (U.S. Bureau of the Census, 1993e).

    As Table 1.4 shows, newcomers from Mexico, El Salvador, Guatemala, Nicaragua, and Honduras constitute larger proportions of the school-age population than they do of the adult population. Hispanic young people who are newcomers or the American-born children of newcomers are very likely to live in households in which most people speak Spanish and in which many people speak English with difficulty. At least 95% of people age 5 and older born in Spanish-speaking countries reported in 1990 that they speak Spanish or another non-English language at home; from three in five of those born in Peru to nearly three-quarters of those born in El Salvador and Mexico acknowledged difficulty speaking English (U.S. Bureau of the Census, 1993e). These data are found in Table 1.5. Among Spanish speakers as a whole, including those born in this country, as shown in Table 1.6, nearly half reported difficulty speaking English in 1990 (U.S. Bureau of the Census, 1993b).

The second largest group of newcomer and linguistically different youth after Hispanics consists of non-Hispanic whites, most of whom are native born, as shown in Table 1.2. This group constituted about a third of the native-born home speakers of non-English languages, and a substantial proportion of the foreign-born who speak only English in their homes, as illustrated in Figure 1.3.

The former Soviet Union, Iran, Germany, Portugal, and Poland are the principal birthplaces of foreign-born linguistically different non-Hispanic white youth. People from these countries are older, on the average, than native-born Americans and, except for people born in Iran, they are older than foreign-born people as a whole, as shown in Table 1.4, meaning that most of them are not recent immigrants.

The home language environments of linguistically different non-Hispanic white young people as well as the available opportunities for them to hear spoken English vary by national origin. The groups with the highest proportions of people speaking their mother tongues at home are those of people born in Portugal and Iran, as shown in Table 1.5. Home speakers of non-English languages born in the Soviet Union and in Portugal are the most likely to have difficulty speaking English (U.S. Bureau of the Census, 1993e).

Not shown in Tables 1.4 or 1.5, because they have no one single birthplace, are the estimated numbers of people from Arabic-speaking countries, who also contribute to the numbers of the non-Hispanic white minority.[2] About 716,000 people claimed Arab ancestry in the 1990 census; 41% of them were foreign-born, of whom 14,000 were age 15 to 19. More than half of the people with Arab ancestry age 5 and older in the entire group and 89% of the newcomers in this age group reported speaking Arabic or another non-English language at home; a third overall, including those born in this country, acknowledged difficulty speaking English (U.S. Bureau of the Census, 1993c).

Youth born in the United Kingdom and Canada are the largest groups among non-Hispanic white newcomers born in English-speaking countries, as indicated in Table 1.4 (U.S. Bureau of the Census, 1993e). However, as many as 3,000 Canadian youth may be linguistically different, most probably speaking French.[3]

Asians and Pacific Islanders are the third largest group among newcomer and linguistically different youth. They numbered an estimated

TABLE 1.4. Estimated Numbers of People, by Age Group, Median Age, Nativity, and Selected Country of Birth of the Foreign-Born: United States, 1990.

Country of birth	Total	Age group				Median age
		5 and under	*5-14*	*15-19*	*20 and over*	
Total	248,710,000	18,264,000	35,278,000	17,654,000	177,514,000	33.0
Native born	228,943,000	18,003,000	34,055,000	16,492,000	160,393,000	32.5
Foreign born	19,767,000	261,000	1,223,000	1,162,000	17,121,000	37.3
Spanish-speaking countries						
Mexico	4,298,000	102,000	359,000	381,000	3,455,000	29.9
Cuba	737,000	2,000	14,000	19,000	702,000	49.0
El Salvador	465,000	7,000	46,000	44,000	369,000	29.1
Dominican Republic	348,000	6,000	29,000	24,000	289,000	33.6
Colombia	286,000	3,000	18,000	12,000	253,000	35.3
Guatemala	226,000	4,000	21,000	18,000	183,000	29.8
Nicaragua	169,000	4,000	25,000	16,000	124,000	30.0
Peru	144,000	2,000	11,000	8,000	124,000	34.9
Ecuador	143,000	2,000	8,000	7,000	127,000	35.8
Honduras	109,000	2,000	10,000	8,000	89,000	31.2
Asian countries						
Philippines	913,000	6,000	51,000	51,000	805,000	38.8
Korea	568,000	6,000	38,000	45,000	479,000	34.9
Vietnam	543,000	4,000	52,000	74,000	413,000	30.3
China	530,000	3,000	19,000	21,000	486,000	44.8
India	450,000	5,000	27,000	24,000	395,000	36.4
Japan	290,000	8,000	19,000	11,000	251,000	37.8
Taiwan	244,000	2,000	20,000	19,000	203,000	33.2
Laos	172,000	4,000	27,000	26,000	115,000	27.0
Hong Kong	147,000	1,000	11,000	12,000	123,000	30.3
Cambodia	119,000	2,000	19,000	16,000	83,000	29.0
Thailand	107,000	5,000	27,000	5,000	70,000	30.4

TABLE 1.4. *Continued*

Other countries in which non-English languages are spoken

Country of birth	Total	5 and under	5-14	15-19	20 and over	Median age
Germany	712,000	3,000	8,000	9,000	692,000	52.8
Poland	388,000	1,000	12,000	8,000	367,000	57.1
Soviet Union	334,000	6,000	24,000	16,000	288,000	54.6
Haiti	225,000	4,000	17,000	13,000	191,000	34.6
Iran	211,000	1,000	16,000	11,000	183,000	35.0
Portugal	210,000	1,000	8,000	9,000	192,000	40.1
English-speaking countries						
Canada	745,000	4,000	20,000	17,000	708,000	52.9
United Kingdom	640,000	4,000	19,000	17,000	601,000	49.7
Jamaica	334,000	3,000	23,000	24,000	284,000	35.7
Guyana	121,000	1,000	11,000	11,000	98,000	33.6
Trinidad/ Tobago	116,000	2,000	7,000	6,000	102,000	35.7

SOURCES: U.S. Department of Commerce, Bureau of the Census, 1990 Census of Population, The Foreign-Born Population in the United States and 1990 Census of Population, Ancestry of the Population in the United States (Washington, D.C.: U.S. Government Printing Office, 1993). NOTE: Numbers may not add to totals because of rounding.

481,000 in 1990. Many Asians have recently arrived in the United States and thus Asian and Pacific Islander youth, as a group, are the most likely to be foreign-born. As depicted in Figure 1.3, they are a substantial proportion of all foreign-born youth who speak their mother tongues at home in this country and they constitute nearly a quarter of foreign-born youth who speak English at home.

Vietnam, the Philippines, and Korea are the principal birthplaces of young newcomers from Asia. The median ages of Asian-born people in 1990, shown in Table 1.4, reveal the shift that has been taking place in this population as older Asian groups are replaced by groups from countries previously little represented in the U.S. population. People born in China and, to a lesser extent, those from the Philippines and Japan are older than the average foreign-born person. All the other Asian newcomer groups are younger. People from Southeast Asia and Hong Kong

TABLE 1.5. Social and Economic Characteristics of the Population, by Nativity and Selected Country of Birth of the Foreign-Born: United States, 1990.

Country of birth	% aged 5+ HSNEL	% HSNEL with Eng. Diff.	% age 15-19 enrolled in school	% high school graduates age 18-24	% high school graduates age 25+	Median family income	% below poverty
Total	13.8	43.9	80.8	76.5	75.2	$35,225	13.1
Native born	7.8	29.4	81.3	78.4	77.0	35,508	12.7
Foreign born	79.1	59.4	74.5	57.1	58.8	31,785	18.2
Spanish-speaking countries							
Mexico	96.1	73.5	55.6	31.3	24.3	21,585	29.7
Cuba	95.0	63.3	78.9	67.8	54.1	32,007	14.7
El Salvador	97.1	74.5	67.8	33.9	32.7	21,818	24.9
Dominican Republic	96.1	71.5	77.0	50.8	41.7	19,694	30.0
Colombia	95.1	64.3	81.4	69.5	66.8	30,342	15.3
Guatemala	96.7	73.1	65.8	38.3	37.5	22,574	25.8
Nicaragua	96.1	68.2	80.6	51.3	58.8	24,416	24.4
Peru	94.6	60.3	83.3	80.0	78.6	31,798	14.6
Ecuador	95.7	64.6	78.8	67.8	60.3	31,133	15.1
Honduras	92.4	65.0	74.0	48.1	49.2	21,735	27.8
Asian countries							
Philippines	88.3	36.1	85.5	83.7	83.5	47,794	5.9
Korea	92.5	67.0	91.7	82.9	80.1	33,406	15.6
Vietnam	96.7	68.4	91.7	68.3	58.9	30,496	25.5
China	96.3	74.9	92.5	68.8	60.6	34,225	15.7
India	88.7	30.6	93.0	88.8	87.2	52,908	8.1
Japan	84.1	66.8	91.5	91.7	86.4	47,034	12.8
Taiwan	96.0	60.3	95.3	89.6	91.6	45,325	16.7
Laos	97.7	73.7	87.2	51.5	37.8	19,615	40.3
Hong Kong	93.2	49.3	95.1	89.6	83.3	49,618	12.7
Cambodia	97.4	74.2	88.5	55.2	35.4	19,043	38.4
Thailand	89.4	63.8	88.5	80.3	74.1	37,100	27.4
Other countries in which non-English languages are spoken							
Germany	57.6	22.7	77.8	84.0	75.9	41,757	7.7
Poland	80.1	59.4	85.8	74.5	58.1	35,742	9.7
Soviet Union	81.1	64.2	84.4	77.8	64.0	28,799	25.0
Haiti	94.7	58.4	87.1	68.4	57.6	25,556	21.7
Iran	91.8	42.3	90.7	87.4	86.7	40,273	15.7
Portugal	92.1	60.8	73.5	60.3	32.1	37,367	7.0
English-speaking countries							
Canada	19.2	25.9	87.3	87.8	72.6	39,995	7.8
United Kingdom	6.8	16.2	85.8	89.2	81.3	45,681	6.6
Jamaica	6.6	26.4	83.5	74.9	67.9	34,338	12.1
Guyana	6.3	32.9	83.0	71.0	69.5	36,278	11.9
Trinidad/Tobago	6.8	25.4	82.0	81.8	74.1	33,319	14.9

Sources: U.S. Department of Commerce, Bureau of the Census, *1990 Census of Population, The Foreign-Born Population in the United States and 1990 Census of Population, Ancestry of the Population in the United States* (Washington, DC: U.S. Government Printing Office, 1993).

HSNEL = speakers of non-English languages.

TABLE 1.6. Social and Economic Characteristics of the Population, by Selected Language or Group of Languages Spoken at Home: United States, 1990.

Language(s)	Percent with English difficulty	Dropout rate, age 16-19	Percent high school grads, age 25+	Median family income (in dollars)	Percent of families in poverty
Total	7.8	11.2	75.2	35,225	10.0
English only	N/A	10.2	77.8	35,842	8.9
Non-English languages	43.9	16.5	56.1	31,773	14.9
American Indian/ Alaska Native languages	38.8	17.8	52.0	*	39.9
Arabic	33.7	10.7	75.7	33,690	16.1
Armenian	51.2	8.3	63.5	36,894	15.1
Asian Indian languages	29.7	4.3	85.2	**	7.1
Chinese languages	59.9	3.6	70.5	40,094	11.6
Czech	29.4	9.0	57.8	32,147	6.5
Dutch	23.7	18.8	71.4	40,237	5.6
Farsi	38.0	4.2	89.1	40,133	12.3
French	27.9	6.5	69.5	36,418	10.0
German	24.9	14.2	70.7	38,371	6.5
Greek	31.5	5.5	65.3	41,761	5.5
Haitian Creole	52.5	8.9	50.9	23,627	14.3
Hebrew	23.5	4.0	84.4	47,819	7.9
Hmong	77.6	12.3	31.5	14,448	61.2
Hungarian	35.0	5.4	65.2	38,306	4.6
Italian	33.2	7.5	50.9	38,447	5.1
Japanese	52.5	3.8	82.6	44,947	4.5
Korean	61.2	4.2	80.4	34,314	12.2
Mon-Khmer	73.3	10.5	35.1	18,391	41.7
Norwegian	21.1	6.5	63.1	34,317	5.3
Polish	37.0	8.7	55.3	34,397	4.9
Portuguese	45.2	12.9	46.2	36,887	7.0
Russian	54.4	8.2	77.0	34,198	18.7
Serbo-Croatian	36.5	6.7	57.8	37,396	4.6
Spanish	47.9	20.9	49.4	27,099	20.1
Swedish	19.1	4.9	73.2	41,017	4.4
Tagalog and Ilocano	35.0	6.9	82.1	***	4.4
Thai and Laotian	62.1	9.2	59.5	31,458	17.8
Turkish	38.7	4.6	77.4	41,032	7.8
Ukrainian	36.9	6.4	60.5	38,651	4.3
Vietnamese	63.3	6.6	62.6	32,336	21.5
Yiddish	29.0	8.0	61.9	45,310	11.4

SOURCE: U.S. Bureau of the Census, 1990 Census of Population and Housing, Detailed Cross-Tabulations of Selected Language Groups for States: 1990 (CD-ROM, STP160) (Washington, DC: Author, 1995).
* Median family income for speakers of American Indian and Alaska Native languages ranged from $10,440 for speakers of Pima to $24,883 for speakers of Eskimo languages and Aleut.
** Median family income for speakers of Asian Indian languages ranged from $44,070 for speakers of Punjabi to $62,986 for speakers of Marathi.
***The median family income for speakers of Tagalog was $46,313 and for speakers of Ilocano, $42,880.

are younger on average than native-born people. They and their off-spring constitute the most rapidly growing element of the Asian new-comer school-age population (U.S. Bureau of the Census, 1993c, 1993e). To the extent that they continue to speak their mother tongues at home, their offspring will contribute to the growth of the linguistically different population in U.S. schools.

Although a majority of Asian/Pacific youth speak non-English languages at home, they are less likely to do so than Hispanics. Some of them come from homes in which proportionally fewer foreign-born people speak non-English languages. As shown in Table 1.5, almost all the newcomers from Laos, Cambodia, Vietnam, China, and Taiwan speak their native languages at home, and many have difficulty speaking English. In contrast, people born in Japan, the Philippines, and India are less likely to speak non-English languages at home and many fewer report difficulty with English. In 1990, the proportions of home speakers of non-English languages among Asian newcomers ranged from 84% of those born in Japan to 98% of those born in Laos.

There were 33,000 Pacific Islanders age 15 to 19 in the United States in 1990. Pacific Islanders are largely native-born, most of them Native Hawaiians, Samoans, or Guamanians. Two-thirds of all Samoans and nearly half of Guamanians speak their mother tongues at home. In contrast, only one in ten Hawaiians speaks Hawaiian or another non-English language at home. Up to a third of home speakers of non-English languages among Pacific Islanders acknowledged difficulty in speaking English (U.S. Bureau of the Census, 1993d).

After non-Hispanic whites, African Americans are the least likely to speak languages other than English at home or to be foreign-born, as shown in Table 1.3. In 1990 there were an estimated 238,000 newcomer and linguistically different African American youth—8% of the African American population age 14 to 19. The majority of these youth are native-born home speakers of non-English languages. However, reflecting the origins of many blacks from the English-speaking countries of the Caribbean, especially Jamaica, Guyana, and Trinidad and Tobago (and as illustrated in Figure 1.3), African American youth constitute the largest portion of foreign-born youth who speak only English at home.

The largest group of black newcomers who speak non-English languages at home consists of youth born in Haiti. Almost all Haitian newcomers speak Haitian Creole, French, or another non-English language at home (U.S. Bureau of the Census, 1993e). More than half of all speakers of Haitian Creole in the United States reported difficulty speaking English in 1990 (U.S. Bureau of the Census, 1993b). This information is shown in Tables 1.5 and 1.6.

FIGURE 1.4. States with at Least 50,000 Linguistically Different and Newcomer Youth, 1990.

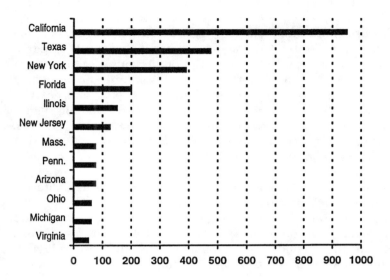

There were an estimated 41,000 American Indian and Alaska Native home speakers of non-English languages age 14 to 19 in 1990. They constituted one in five of American Indian/Alaska Native youth in their age group. Among speakers of American Indian and Alaska Native languages of all ages in 1990, about 39% acknowledged English-speaking difficulty (U.S. Bureau of the Census, 1993b).

GEOGRAPHIC DISTRIBUTION OF NEWCOMER AND LINGUISTICALLY DIFFERENT YOUTH

Youth who speak languages other than English at home, were born in foreign countries, or both are found in all states. Nevertheless, the impact of this population is much greater in some states than in others. In 1990, the numbers of newcomer and linguistically different youth ranged from nearly a million in California to about 3,000 each in North Dakota, Vermont, and Wyoming. Their proportions of the total population age 14 to 19 ranged from two in five in California to fewer than one in twenty in the southern states of Alabama, Arkansas, Kentucky, Mississippi, Tennessee, and West Virginia, and in North Dakota.

As depicted in Figure 1.4, there are five states in addition to California with at least 100,000 newcomer and linguistically different youth and six states with from 50,000 to 100,000 members of this group. Newcomer and linguistically different youth in these states totaled an estimated 2.7 million, or 8 out of 10 members of this population in the nation in 1990.

Native-born youth who speak languages other than English at home are a substantial majority of the newcomer and linguistically different group in most states. This is the case in two of the states with the largest proportions of these youth: New Mexico and Texas. In 1990, more than 3 in 10 of all young people age 14 to 19 in New Mexico and nearly a quarter of those in Texas were native-born home speakers of non-English languages, while very few were foreign-born. In contrast, in California, the state with the largest number of newcomer and linguistically different youth, foreign-born youth who speak languages other than English at home predominate.

Linguistically different newcomers who have settled in California form the largest single group in any state. They constitute 15% of newcomer and linguistically different young people in the whole country and 45% of all foreign-born youth who speak non-English languages at home. California has the second largest numbers and the second-highest proportion of newcomer youth who speak only English at home, after New York.

Table 1.7 provides the estimated numbers of young people age 14 to 19 in each state and the District of Columbia according to the categories defined for this study. Table 1.8 gives the distribution.

LINGUISTIC DIVERSITY, NATIVITY, AND EDUCATIONAL STATUS

Youth age 14 to 19 who speak languages other than English at home or who are foreign-born or both are less likely than native-born youth who speak only English at home to be high school graduates. If they are not high school graduates and not enrolled, they complete fewer years of schooling before leaving school than majority youth in similar circumstances. If they are enrolled in the intermediate or secondary grades, they are somewhat more likely than other students to be enrolled in grades 10 to 12 than in grades 6 to 9, possibly because those who are still enrolled are older than their majority classmates due to delayed education.[4] Native-born linguistically different students are frequently held back, and foreign-born students from certain backgrounds come to U.S. schools with fewer years of education than their U.S.-born monolingual English-speaking peers. Thus, these two groups routinely need more time to catch up. There are considerable differences in educational participation and attainment related to home language usage and nativity.

About 700,000 of the linguistically different and newcomer youth were high school graduates in 1990, as shown in Table 1.9. Three in five were native-born and the majority of the rest were foreign-born home speakers of non-English languages. However, foreign-born youth who speak only English at home are the most likely to be high school graduates by age 19. Their 1990 graduation rate surpassed that of native-born English monolinguals (30% compared with 24%) and those of linguistically different native-born and newcomer youth (20% and 19%, respectively). These differences are highlighted in Table 1.10.

Most of the newcomer and linguistically different students age 14 to 19 who are enrolled in school, like native-born students in that age group who speak only English at home, are enrolled in grades 10 to 12: they have completed 9 to 11 years of schooling, as shown in Table 1.10. However, more, proportionally, of the former than the latter are in those grades. In 1990, 74% of newcomer and linguistically different youth who were enrolled had completed 9 to 11 years of schooling and 26% had completed 5 to 8 years. In comparison, 69% of enrolled native-born students who speak only English at home had completed 9 to 11 years and 31% had completed 5 to 8 years.

An estimated 441,000 of the newcomer and linguistically different youth, or about 13%, either had never been enrolled in U.S. schools or had left before completing high school. About 4% of them were foreign-born monolingual English speakers. The remainder were evenly divided between native-born and foreign-born home speakers of non-English languages.

There is a considerable difference between the dropout rates of native-born home speakers of non-English languages and foreign-born home speakers of English on the one hand and that of the foreign-born non-English home speakers on the other. One in 10 of the former, in comparison with less than 1 in 5 of the latter, was a dropout in 1990. The dropout rate of monolingual English-speaking native-born youth was 1 in 12.

Foreign-born, out-of-school youth are considerably more likely than native-born home speakers of non-English languages to have low levels of schooling, and native-born youth who speak non-English languages at home are likely to have lower levels than native-born youth who speak only English. In 1990, there were 101,000 young people, age 14 to 19, who had completed fewer than five years of schooling; half of them—52,000—were linguistically different or newcomer youth, and 38,000, nearly two in five of the total, were foreign-born home speakers of non-

TABLE 1.7. Estimated Numbers of Youth, Age 14 to 19 by Nativity, Language Spoken at Home, and State: United States, 1990.

State	Total	NB, English only	Newcomer and linguistically different			
			Total	NB, non-English	FB, English only	FB, non-English
Total	20,876,000	17,455,000	3,421,000	2,102,000	174,000	1,146,000
Alabama	375,000	359,000	17,000	14,000	*	2,000
Alaska	45,000	40,000	5,000	4,000	*	1,000
Arizona	310,000	232,000	78,000	57,000	2,000	19,000
Arkansas	212,000	203,000	10,000	8,000	*	1,000
California	2,395,000	1,448,000	947,000	399,000	38,000	510,000
Colorado	266,000	236,000	30,000	21,000	1,000	8,000
Connecticut	248,000	205,000	43,000	31,000	3,000	9,000
Delaware	54,000	49,000	5,000	4,000	*	1,000
District of Columbia	46,000	39,000	7,000	3,000	1,000	3,000
Florida	940,000	744,000	196,000	108,000	17,000	70,000
Georgia	588,000	548,000	41,000	28,000	3,000	10,000
Hawaii	86,000	67,000	19,000	9,000	1,000	9,000
Idaho	96,000	87,000	8,000	7,000	*	1,000
Illinois	958,000	802,000	156,000	100,000	4,000	52,000
Indiana	506,000	472,000	33,000	29,000	1,000	3,000
Iowa	234,000	219,000	15,000	12,000	*	3,000
Kansas	206,000	191,000	15,000	10,000	1,000	5,000
Kentucky	333,000	319,000	14,000	12,000	1,000	1,000
Louisiana	397,000	370,000	27,000	21,000	1,000	5,000
Maine	103,000	95,000	7,000	6,000	*	1,000
Maryland	365,000	321,000	44,000	25,000	5,000	14,000
Massachusetts	478,000	396,000	82,000	51,000	5,000	26,000
Michigan	821,000	762,000	60,000	46,000	2,000	11,000
Minnesota	358,000	331,000	27,000	19,000	1,000	7,000
Mississippi	265,000	253,000	12,000	10,000	*	1,000
Missouri	431,000	408,000	23,000	18,000	1,000	3,000
Montana	70,000	66,000	4,000	4,000	*	*
Nebraska	137,000	129,000	7,000	6,000	*	1,000
Nevada	89,000	76,000	13,000	7,000	1,000	6,000
New Hampshire	87,000	81,000	6,000	4,000	*	1,000
New Jersey	598,000	468,000	130,000	83,000	8,000	39,000
New Mexico	134,000	85,000	49,000	43,000	1,000	6,000
New York	1,428,000	1,037,000	391,000	236,000	42,000	113,000
N. Carolina	575,000	544,000	32,000	25,000	2,000	5,000

TABLE 1.7. *Continued*

			Newcomer and linguistically different			
		NB,		NB, non-	FB, English	FB, non-
State	*Total*	*English only*	*Total*	*English*	*only*	*English*
North Dakota	58,000	56,000	3,000	2,000	*	*
Ohio	938,000	876,000	62,000	53,000	2,000	6,000
Oklahoma	278,000	261,000	16,000	12,000	1,000	4,000
Oregon	227,000	205,000	22,000	12,000	2,000	9,000
Pennsylvania	965,000	884,000	81,000	63,000	4,000	14,000
Rhode Island	81,000	66,000	14,000	8,000	*	5,000
S. Carolina	324,000	306,000	17,000	15,000	1,000	1,000
South Dakota	62,000	58,000	4,000	4,000	*	*
Tennessee	429,000	408,000	21,000	17,000	1,000	3,000
Texas	1,538,000	1,061,000	477,000	355,000	9,000	113,300
Utah	186,000	169,000	17,000	13,000	1,000	3,000
Vermont	49,000	46,000	3,000	2,000	*	*
Virginia	510,000	460,000	50,000	28,000	4,000	18,000
Washington	381,000	336,000	45,000	25,000	3,000	17,000
W. Virginia	167,000	159,000	8,000	7,000	*	1,000
Wisconsin	410,000	381,000	29,000	23,000	1,000	5,000
Wyoming	41,000	38,000	3,000	2,000	*	*

Source: 1990 census of population.

Note: Numbers may not add to totals because of rounding.

NB = native born; FB = foreign born.

*Fewer than 1,000 young people.

English languages. In contrast, there were about 1.4 million youth who had left school after completing 9 to 11 years, and four out of five of them were native-born monolingual English speakers. Both of the foreign-born groups had completed fewer years of schooling than either native-born linguistically different youth or majority youth.

Since the census did not ask where individuals attended school, it is impossible to determine whether the foreign-born youth had ever been enrolled in U.S. schools or, if they were, how much time they spent before leaving. If they enroll, newcomers may fall behind or fail to find programs to meet their needs. Many may simply have to leave school to begin working.

Older foreign-born youth and foreign-born adults, like the 14-to-19-year-olds in the special study, are less likely to be high school graduates. Newcomer youth age 15 to 19 are less likely to be enrolled in educational

TABLE 1.8. Percentage Distribution of Youth Age 14 to 19 in Each State by Nativity and Language Spoken at Home: United States, 1990.

| | | | Linguistically different and newcomer | | | |
| | | NB, | | NB, non- | FB, | FB, non- |
State	Total	Eng. only	Total	English	Eng. only	English
Total	100.0	83.6	16.4	10.1	0.8	5.5
Alabama	100.0	95.6	4.4	3.7	0.1	0.6
Alaska	100.0	88.3	11.7	10.0	0.3	1.4
Arizona	100.0	74.9	25.1	18.5	0.6	6.0
Arkansas	100.0	95.5	4.5	3.9	0.1	0.5
California	100.0	60.5	39.5	16.7	1.6	21.3
Colorado	100.0	88.8	11.2	7.8	0.5	2.8
Connecticut	100.0	82.6	17.4	12.6	1.2	3.5
Delaware	100.0	91.5	8.5	6.7	0.8	1.0
DC	100.0	84.3	15.7	7.4	1.6	6.7
Florida	100.0	79.2	20.2	11.5	1.8	7.5
Georgia	100.0	93.1	6.9	4.8	0.5	1.7
Hawaii	100.0	77.8	22.2	10.6	1.7	10.0
Idaho	100.0	91.4	8.6	6.9	0.4	1.4
Illinois	100.0	83.7	16.3	10.4	0.4	5.4
Indiana	100.0	93.4	6.6	5.8	0.2	0.6
Iowa	100.0	93.5	6.5	4.9	0.2	1.4
Kansas	100.0	92.7	7.3	4.7	0.3	2.2
Kentucky	100.0	95.8	4.2	3.7	0.3	0.3
Louisiana	100.0	93.1	6.9	5.3	0.3	1.3
Maine	100.0	92.9	7.1	6.0	0.4	0.6
Maryland	100.0	88.0	12.0	6.7	1.3	4.0
Massachusetts	100.0	82.9	17.1	10.7	1.0	5.4
Michigan	100.0	92.8	7.2	5.6	0.2	1.4
Minnesota	100.0	92.5	7.5	5.2	0.3	2.0
Mississippi	100.0	95.7	4.3	3.8	0.1	0.4
Missouri	100.0	94.7	5.3	4.2	0.3	0.8
Montana	100.0	94.0	6.0	5.2	0.2	0.6
Nebraska	100.0	94.6	5.4	4.4	0.2	0.8
Nevada	100.0	85.2	14.8	7.4	0.6	6.8
New Hampshire	100.0	93.6	6.4	5.1	0.5	0.8
New Jersey	100.0	78.3	21.7	13.8	1.4	6.5
New Mexico	100.0	63.4	36.6	31.9	0.4	4.3
New York	100.0	72.6	27.4	16.5	2.9	7.9
North Carolina	100.0	94.5	5.5	4.4	0.3	0.8
North Dakota	100.0	95.3	4.7	4.2	0.3	0.1
Ohio	100.0	93.4	6.6	5.6	0.3	0.7
Oklahoma	100.0	94.2	5.8	4.3	0.2	1.3
Oregon	100.0	90.2	9.8	5.3	0.7	3.8
Pennsylvania	100.0	91.6	8.4	6.5	0.4	1.4
Rhode Island	100.0	82.2	17.8	10.4	0.6	6.7
South Carolina	100.0	94.7	5.3	4.6	0.3	0.4
South Dakota	100.0	93.7	6.3	5.7	0.4	0.2
Tennessee	100.0	95.2	4.8	4.0	0.2	0.6
Texas	100.0	69.0	31.0	23.1	0.6	7.3
Utah	100.0	91.0	9.0	6.9	0.4	1.7
Vermont	100.0	94.5	5.5	4.8	0.3	0.5
Virginia	100.0	90.3	9.7	5.6	0.7	3.4
Washington	100.0	88.1	11.9	6.6	0.8	4.5
West Virginia	100.0	95.4	4.6	4.0	0.2	0.4
Wisconsin	100.0	93.0	7.0	5.5	0.2	1.3
Wyoming	100.0	93.5	6.5	5.3	0.4	0.8

SOURCE: 1990 census of population.
NOTE: Percentages may not total 100.0 because of rounding.
NB = native born; FB = foreign born.

TABLE 1.9. Estimated Numbers of Youth Age 14 to 19 by Nativity, Language Spoken at Home, and Educational Status: United States 1990.

Educational status	Total	NB, English only	Newcomer and linguistically different			
			Total	NB non-English	FB, English only	FB, non-English
Total	20,876,000	17,455,000	3,421,000	2,102,000	174,000	1,146,000
High school graduates	4,946,000	4,250,000	697,000	426,000	51,000	219,000
Enrolled	14,077,000	11,793,000	2,284,000	1,465,000	105,000	713,000
Years completed:						
Fewer than 5	36,000	30,000	6,000	3,000	*	3,000
5-8	4,209,000	3,618,000	592,000	382,000	25,000	185,000
9-11	9,831,000	8,145,000	1,686,000	1,080,000	80,000	526,000
Not enrolled	1,853,000	1,412,000	441,000	211,000	17,000	213,000
Years completed:						
Fewer than 5	101,000	50,000	52,000	10,000	3,000	38,000
5-8	377,000	249,000	127,000	52,000	4,000	71,000
9-11	1,375,000	1,113,000	262,000	148,000	10,000	104,000

Source: 1990 census of population.

Note: Numbes may not add to totals because of rounding.

NB = native born; FB = foreign born. *Fewer than an estimated 1,000 young people.

institutions at any level than native-born youth. In 1990, 57% of young adult newcomers, compared with 78% of native-born young adults, and 59% of newcomers age 25 and older, compared with 77% of native-born adults, were high school graduates. Three-quarters of newcomer youth age 15 to 19, compared with 81% of native-born youth, were enrolled in educational institutions, including institutions of higher education and other post-secondary institutions (U.S. Bureau of the Census, 1993c, 1993e), as shown in Table 1.5. Adults who speak languages other than English at home, regardless of birthplace, are less likely to be high school graduates than adults who speak only English at home. Sixteen-to-nineteen-year-olds who speak non-English languages at home are more likely to be high school dropouts than their monolingual English peers (U.S. Bureau of the Census, 1995).

As with the information on language usage and English-speaking difficulty, the information on educational participation and attainment, examined by national origin, demonstrates that generalization is mis-

TABLE 1.10. Percentage Distribution of Youth Age 14 to 19 by Nativity, Language Spoken at Home, and Educational Status: United States, 1990.

| | | | | Newcomer and linguistically different | | |
Educational status	Total	NB, English only	Total	NB, non-English	FB, English only	FB, non-English
Total	100.0	100.0	100.0	100.0	100.0	100.0
High school graduates	23.7	24.3	20.4	20.3	29.6	19.1
Enrolled	67.4	67.6	66.8	69.7	60.6	62.3
Percentages of enrollees who have completed:						
Fewer than 5 years	0.3	0.3	0.3	0.2	0.4	0.4
5-8 years	29.9	30.7	25.9	26.0	23.7	25.9
9-11 years	69.8	69.1	73.8	73.7	75.9	73.7
Not enrolled	8.9	8.1	12.9	10.0	9.8	18.6
Percentages of non- enrollees who have completed:						
Fewer than 5 years	5.5	3.5	11.7	5.0	15.9	18.0
5-8 years	20.3	17.7	28.8	24.8	24.3	33.2
9-11 years	74.2	78.8	59.4	70.2	59.8	48.8

SOURCE: 1990 census of population.
NOTE: Percentages may not total 100.0 because of rounding.
NB = native born; FB = foreign born.

leading. As a group, Asians are generally perceived to be successful, graduating from high school and moving on to higher education at higher rates than their proportion in the college-age population, whereas Hispanics are seen to be dropping out and those who graduate enrolling in college at rates lower than their proportion of the population. The reality is that both groups are diverse: within each group, newcomers (both youth and adults) from certain countries fare better than others. They become economically successful sooner and have lower poverty rates.

Consistent with the perception of Asians as valuing education and taking advantage of the available educational opportunities, 15-to-19-year-old Asian newcomers in all groups are enrolled in school at higher rates than native-born Americans, and 16-to-19-year-old speakers of Asian languages, except for speakers of Mon-Khmer and Hmong, are much less likely to have dropped out of school than English monolingual youth (U.S. Bureau of the Census, 1993d, 1993e, 1995). These data are also shown in Tables 1.5 and 1.6.

Some Asian newcomers are very well educated. Adults born in India and Taiwan were three times as likely, and people born in Hong Kong and the Philippines more than twice as likely, to be college graduates as native-born Americans in 1990. College graduates constituted 65% of Indian-born newcomers, 62% of Taiwanese newcomers, and at least two-fifths of those born in Hong Kong and the Philippines. In comparison, one in five native-born adults was a college graduate in 1990 (U.S. Bureau of the Census, 1993c, 1993e).

The information on the educational attainment of people born in Spanish-speaking countries presents a different picture. It reflects to a large extent the characteristics of the dominant group—people born in Mexico and in some of the Central American countries. People from some of the other Spanish-speaking countries, especially the South American countries, are much better educated in general.

About a third of all newcomers age 15 to 19 were born in Mexico, and Mexican-born youth are considerably less likely to be enrolled in school than foreign-born youth as a whole. Mexican-born newcomers are also much less likely to be high school graduates, and a substantial proportion of the adults age 25 and older have very limited schooling. In 1990, both their enrollment rates and their high school graduation rates were the lowest of any of the newcomer groups examined: 56% of 15-to-19-year-old Mexican-born youth were enrolled; 31% of young adults age 18 to 24 and 24% of adults age 25 and older were high school graduates. Nearly three in ten adults born in Mexico had completed fewer than five years of schooling in all. This rate was two and a half times that of foreign-born people as a whole and sixteen times the rate of native-born Americans in 1990 (U.S. Bureau of the Census, 1993c, 1993e).

The educational participation and high school graduation rates of youth born in Peru are higher than those of native-born youth, and the high school graduation rate of Peruvian-born adults exceeds that of native-born adults. Young people born in Colombia, Nicaragua, Ecuador, Cuba, and the Dominican Republic are more likely to be enrolled, and adults born in Colombia and Ecuador are more likely to be high school graduates, than their foreign-born peers in general (U.S. Bureau of the Census, 1993e).

Spanish-speaking adults are less likely to be high school graduates than home speakers of non-English languages as a whole (49% compared with 56%), and 16-to-19-year-olds who speak Spanish at home are more likely not to have completed high school than the average of all home speakers of non-English languages (21% compared with 17%) (U.S. Bureau of the Census, 1995).

Among the newcomers from other countries in which non-English languages are spoken, the 1990 high school graduation rates ranged from 32% of adults age 15 and older born in Portugal to 87% of adults born in Iran and 89% of home speakers of Farsi. The 1990 enrollment rates of youth age 15 to 19 ranged from 74% of those born in Portugal to 91% of those born in Iran. Although the dropout rate of Portuguese-speaking youth is three times that of Farsi-speaking youth, it is still less than the rate of home speakers of non-English languages in general (U.S. Bureau of the Census, 1993e, 1995).

People born in Haiti and home speakers of Haitian Creole are less likely to be high school graduates than foreign-born people or home speakers of non-English languages as a whole (58% and 51% compared with 59% and 56%), but the young people are more likely to be in school and not to be dropouts than native-born or English monolingual youth (U.S. Bureau of the Census, 1993d, 1993e, 1995).

Young people age 15 to 19 born in the English-speaking countries for which data were examined were enrolled at higher rates than native-born youth in their age group in 1990, and older members of these groups exceeded the average foreign-born person in educational attainment. In 1990, better than four out of five of the young people from these countries were enrolled, and the high school graduation rates for adults ranged from 68% of those born in Jamaica to 81% of those born in the United Kingdom (U.S. Bureau of the Census, 1993c, 1993e).

The differences in educational participation and attainment shown for the foreign-born in Table 1.5 reflect the different backgrounds of immigrants from various countries, their reasons for coming to the United States, and their varying immigrant experiences. Educational attainment is closely tied to the economic status of different groups. Some newcomers easily make the transition to life in this country and do well. They may only need additional help with English and recertification in the professions they practiced in their home countries. Their children come to the U.S. literate and educated in their own languages and need only to master English language skills to graduate from high school and go on to higher education. Other newcomers with limited education, and some native-born minorities who are the products of past educational failure, find only low-paying jobs and struggle with English. Their children frequently must leave school to work to supplement the family income. The information on economic status will be examined in the next section.

TABLE 1.11. Estimated Numbers of Youth Age 14 to 19 for Whom Poverty Status Is Determined, and Numbers and Percentages in Poverty by Nativity and Language Spoken at Home: United States, 1990.

			Newcomer and linguistically different			
	Total	*NB, English only*	*Total*	*NB, non-English*	*FB, English only*	*FB, non-English*
Youth for whom poverty status is determined	19,455,000	16,199,000	3,256,000	2,003,000	156,000	1,097,000
Youth in poverty	3,294,000	2,445,000	849,000	467,000	31,000	350,000
Percentage	16.9	15.1	26.1	23.3	20.1	31.9

Source: 1990 census of population.
Notes: Poverty status is not determined for youth living in group quarters and unrelated 14-year-olds. Percentages calculated on unrounded numbers. Numbers may not add to totals because of rounding.

NB = native born; FB = foreign born.

LINGUISTIC DIVERSITY, NATIVITY, AND POVERTY

Newcomer and linguistically different youth, as a group, are more likely to be poor than majority youth; those who are foreign-born and speak languages other than English at home are the most likely to be poor. About 849,000 newcomer and linguistically different youth, among the estimated 3.3 million for whom poverty was determined, were from families with incomes below the poverty level.[5] These included, as shown in Table 1.11, 467,000 native-born home speakers of non-English languages, 31,000 foreign-born English speakers, and 350,000 linguistically different newcomers. Nearly a quarter of the native-born home speakers of non-English languages, one in five English-speaking newcomers, and three in ten foreign-born non-English home speakers were poor. In contrast, only one in seven majority youth was poor.

The averages for the foreign-born as a whole and for home speakers of non-English languages mask considerable differences among the various national origin and language groups that roughly parallel the differences in educational attainment as illustrated in the tables. The groups with the highest educational attainment also have the highest median family incomes and the lowest poverty rates.

The highest median family income in 1989 among the groups examined was that of speakers of Marathi, an Asian Indian language, $62,986. People from Hong Kong, the Philippines, Japan, and Taiwan also had median incomes of at least $45,000. Considerably worse off, although not the lowest in educational attainment, are some of the Southeast Asians, especially Hmong and Mon-Khmer speakers and people born in Cambodia and Laos. They had the lowest median family incomes of all the groups studied and the highest poverty rates.

The family incomes and likelihood of poverty also vary among people born in Spanish-speaking countries but to a lesser extent than among the Asian groups. In 1989, the median family income ranged from under $22,000 for people born in Mexico, Honduras, and El Salvador to $32,007 for people born in Cuba. The poverty rate for individuals born in Spanish-speaking countries ranged from 30% of people born in Mexico and the Dominican Republic to half that for those born in Peru, Cuba, Ecuador, and Colombia (U.S. Bureau of the Census, 1993e).

Among the other groups from countries speaking non-English languages, those born in Germany and Iran have the highest median family incomes. The groups faring less well economically are those born in Haiti and the former Soviet Union: their median family incomes are lower than the average of all the foreign-born, and about a fifth of them are poor (U.S. Bureau of the Census, 1993e, 1995).

All of the newcomers from the English-speaking countries for which data were examined are faring better economically than the foreign born as a whole. Those born in the United Kingdom, Canada, and Guyana had median family incomes which exceeded that of native-born people and only newcomers from Trinidad and Tobago were more likely to be poor than the average native-born person (U.S. Bureau of the Census, 1993c, 1993e).

IMPLICATIONS

The growth of linguistically different populations and the influx of newcomers bringing languages and cultures previously almost unknown in the United States have changed the composition of the school-age population. Already one in every six middle school and high school students speaks a non-English language at home, is a newcomer, or both. There were about 2.3 million of these youth in the schools in 1990 and 441,000 more who were out-of-school non-high-school graduates. Altogether, there were about 3.4 million 14-to-19-year-old newcomer and linguistically different youth in 1990 (see Table 1.9). Because linguistically different and newcomer populations are younger on average than the majority population, the population of newcomer and linguistically different youth will continue to increase faster than the majority population. Even if immigration ceases, this population will grow. The increasing presence of these youth in our midst presents new challenges to school administrators and teacher educators.

First, more teachers must be prepared to teach limited English-proficient (LEP) students. The National Education Goals Panel (1995) reported that 43% of secondary teachers had LEP students in their classes in 1994 and that only half of them had received any training to teach them. Teachers with specific preparation to teach English as a second language should be a part of the language arts staff at every middle or secondary school with LEP students. Moreover, all teachers should have some preparation in ESL techniques to enable them to recognize language problems and modify instruction accordingly.

Second, all teachers should have some preparation in understanding cultural differences and differences in the educational backgrounds of their students. This has always been important for teachers of minority students. It is much more important now that many students come from unfamiliar parts of the world.

Third, schools must do a much better job of identifying and testing linguistically different students. The National Center for Education Statistics (1992) found that teachers failed to recognize many language-minority eighth graders and that they failed to identify for special language services many language-minority students who rated their own English proficiency as low or moderate. Appropriate educational programs to meet the needs of diverse student bodies must begin with identification of all language-minority students for testing in English language proficiency. This will require the training and hiring of evaluators specialized in working with language-minority students.

Fourth, schools must actively enlist parents and other members of the minority communities to help in planning programs and making decisions for their youngsters and to assist teachers and other staff in understanding cultural and other differences. Schools must accommodate the schedules of parents to assure maximum parental involvement.

Fifth, teacher education institutions must make greater efforts to recruit personnel and students from among the linguistically different and newcomer communities. Schools must hire members of these communities to work as paraprofessionals and community liaisons. More importantly, however, educational institutions at all levels must actively seek individuals from these communities to fill professional positions. Staffing must match the diversity of student bodies in the 21st century.

Finally, research beyond demographics is needed to develop profiles of specific newcomer and linguistically different communities to serve as guides for program planning.

The 21st century will offer few opportunities for those with limited education. Newcomers and linguistically different youth have much to offer our country, but only if they have educational opportunities that will enable them to realize their full potential.

NOTES

1. The reader will notice that there are two age groups for the youth of interest: 14–19 and 15–19. This is due to the use of different data sources to compile the information for this chapter. The supplementary information in this chapter comes from published Census sources, which provide data only for 15-to-19-year-olds.

2. Note that some Arabic-speaking youth and Arab newcomers, especially those from North Africa, may be dark-complexioned, but are still defined as "white" in the federally mandated racial/ethnic categories.

3. The number of linguistically different Canadian-born youth was obtained by applying the percentage of the total Canadian-born population reporting that they speak a non-English language at home to the number of youth age 15 to 19 (U.S. Bureau of the Census, 1993g).

4. The extent of delayed education cannot be determined from the 1990 census data because the 1990 question on years of schooling completed did not ask for a separate response for each year completed, and thus year of age cannot be matched with year of schooling completed, as in the past.

5. The poverty level in 1990 was defined as a 1989 average income of $12,674 for a family of four persons. Poverty was not determined for people living in group quarters, including college dormitories, military barracks, and migrant camps; institutionalized people; and unrelated individuals under 15 (U.S. Bureau of the Census, 1993f, pp. B-28–29). To the extent that some of the poorest, predominantly minority youth may have been living in migrant camps on April 1, 1990, and that economically advantaged, predominantly majority 18- and 19-year-olds tended to be in college, the findings in this study may understate the differences in poverty rates among the groups.

REFERENCES

National Center for Education Statistics, U.S. Department of Education. (1992). *Language characteristics and academic achievement: A look at Asian and Hispanic eighth graders in NELS:88,* by Denise Bradby, Jeffrey Owings, and Peggy Quinn. Washington, D.C.: U.S. Government Printing Office.

National Education Goals Panel. (1995). *Data for the National Education Goals report, Volume One: National data.* Washington, D.C.: U.S. Government Printing Office.

Undercount or overcount? Census Bureau announces preliminary findings from follow-up studies. (1991). *Numbers and Needs.* May–June, 1(2).

U.S. Bureau of the Census. (1984). *1980 census of population, detailed population characteristics, United States summary.* Washington, D.C.: U.S. Government Printing Office.

U.S. Bureau of the Census. (1993a). *The foreign-born population in the United States: 1990, by Susan J. Lapham* (CPH-L-98). Washington, D.C.: Author.

U.S. Bureau of the Census. (1993b). *Language spoken at home and ability to speak English for the United States, regions and states: 1990* (CPH-L-133). Washington, D.C.: Author.

U.S. Bureau of the Census. (1993c). *1990 census of population, ancestry of the population in the United States.* Washington, D.C.: U.S. Government Printing Office.

U.S. Bureau of the Census. (1993d). *1990 census of population, Asians and Pacific Islanders in the United States.* Washington, D.C.: U.S. Government Printing Office.

U.S. Bureau of the Census. (1993e). *1990 census of population, the foreign-born population in the United States.* Washington, D.C.: U.S. Government Printing Office.

U.S. Bureau of the Census. (1993f). *1990 census of population and housing, public use microdata samples, United States.* Washington, D.C.: Author.

U.S. Bureau of the Census. (1993g). *1990, profiles of the foreign-born population, selected characteristics by place of birth, by Susan J. Lapham* (CPH-L-148). Washington, D.C.: Author.

U.S. Bureau of the Census. (1995). *1990 census of population and housing, detailed cross-tabulations of selected language groups for states: 1990* [CD-ROM]. Washington, D.C.: Author.

U.S. Bureau of the Census. (1996). *Population projections of the United States by age, sex, race, and Hispanic origin: 1995 to 2050,* by Jennifer Cheeseman (Current Population Reports, P25-1130). Washington, D.C.: U.S. Government Printing Office.

CHAPTER 2

THE ESL LEARNING ENVIRONMENT IN SECONDARY SCHOOL

Linda Harklau

UNIVERSITY OF GEORGIA

Those wishing to characterize the nature of language acquisition and content learning in secondary schools face unique challenges. Unlike students in college-level intensive English programs or elementary school, adolescent language learners in America's high schools are likely to be in several different classroom settings with several different teachers every day. Moreover, while most studies have focused on classrooms where language learning is the specific focus of instruction, high school classes geared specifically to language learners—such as ESL—usually account for only a portion of the learners' day. They spend just as much or more of their time in mainstream content-area classrooms. Because of the compartmentalized nature of high school instruction, mainstream instruction itself is quite diverse, spanning different subject matter specializations, different expectations for participation structures and literate behaviors, and different levels of academic expectations.

This chapter provides an overview of language learners' experiences with American high schools, and the language learning opportunities they afford. I argue that high schools can best be understood as a series of instructional niches that students traverse over the course of a school day. Each of these niches carries certain assumptions and expectations for student performance, and each provides a unique linguistic and academic environment in which to learn language and content-area concepts. At the same time, most educators, including ESL instructors, work in only one of these environments, and may have little opportunity to see how what they do in their classroom compares with the other instructional experiences students have over the course of a school day. Thus, if one is to gain an overall sense of the nature of second language acquisition in a high school, it is necessary to draw explicit comparisons among these environments.

The discussion in this chapter draws upon data collected in a three-and-a-half-year ethnography of second language learning in high school (Harklau, 1994a, 1994b, 1994c). The study took place at a suburban, racially and ethnically diverse northern California high school where limited English proficient students constituted fewer than 100 of the 1,600 students. Like many U.S. high schools outside the urban centers where large language minority enrollments have long been the norm, Gateview High School was experiencing recent growth in its language minority and Limited English Proficient (LEP) population. Gateview's[1] response, not atypical in these settings, was to develop an unintegrated ESL curriculum supplemental to an unaltered mainstream curriculum. One teacher, Maureen Carson, was given sole responsibility for transforming these students into proficient English speakers capable of functioning in mainstream classrooms at the school.

The study focused on the sizable Chinese American immigrant student community at Gateview, featuring in-depth case studies of four students from Taiwan and Hong Kong who had immigrated to the United States after attending elementary schools in their native countries. Like other LEP students at the school, they were placed in one of three levels of ESL on the basis of oral proficiency test scores when they first entered Gateview. Students in ESL 1 and 2 were usually also enrolled in a social studies course designed specifically for ESL students. Within 2 to 3 years, most students progressed out of the ESL course sequence and into full-time mainstream coursework. I traced students' paths through this transition, observing their ESL and mainstream classes, interviewing them about their language learning experiences, talking with their teachers, and collecting their schoolwork.

In this chapter, instructional environments and implications for learners of the school language are compared in two ways. In the first section, I compare the experiences of learners in ESL and mainstream classroom environments. This examination extends not only to the spoken interactional patterns that have been emphasized in classroom research on second language acquisition, but also to the vital role of written language as a means of interaction and subject matter learning in high school classroom contexts. I also compare instructional goals and curricula, and consider the nature of peer relationships in ESL and "regular" classes.

The second section explores the role of ability grouping, or "tracking," in creating different instructional environments and different linguistic opportunities for learners within mainstream instruction. Dominant themes in the current debate around tracking and ability grouping are reviewed, and particular implications for language-minority students are discussed. I examine how opportunities for speaking and writing English differ in high- and low-track classrooms, and how these differences affect students' preparation to pursue further educational and occupational goals after high school. Differences in interactional patterns with native English-speaking peers are also related to track levels.

ESL AND MAINSTREAM CLASSES

Many studies have explored the nature of mainstream high school classroom activities and the participation structures they engender (Applebee with Auten, 1981; Boyer, 1983; Goodlad, 1984; Sirotnik, 1983; Sizer, 1984). These studies show that there is an abundance of teacher talk in high school classrooms.

Spoken Language Use

Much of the mainstream classroom time at Gateview was taken up in teacher-led presentations followed by some discussion. Such discussions often seemed to be equal parts lecture and initiation-reply-evaluation (or "IRE"; see Mehan, 1979), with the teacher controlling the conversation and soliciting student responses only as a means of assessing comprehension. This pattern was especially prevalent in math classes, where much of class time focused around teacher lectures on concepts in the course text and teacher demonstration of problem-solving. It was less frequent, although still the predominant participation structure, in English and social studies classes, where it often took the form of review and discussion of reading assignments. Teacher-led discussions can provide English learners with a plentiful source of input from a native speaker. It is good input in the sense that students are highly motivated to listen to and understand it, since it relays content-area concepts that they need to know. In this sense, it serves an authentic communicative purpose (Krashen, 1981). However, because the majority of their audience is native English-speaking, teachers tend not to make the adjustments in input that they might if they were speaking exclusively with non-native speakers; for example, reducing the speed or complexity of talk; increasing repetition and pausing; or contextualizing abstract concepts through the use of nonverbal cues such as pictures, demonstrations, or gestures

(Chaudron, 1988; Hatch, 1983; Wong Fillmore, 1985). In addition, some teachers' talk contained features such as puns or asides that made it even more difficult for non-native-speaking learners to understand.

As a result, a great deal of the teacher-generated input in mainstream classes at Gateview was incomprehensible to learners and caused them considerable frustration. One ESL student remarked, "Like, sometimes I know I won't understand, so I just don't listen to him [the teacher]." In addition, research suggests that first-language socialization patterns of some English learners render teacher-directed participation structures relatively ineffective as a means of engaging students in learning (Heath, 1986; Trueba, Guthrie, & Au, 1981; Wong Fillmore, 1985).

What about opportunities for "output" (Swain, 1985), for students to negotiate meaning through spoken discourse in these classrooms? Such opportunities were hampered by the large size of mainstream high school classes, which gave learners only a 1 in 25 or 1 in 30 chance of being designated by the teacher to speak (Knott, 1987). Learner participation tended to be further limited by teachers' fears of embarrassing non-native speakers by calling on them when they were not prepared to speak, and by learners' own apprehensions about their competence as English speakers. One student commented, for example, "I don't like to talk because of lack of confident [*sic*]." Even when opportunities for output came students' way, much of the student talk in teacher-directed discussions was expected to take the form of word- or phrase-level responses to display questions from the teacher, rather than authentic negotiation of meaning.

Student-led or student-generated discussion activities offered greater potential for learner output. These activities were most likely to occur in English and social studies classes, where they took forms such as peer-editing compositions or preparing for a team debate. Overall, however, they were relatively rare at Gateview and have been reported to constitute an average of only 5% of class time in high schools (Applebee with Auten, 1981). Taken together, it is perhaps not surprising that in 12 days of observing these students through entire school days, I noted that they interacted with teachers on the average of once a day in mainstream classes. One teacher told me he wasn't even sure he would recognize the voice of an ESL student in his class.

In ESL classes, on the other hand, opportunities for spoken language interaction and use were specifically tailored to learners. Maureen Carson arranged the desks in a semicircle in the middle of the room. Sitting at the open end of the semicircle with a board propped up on a chair next to her, Carson scanned students' faces as she spoke and made adjustments in input as necessary. ESL classes also provided students with considerably more opportunities for spoken language output than their mainstream classes. Students agreed that they spoke the most in ESL. As one student said, "And here [ESL class], I dare to talk more, and gradually I will rather ask more question." Carson frequently asked open-ended questions and modeled a response before asking students to respond (e.g., "If you had to think of one picture from the eighties that you would remember, what would it be? Mine would be . . ."). Rather than allowing the loudest or most persistent students to do most of the talking, as frequently happened in mainstream classes, Carson called upon every student in her classes several times over the course of a class. Smaller class sizes and students' greater comfort in speaking in front of fellow non-native speakers facilitated discussions. Unlike mainstream classes, where ESL students seemed cowed and rarely spoke, students in the ESL classes engaged in extended interactions about everything from how fax machines work to why Truman authorized the use of atom bombs.

Written Language Use

Research on second language acquisition in classroom settings evidences a pervasive and often implicit bias toward spoken language and interaction. The origins of this bias may be traced in part to the primacy of speech in the structuralist and subsequent Chomskyan traditions in American linguistics, and in part to reaction against the predominantly written format of grammar translation in language pedagogy. The pervasiveness of this bias may not be fully appreciated until one encounters the contexts of North American public schools, which carry an equally pervasive bias toward written forms of communication. Second language researchers in these contexts have shown written language to be integral to academic learning (Adamson, 1993; Cummins & Swain, 1986; Saville-Troike, 1984).

Since most high school students are presumed to be literate, and since written media are an efficient means of communicating information, virtually every activity in high school classrooms involves literacy. One distinct advantage of the written mode as input for non-native speakers is that unlike spoken language, print is reviewable. It allows students to adjust the input to their own pace and proficiency level. Students at Gateview, for example, often relied heavily on textbooks and verbatim notes from the board to help them to "decode" what the teacher said in class. For example, one student described how she studied:

> Like when the test comes, so I just, like, open my book and read through all the pages . . . when the class, I copy down all the notes and the homework,

so when I don't understand, I just [take] my books [home] to solve it by myself.

Print is also a rich source of academic and technical vocabulary (e.g., "kinetic energy," "molecule," "tangent," "acquiesce," "culminate," "complacent," "augment") that learners must acquire in order to function in content-area classrooms.

Literacy events in American high school classrooms, however, vary considerably in extent and authenticity of interactions with print. Reading materials at Gateview, for example, ranged from literary and news sources (e.g., novels such as Fitzgerald's *The Great Gatsby,* short stories such as Wright's "The Rockpile," and magazine and newspaper articles) and textbooks (e.g., biology, chemistry, and math texts) to mechanical worksheets (e.g., identifying and correcting run-on sentences, matching vocabulary to definitions). Likewise, activities including writing varied from literary and social analysis (e.g., how Hardy's *Tess of the d'Urbervilles* reflects contemporary social values, how the U.S. might reduce the trade deficit) to fill-in-the-blank, multiple-choice, and other discrete item formats (e.g., biology tests, word root worksheets, short-answer exercises at the end of history textbook chapters). While every subject area made use of such discrete item activities to some extent, they were most prevalent in math courses, where solving assigned problems from the text and copying notes from the board were often students' sole experiences with print. Not surprisingly, students' most extensive and meaningful interaction with writing in content-area classrooms came in English and social studies. Even when work was intended to engage students in meaningful activities, however, ESL learners often developed academic survival strategies that turned such tasks into rote memorization and repetition of material. For example, when one student was asked to generate original sentences for vocabulary words, he simply copied sentences from his bilingual dictionary. In other cases, teachers' efforts to teach note-taking skills became exercises in verbatim copying from the board.

Because ESL teachers tend to have wide latitude in terms of curriculum and methodology, it is more difficult to draw generalizations about the uses of writing in their classrooms. At Gateview, for example, Carson and her successor, Mrs. Malone, evidenced quite different orientations to reading and writing in the ESL curriculum. Carson, drawing on a background in English, social studies, and gifted instruction, was inclined to teach language through English literature and history. Accordingly, she emphasized extensive reading of both authentic and abridged literary sources (e.g., *The Count of Monte Cristo, The Secret Garden,* "The Devil and Daniel Webster"), global and American history texts, and newspaper and magazine articles. Students wrote on a variety of topics, including autobiography, fairy tales, research papers incorporating source materials, and essays in which they were expected to demonstrate an understanding of readings and use them to formulate and defend their own opinions. As one counselor observed, "She makes a situation a seed bed, where opinionation can grow. That's what she likes to foster." Carson was aware that students could often get by copying material that they did not fully understand in mainstream classes. When students did the same in ESL, she called their bluff, asking them to explain concepts in their own words. As she warned one new student, "Jane, you're new here, but what we do is, we never write down words we don't understand."

The curricula and goals of Malone's classes reflected a different theoretical orientation to second language literacy instruction. She emphasized language fluency and comfort with using the interpersonal linguistic competence students had already acquired. As she put it, she felt her goal was to "get some of the soul of the language into them." As a result, she tended to focus on productive use of basic vocabulary and structure in written work through activities such as poetry and expressive writing (e.g., love poems for Valentine's Day, essays on "my friend").

Explicit Focus on Linguistic Form

Explicit instruction and feedback in the dynamics of English grammar and usage were quite rare in mainstream classrooms at Gateview. Since the ESL students seldom spoke and were surrounded by competent speakers of English, there was no appropriate occasion for content-area teachers to provide ESL students with feedback on pronunciation or grammar in spoken interaction. In ESL classes, on the other hand, Carson and Malone not only organized their classes so that students spoke frequently, but they also built in evaluations of *how* students said things: asking them explicitly to speak more loudly, more clearly, or to maintain eye contact while speaking. They corrected pronunciation when necessary, and used poetry to develop students' sense of English cadence and rhythm. ESL classes included dictations to hone listening skills, sometimes focusing on homonyms or contrasting vowel sounds. Class activities were sometimes audio- or videotaped so that students could evaluate their own language performance. Even though an aide reported that they sometimes winced as they heard or saw themselves on tape, ESL students nevertheless seemed to appreciate the feedback provided by tapes.

Feedback on learners' written language differed considerably in mainstream and ESL classrooms as well. In mainstream classes, explicit grammar instruction took place exclusively in English. Its purpose was to formalize and label intuitions that students were already expected to possess as native speakers of English. As such, it did not provide the sorts of grammatical rules and principles that non-native speakers might rely on in lieu of those intuitions. For example, one class exercise focused on correct apostrophe placement in "possessive nouns" (*brother's shoes*), "contractions" (*they're, can't*), and "possessive pronouns" (*its*). The exercise was accompanied by a few cursory sentence examples, and no explanation was offered for how these items differ in function or usage. Another class focused on sentence fragments and run-ons, errors that native language writers make in greater proportion than non-native language writers (Raimes, 1979; Silva, 1993).

Mainstream teachers at Gateview were not trained in meeting the special linguistic needs of second language learners, and some commented that they were uncertain how best to give non-native language writers feedback. Students' work showed that many teachers ignored errors completely. Others marked errors inconsistently, randomly correcting an article error in one line, word choice in the next, and complementation in the third. Vocabulary and word choice were particular problem areas for non-native language writers in mainstream classes. Since most of learners' vocabulary was assimilated through high school–level reading material and vocabulary exercises, their vocabulary tended to have an academic flavor—they were more likely to know the word "silhouette" than "shadow," "timorous" than "shy." The bilingual dictionaries to which students often resorted gave them little information regarding the particular connotations or usage associated with the words they learned. As a result, language learners at Gateview made frequent errors in word choice. One student, for example, pretending she was Hamlet writing to his mother, wrote, "I wish you hadn't *spared* my birth." Another, in a vocabulary exercise, wrote, "In the *transient* time, the weather changed from the sunny sky to the rainny [*sic*] sky." Mainstream teachers often assumed, incorrectly, that simply marking the word or putting a question mark next to it would be enough for students to edit such errors by ear.

As one might expect, ESL classes provided instruction that was tailored to meet ESL students' special needs as readers and writers. Mrs. Carson kept a store of both bilingual and learner dictionaries readily accessible to students. She provided explicit instruction on reading skills and strategies, such as guessing the meaning of words from context ("What do you think the word 'discrepancy' means in that sentence?"), focusing students' attention on how implicit meanings are conveyed in texts ("On page 115 I see two indicators of nervousness"), and predicting content by looking at subject headings, maps, and pictures. When giving feedback on compositions, Carson marked grammatical errors on ar-

ticles, prepositions, and verb tenses, as well as mechanical errors such
as faulty spelling. Carson also included proofreading and peer-editing
exercises. Worksheets and tests incorporated language as a criterion
("Write five good sentences about . . .").

Peer Interaction and Socialization

Many in the general public as well as many educators in American public
schools hold a folk belief that ESL students will learn English simply by
surrounding them with native English-speaking peers. The underlying
premise is that ESL students will inevitably interact with and learn from
peers. At Gateview, however, the reticence of Chinese American immigrant students in interactions with mainstream teachers extended to their
peers as well. While talk occurred between learners and native English-
speaking peers during class, it was generally initiated by the native
speaker and seldom lasted over more than three or four turns. Almost all
peer talk between learners and native speaker peers was on school topics;
there was little social chatter in these exchanges.

Learners perceived a social wall between themselves and American-
born peers. They felt that their language ability and immigrant background profoundly affected their social lives. One student wrote of her
frustration with self-expression in English:

> I have no way to project, reveal my persona. Speech is an important part of
> a person's image. All ESL kids when they first come to this country their im-
> age become: "The foreign students" and that's their persona, all the rest are
> not revealed, are forgotten. For me I cannot stand not to be able to say
> things I want to say.

Another remarked on the lack of common cultural ground to serve as a
basis for social interaction:

> Like, if you talk to an American, a girl from America, I don't know what we
> can talk about, because they have their life, is different from me.

So even though they were surrounded by native speakers most of the day,
ESL students seldom found interactions with these peers easy or comfortable.

Although students spoke of ESL as just another school subject, it
played a vital role in their social adjustment in American schools and
society as well. The ESL room was a haven for non-native speakers, where
they could be among peers who understood the immigrant experience,

what they had left behind and what they were going through at home and at school. It was a retreat from the overwhelming monolingual environment of the mainstream, a place where students' multiple linguistic and cultural affiliations were understood and appreciated. Mrs. Carson and the aides provided the assistance that newcomers sometimes needed in negotiating the American schooling system and life in the U.S. more generally. They were counselors, social workers, confidantes, tutors, and mentors, dealing with everything from school paperwork to changing students' course placements, to stopping an illegal chain letter circulating among students, to straightening out a student's draft registration, to filling out college admission and financial aid forms, to monitoring and reporting student abuse or abandonment at home. Blackboards and walls in the ESL room were covered with information about the school calendar, test dates, and other events that mainstream students were generally assumed to know. Carson also kept students informed about extracurricular activities in the school. ESL thus provided a vital link in students' adjustment to American high schools and in developing a support system and peer network.

In sum, then, ESL and mainstream classrooms differed considerably as contexts for second language acquisition. They operated under different assumptions about appropriate curricula and student needs, and they invited different patterns of student behavior and patterns of language use.

INSTRUCTIONAL NICHES CREATED BY TRACKING

Tracking is a major force in the differentiation of linguistic and academic environments encountered by adolescent language learners in American high schools. Tracking is a form of ability grouping, the process through which schools separate students into groups based on perceived differences in ability and needs, and apply different curricula to those groups. While ability grouping begins in the early levels of the educational system through practices such as reading groups, tracking at the high school level formalizes and institutionalizes this process, separating students into completely different classrooms where they often work with completely different teachers and curricula.

Language-minority students are adversely affected by ability grouping practices in American schools. Researchers (Braddock, 1990; Medina, 1988; Mehan, Hubbard, & Villaneuva, 1994) have noted that language-minority students are overrepresented in the low rungs of the system. Cummins (Cummins & Swain, 1986) has noted that limited English pro-

ficiency is often confounded with a lack of academic and intellectual ability. At Gateview, ESL students were often placed in low-track mainstream
classes out of an apprehension that their language proficiency was not
sufficient to compete in high-track courses (Harklau, 1994b, 1994c).
However, such placements carry with them potential long-term consequences for the linguistic and academic environments in which ESL students will learn, and for the literate practices into which they are socialized.

In recent years, a number of studies have documented significant
differences in the curriculum, activities, and participation structures of
high- and low-track classes (cf. Gamoran, Nystrand, Berends, & LePore,
1995; Oakes, 1985; Oakes, Gamoran, & Page, 1992; Page, 1991), differences in evidence at Gateview. Classes differed, first and most fundamen-
tally, in terms of on-task time and the work students were expected to
complete. One student, for example, reported that in her low-track biology class the teacher planned instruction for only three of five days per
week. The other two days, she reported, ". . . we can do anything we want.
And no homework." The following year, the same student observed that
in her low-track English class,

> . . . we don't have to do homework. . . And sometimes we just talk for the
> whole period. . . . not about English. It's about the outside of students. It's
> about where they work, they get upset, all this stuff about the students.

In high-track classes, on the other hand, students were not only assigned
more work, but were often expected to find and prepare additional material independently for class projects such as a debate on economic policy
or a mock trial of a historical character. Discussion in these classes rarely
veered off of the instructional agenda at hand. Overall, then, ESL students in high-track classes had more copious linguistic interaction with
academic, content-area material.

Workload and expectations for achievement were not the only dimensions on which high- and low-track classrooms differed. Substantial
differences existed in the quality of spoken and written language interactional opportunities available to ESL students as well. In terms of spoken
language, high- and low-track classes differed in the level of student participation that was allowed or encouraged. Students in high-track classes
tended to share the teacher's instructional agenda. Because teachers were
generally confident that student-led activities would further their agenda,
what few student-directed activities there were in mainstream classrooms
tended to occur in high-track classrooms. Such activities provided rich
potential for ESL students to engage in extended interactions on aca-

demic topics of mutual interest. In fact, high-track teachers encouraged ESL students to speak up more in class, making comments such as, "You really should have participated a lot more during the hearings (ask more questions)."

Students in low-track classes, on the other hand, were likely to be ambivalent about schooling and sometimes resistant to the classroom agenda. Their ambivalence can be understood as the product of the mutually constitutive forces of the school's successive negative evaluations of their ability, and their simultaneous internalization and rejection of those evaluations and the schooling system (Collins, 1988; McDermott, 1977; Page, 1991). Low-track students' "uncertain engagement with schooling" (Page, 1990) manifested itself in resistance and challenges to the teacher's agenda. Students at Gateview, for example, might be sullen and unresponsive: arriving late for class, slouching back in their seats, doodling, inattentive. Alternately, they could be disruptive. For example, in one particularly memorable English class I observed, two ESL students looked on as their classmates shouted over the teacher and then, tapping on their desks, broke into choral song.

Low-track students' resistance and ambivalence about schooling exercised profound effects on opportunities for learners to speak in the classroom. Teachers tended to structure class activities in ways that limited student participation. Wary of discussions that could quickly become off-topic or adversarial, teachers tended to avoid open-ended questions about the material at hand, asking questions that called only for short-word or phrase responses. ESL students' reticence was regarded as orderly behavior and evaluated positively. Low-track students often intimidated ESL students, who complained that their peers were too noisy. In addition, American-born low-track students were much more likely than their high-track counterparts to be overtly hostile toward ESL students. As a result, low-track classes tended to heighten ESL students' social isolation and limit their opportunities to engage in spoken interaction.

Substantially different literate behaviors are rewarded in high- and low-track classrooms (Gamoran et al., 1995; Oakes, 1985; Oakes et al., 1992). For low-track students, reading tended to consist exclusively of textbooks in which language was abridged and excerpted into texts rarely more than a few pages in length. The principle underlying these texts was to render reading shorter and "conceptually simplified" (Gamoran & Berends, 1987), and thus easier to comprehend. However, by extracting readings from authentic contexts—for example, one chapter from the middle of Frederick Douglass's autobiography—textbooks arguably make comprehension more difficult (Knott, 1987) and place increased emphasis on mechanical skills such as sight-reading and vocabulary (Goodman,

Shannon, Freeman, & Murphy, 1987; Tierney, 1990). Accompanying multiple-choice and fill-in-the-blank exercises in textbooks and workbooks further reinforced reading as the transmission of discrete portions of knowledge. High-track students, on the other hand, were more likely to be assigned extensive reading from authentic sources such as novels (e.g., *The Great Gatsby,* Morrison's *Sula*), poetry, and short stories in English; and newsmagazine articles and biographies in social studies. While high-track classes made use of some discrete point exercises as well (most typically, vocabulary study), students were also asked to synthesize, analyze, and interpret reading material.

Extended writing was rare in low-track classrooms at Gateview. When it occurred, it seldom went beyond requests to recount factual information or to write about personal experience in a journal. Pre-writing activities such as class discussion or brainstorming were infrequent. In terms of teacher response, one student's low-track social studies teacher stamped his work "CHECKED" plus the date, checked or crossed off incorrect items, and wrote a grade. His English teacher, he reported, never asked him to revise his work, and generally encouraged him to "be as brief as possible. Don't write, like, too long sentence. [*sic*]" ESL students in high-track classes, on the other hand, had a number of opportunities to write at length, grappling with discourse features such as appropriate tense usage, cohesive devices, and organization. One student noted that while her low-track writing assignments had allowed her to simply locate answers and repeat them (sometimes with the exact wording) in her work, her Advanced Placement English class demanded that she have a fundamental understanding of the text so that she could synthesize the information. High-track teachers responded not only to the technical details of students' writing, but also to students' ideas and how they were organized and presented; e.g., "Explain more fully in the analysis section" or "Do you expect this trend to continue? Why?" Students were often expected to incorporate feedback into a subsequent draft.

Of course, while for the purposes of this discussion I have focused on the extremes of tracking, it must be acknowledged that tracking does not create the neat dichotomy depicted here, but rather a messy and inexact continuum. Some low-track teachers fostered extensive and authentic interactions with texts, and some high-track teachers taught largely through rote memorization of discrete information. Overall, however, the patterns described here are widespread not only at Gateview, but at secondary schools nationwide (Oakes, 1985).

From this discussion, it is clear that tracking creates variant experiences for ESL students in high school classrooms. Track assignment has considerable implications not only for ESL students' academic environment but also, because classroom language and academic learning are tightly interwoven in American high school contexts, for their language acquisition as well. Instruction in low-track classes socializes ESL students into language behaviors and practices that are not only different from those in high tracks, but also differentially valued and rewarded in the educational system beyond high school. Thus, low-track academic training may effectively limit language-minority students' access to future educational and occupational goals. Because of the tracking system, school personnel are left with a difficult decision, to either place ESL students in academically limiting low-track classes that nonetheless offer greatest chance of school success, or to place them in high-track classes that will offer education in more valued linguistic and academic skills, but that also carry considerable risk that ESL students will not be able to compete with native English speaking peers (see Harklau, 1994b, for the dynamics of this process). Neither option is entirely appropriate, and the system forces school personnel to confound language proficiency with purported academic ability.

ESL students' language proficiency continues to grow over the course of schooling. Yet, the nature of academic and linguistic socialization in low-track classes does not easily articulate with what is valued in higher tracks, and the dynamics of the system make it unlikely for students to move upward once placed. Thus, low-track placements, at first a pragmatic and ostensibly temporary solution to students' limited English proficiency and ability to compete, easily lead to low-track placement throughout their high school careers.

RECOMMENDATIONS

This discussion relies on examples from one high school to exemplify the linguistic environment provided to second language learners in American high schools, and high schools of course vary widely in program structure and student population. Furthermore, as we have seen, even within Gateview, learners experience a series of widely differing linguistic and academic niches over the course of a school day. In ESL classrooms, they experience plentiful opportunities for spoken interaction, explicit focus on language form, assistance with negotiating American schooling, and immigrant peer social support. They spend more of their time in mainstream classes, where spoken interaction with teachers is limited, and linguistic and cultural dynamics work for the most part against extended interaction with native English-speaking peers as well. Students experience copious interactions with print, but those interactions may nonetheless be limited by a lack of attention to the specific instructional needs of second language learners.

Mainstream classrooms are further differentiated in activities and participation structures by subject area and more significantly by ability grouping. The tracking system in place at most American high schools results in varying opportunities for student participation and speaking, for authentic and extensive interactions with print, and for peer interaction. Given such broad variation across and within high school instructional environments, what general statements can be made about improving the overall quality of adolescents' experiences with language and academic concept learning?

One recommendation concerns communication between ESL and mainstream educators. Because of the compartmentalization of instruction that already exists in high schools, it is perhaps easiest for schools to think of ESL as one more subject area to be affixed to students' schedules until they can function in mainstream classrooms. Nonetheless, the experiences of Gateview ESL students reveal the weaknesses of such a system—little support for students' special linguistic needs outside the confines of ESL classrooms, little recognition of fostering of linguistic and ethnic diversity in the school at large, and a strong tendency to confound bilingualism with academic deficiency. These weaknesses are especially significant given that students' stay in ESL is relatively brief, and the majority of their time as language learners is spent in mainstream classrooms.

The education of language learners in high schools is enhanced by coordination of efforts among mainstream and ESL educators, with all taking responsibility for students' linguistic and academic learning in their classrooms. Coordination demands considerably more than a one-day workshop on teaching LEP students, however. It requires strong administrative support for recognizing and including language-minority students' perspectives in the life of the school and promoting ethnic and linguistic diversity (e.g., multilingual school literary publications, multiethnic English and social studies curricula, bilingual and bicultural teachers who can serve as role models) (Lucas, Henze, & Donato, 1990). Administrators also need to provide appropriate ongoing training and support and, above all, time for ESL and mainstream educators to collaborate. Content-area teachers must be encouraged to develop realistic understandings of the purpose and scope of ESL instruction. On their part, ESL teachers at the high school level need to be informed about curricula in subject areas if they are to support content-area learning while developing language skills (Short, 1991; see also Chapter 5).

This examination of the multiple linguistic environments of high school classrooms has also shown the particularly deleterious and far-reaching effects of tracking on the educational opportunities for adolescents learning English in American high schools. Recent efforts to "un-track" high schools hold particular potential to make high school class-rooms more inclusive and welcoming for language-minority students, and to make their educational experiences more equitable. Proponents of "untracking" have suggested that heterogeneous grouping in classrooms creates learning environments that are as good or better for many students as tracked classes (Goodlad, 1984; Goodlad & Oakes, 1988; Oakes, 1986; Wheelock, 1992). They caution, however, that untracking must consist of more than simply mixing ability groups. To be effective, it demands fundamental shifts in the curriculum, philosophy, and goals of instruction. Changes suggested by advocates of untracking are in many ways compatible with ESL student needs in mainstream classrooms: increased use of cooperative learning techniques (McGroarty, 1992; Sagan, 1986) and other forms of student-directed group work; curricula organized around central concepts or themes, and linked to hands-on activities (Wheelock, 1992) and real-life experiences of students (Goodlad & Oakes, 1988); authentic, individualized forms of assessment (Chapter 7, this volume; Goodlad & Oakes, 1988; Oakes, 1986); modeling tasks (Cone, 1991); and collaborative teams of teachers who work together to plan and implement instruction for a cluster of students within the school (Wheelock, 1992).

At the same time, it must be acknowledged that such changes are not in themselves panaceas, and their effects on ESL student instruction are not self-evident. The potential of current efforts to restructure schools, which include not only untracking but also site-based management and increased integration across subject areas, is dependent on the level of awareness and understanding of language-minority students' educational needs that is present in the faculty and administrators making those changes (Jones, 1993). Undertaken by those who operate under the folk belief that language-minority students will learn best when "submersed" in mainstream classrooms without ESL or bilingual instructional support, restructuring efforts can erode the safeguards that ensure that special assistance is provided to language-minority students (Miramontes, 1993). Thus, ESL educators in schools undergoing such changes need to ensure that colleagues are educated about the nature of second language learning and about the legal and ethical rights of language-minority students. When implemented thoughtfully by schools that are educated about the needs of language learners, restructuring efforts hold great promise for changing American high schools in ways that will offer linguistic-minority adolescents significantly enriched contexts in which to learn the language of American schooling and the academic concepts communicated through it.

NOTE

1. All names are pseudonyms.

REFERENCES

Adamson, H. D. (1993). *Academic competence: Theory and classroom practice: Preparing ESL students for content courses.* White Plains, NY: Longman.

Applebee, A. N., with Auten, A. (1981). *Writing in the secondary school: English and the content areas.* Urbana, IL: National Council of Teachers of English.

Boyer, E. L. (1983). *High school: A report on secondary education in America.* New York: Harper & Row.

Braddock, J. H. (1990). *Tracking: Implications for student race-ethnic subgroups* (No. 1). Baltimore, MD: Center for Research on Effective Schooling for Disadvantaged Students, Johns Hopkins University. (ERIC Document Reproduction Service No. ED 325 600)

Chaudron, C. (1988). *Second language classrooms: Research on teaching and learning.* New York: Cambridge University Press.

Collins, J. (1988). Language and class in minority education. *Anthropology and Education Quarterly, 19*(4), 299–326.

Cone, J. R. (1991). Untracking advanced placement English: Creating opportunity is not enough. *Phi Delta Kappan, 712–717.*

Cummins, J., & Swain, M. (1986). *Bilingualism in education: Aspects of theory, research, and practice.* New York: Longman.

Gamoran, A., & Berends, M. (1987). The effects of stratification in secondary schools: Synthesis of survey and ethnographic research. *Review of Educational Research, 57*(4), 415–435.

Gamoran, A., Nystrand, M., Berends, M., & LePore, P. C. (1995). An organizational analysis of the effects of ability grouping. *American Educational Research Journal, 32*(4), 687–715.

Goodlad, J. I. (1984). *A place called school: Prospects for the future.* New York: McGraw-Hill.

Goodlad, J. I., & Oakes, J. (1988). We must offer equal access to knowledge. *Educational Leadership, 45*(5), 1622.

Goodman, R. S., Shannon, P., Freeman, Y., & Murphy, S. (1987). *Report card on basal readers.* Katonah, NY: Richard C. Owen Publishers.

Harklau, L. (1994a). ESL and mainstream classes: Contrasting second language learning contexts. *TESOL Quarterly, 28*(2), 241–272.

Harklau, L. A. (1994b). Jumping tracks: How language-minority students negotiate evaluations of ability. *Anthropology and Education Quarterly, 25*(3), 347–363.

Harklau, L. A. (1994c). Tracking and linguistic minority students: Consequences of ability grouping for second language learners. *Linguistics and Education, 6,* 221–248.

Hatch, E. M. (1983). *Psycholinguistics: A second language perspective.* Rowley, MA: Newbury House.

Heath, S. B. (1986). Sociocultural contexts of language development. In California State Department of Education, Bilingual Education Office (Ed.), *Beyond language: Social and cultural factors in schooling language minority students* (pp. 143–186). Los Angeles: California State University, Evaluation, Dissemination and Assessment Center.

Jones, T. G. (1993). The connection between urban school reform and urban student populations: How are urban school reform efforts addressing the needs of language minority students? *Journal of Educational Issues of Language Minority Students, 12* (Special issue), 61–75.

Kagan, S. (1986). Cooperative learning and sociocultural factors in schooling. In California State Department of Education (Ed.), *Beyond language: Social and cultural factors in schooling language minority students.* Los Angeles: California State University, Evaluation, Dissemination, and Assessment Center.

Knott, G. (1987). Literacy instruction in secondary school classroom contexts. In D. Bloome (Ed.), *Literacy and schooling* (pp. 354–371). Norwood, NJ: Ablex.

Lucas, T., Henze, R., & Donato, R. (1990). Promoting the success of Latino language-minority students: An exploratory study of six high schools. *Harvard Educational Review, 60*(3), 315–340.

McDermott, R. P. (1977). Social relations as contexts for learning in school. *Harvard Educational Review, 47*(2), 198–213.

McGroarty, M. (1992). Cooperative learning: The benefits for content-area teaching. In P. A. Richard-Amato & M. A. Snow (Eds.), *The Multicultural classroom: Readings for content- area teachers* (pp. 58–69). New York: Longman.

Medina, M. (1988). Hispanic apartheid in American public education. *Educational Administration Quarterly, 24*(3), 336–349.

Mehan, H. (1979). *Learning lessons.* Cambridge, MA: Harvard University Press.

Mehan, H., Hubbard, L., & Villaneuva, I. (1994). Forming academic identities: Accommodation without assimilation among involuntary minorities. *Anthropology and Education Quarterly, 25*(2), 91–117.

Miramontes, O. B. (1993). ESL policies and school restructuring: Risks and opportunities for language minority students. *Journal of Educational Issues of Language Minority Students, 12*(Special Issue), 77–96.

Oakes, J. (1985). *Keeping track: How schools structure inequality.* New Haven: Yale University Press.

Oakes, J. (1986). Keeping track, part 2: Curriculum inequality and school reform. *Phi Delta Kappan, 68*(2), 148–154.

Oakes, J., Gamoran, A., & Page, R. N. (1992). Curriculum differentiation: Opportunities, outcomes, and meanings. In P. W. Jackson (Ed.), *Handbook of research on curriculum* (pp. 571–608). New York: Macmillan.

Page, R. N. (1990). Games of chance: The lower-track curriculum in a college-preparatory high school. *Curriculum Inquiry, 20*(3), 249–281.

Page, R. N. (1991). *Lower-track classrooms: A curricular and cultural perspective.* New York: Teachers College Press.

Raimes, A. (1979). *Problems and teaching strategies in ESL composition (If Johnny has problems, what about Juan, Jean, and Ywe-Han?).* Washington, D.C.: Center for Applied Linguistics.

Saville-Troike, M. (1984). What really matters in second language learning for academic achievement? *TESOL Quarterly, 18,* 199–219.

Short, D. J. (1991). How to integrate language and content instruction: A training manual. Washington, DC: Center for Applied Linguistics. (ERIC Document Reproduction Service No. ED 359 780)

Silva, T. (1993). Towards an understanding of the distinct nature of L2 writing: The ESL research and its implications. *TESOL Quarterly, 27,* 657–678.

Sirotnik, R. A. (1983). What you see is what you get: Consistency, persistency, and mediocrity in classrooms. *Harvard Educational Review, 53*(1), 16–31.

Sizer, T. R. (1984). *Horace's compromise: The dilemma of the American high school.* Boston: Houghton Mifflin.

Swain, M. (1985). Communicative competence: Some roles of comprehensible input and comprehensible output in its development. In S. M. Gass & C. G. Madden (Eds.), *Input in second language acquisition* (pp. 235–253). Rowley, MA: Newbury House.

Tierney, R. J. (1990). Redefining reading comprehension. *Educational Leadership, 47*(6), 37–42.

Trueba, H. T., Guthrie, G. P., & Au, R. H.-P. (Eds.). (1981). *Culture and the bilingual classroom: Studies in classroom ethnography.* Rowley, MA: Newbury House.

Wheelock, A. (1992). *Crossing the tracks: How "untracking" can save America's schools.* New York: New Press.

Wong Fillmore, L. (1985). When does teacher talk work as input? In S. M. Gass & C. G. Madden (Eds.), *Input in second language acquisition* (pp. 17–50). Rowley, MA: Newbury House.

CHAPTER 3

Educating Latino High School Students with Little Formal Schooling

Ofelia García

Long Island University

In a large New York City high school sits 16-year-old Marcos, with almost a mustache, struggling to print on his paper the few Spanish words that are written on the blackboard. Dora, a pretty 17-year-old with lots of eye makeup, sits to his left, carefully copying into a notebook while she reads to herself, loud enough for everyone to hear. Many of the other 17 students in the class toil over their work just as carefully. All of them ask for help continuously from the one teacher in the room. When the teacher doesn't respond immediately, they're up. They walk around, look at someone else's work, talk to them, kid them in a grown up or adolescent way, and then go back to their childish work. There's something odd about this class, having to do with the incongruence between the physical maturity of the young people in this class and their immaturity in handling the classroom script and other academic tasks. There's also a marked difference between their bright and quick dialogue with each other and their slow reading and careful writing.

This is but one of many classrooms in the New York City high school system that are struggling with yet another kind of student whose numbers have been increasing since the early 1970s. Like other immigrant students of the past, Marcos and Dora lack English proficiency. And like other immigrant students of the past, they have to adjust to a new school system in a new society. But many of the bilingual and ESL programs that New York City high schools have developed for immigrant students are inadequate for these students.[1]

The focus of most high school bilingual programs in New York City is on encouraging the acquisition of English while continuing the students' education in their native language. But in the case of Marcos and Dora, there is little to continue. Their lives have been disrupted by a trip that has taken them away from the intimacy of extended family in the Dominican Republic (where they had gone sporadically to a loosely organized small school), to mothers whom they hardly know and who send them every day to a school with over 3,000 students and a highly structured academic curriculum.

Marcos and Dora, bright adolescents with little formal school experience, inadequate literacy skills for U.S. society, and no English, seem lost in the large high school, just as they feel lost in the new urban environment. But beyond school and society, these adolescents also feel lost at home, a product of having to play the role of son and daughter to women who left their young children in the care of grandmothers to come to the United States. In a poetic metaphor that turns out to be characteristically present in most students who share Marcos's and Dora's lot, Dora explains the alienation she feels not only from people, but also from the "new" family with whom she now lives: *"Allá, uno estaba con la gente de uno. Aquí, nada más está con la familia de uno. Y a veces la de uno es sólo por aquello de la sangre."* ["There, one was with one's people. Here, one is only with one's family. And sometimes one's family is only because of a blood relationship."] Dora's father died when she was a year old and her mother left for Puerto Rico shortly afterwards. Dora and her three older siblings stayed with their maternal grandmother, whom they called "Mamí," in Jaina, a town in the Dominican Republic. Dora's mother sent money, toys, and clothes from Puerto Rico and later from the United States. She wrote frequently but never visited, since she had no immigration papers. And then, a few years ago, as a result of the amnesty program, Dora's mother was able to claim her children. Dora and the youngest brother came to the United States. The other two were married by then and stayed behind. And "Mamí" stayed in Jaina while the stranger in New York usurped the "Mamí" title. The relationship has been strained from the beginning. The new "Mamí" is a youngish secretary who lives with a man and speaks English as well as Spanish. The "Mamí" Dora knew was an older Spanish-speaking woman who hardly left her home.

This chapter provides some insights into the past and present school lives of others like Marcos and Dora. It also describes efforts being made in two New York City high schools to educate these adolescents, including the curriculum and teaching strategies used. It looks at what works and what doesn't in these contexts. And it offers recommendations for the future, a future that will bring an increasing number of students like Marcos and Dora to U.S. high schools.

THE EMERGENCE OF DUAL LITERACY PROGRAMS

Throughout the 1970s and 1980s, New York City high schools developed bilingual and ESL programs to educate the increasingly large number of students coming from non-English-speaking countries. In particular, spurred by the Aspira Consent Decree of August 29, 1974, and by the large number of Latino students and professionals in New York City, the high schools were able to institute Spanish–English bilingual programs. These bilingual programs consist of courses in ESL and courses in the different academic subjects taught in Spanish. Students remain in the bilingual program until they acquire enough English to score beyond the 40th percentile in the Language Assessment Battery, the standardized test used in New York State to exit students from transitional bilingual programs. Of the total enrollment of 167,602 students with Limited English Proficiency in New York City in 1995–1996, 42,599 were high school students, and over two-thirds were Latino students (Board of Education of the City of New York, 1995–1996).

Whereas Puerto Rican students who lacked English proficiency were the main target of the Aspira Consent Decree, the Latino students in the 1980s and 1990s have come not only from Puerto Rico, but increasingly from the Dominican Republic, Central America, South America, and Mexico (for more on Spanish and Latinos in New York, see especially García, 1997; García & Otheguy, 1997; Zentella, 1997). Bilingual programs that focused on continuing an education while teaching English were clearly inadequate for many students whose education had been interrupted by sociopolitical fragmentation and even civil war. But beyond sociopolitical difficulties encountered lay the various expectations that different societies have for the children of the poor. Many of the poor families who have arrived in New York City recently have clearly been excluded from Latin American educational systems, which focus on educating only the elite. Whereas at the elementary level the difficulties have begun to be felt, it is at the high school that the situation has become desperate.

In New York City students who are 15 years old are automatically placed in the 9th grade. But departmentalized high school bilingual programs cannot be of help to students with little formal schooling. These students regularly fail not only the ESL class, but also the Spanish-language class and the subject classes taught in Spanish. In addition, they are considered discipline problems and many are referred to special education programs (Dual Literacy Programs, 1993).

In order to alleviate this situation, the Office of High School Bilingual/ESL Programs in the New York City Board of Education recommended the establishment of what are broadly known as Dual Literacy Programs for Limited English Proficient Students (for an extensive study of one such Dual Literacy Program, see Marsh, 1995). Dual Literacy Programs grew steadily throughout the 1980s and early 1990s, and are now available in New York City not only in Spanish, but also in Chinese and Haitian Creole. By spring 1993, there were programs in 18 high schools serving a total of almost 700 students, 85% of whom were Latinos (Dual Literacy Programs, 1993). Cuts in the budget for such programs brought the number down to nine in 1996. But by 1997, because of increased funding through the new Emergency Immigrant Program and a surge in the number of students in need of such programs, there were Dual Literacy Programs in 32 schools.

WHO ARE THESE STUDENTS AND WHAT HAS BEEN THEIR PAST SCHOOL EXPERIENCE?

The portrayal of students in Dual Literacy Programs that follows is based on my intensive observations and data-gathering in two Dual Literacy Programs in two New York City high schools. These two settings give us but a glimpse of the lives of students with little formal schooling.

In the two settings studied, the typical student (84%)[2] was born in the Dominican Republic, arrived in the United States in the last 2 years (72% had lived in the United States for less than 2 years), and was older than the typical ninth grader (61% of them were 17 years old or older). In addition, and extremely important, three-fourths of the students (72%) had been raised by relatives other than the parents.

Although all these students were placed in the 9th grade upon entering high school, only 26% had finished the 8th grade in their countries. Over half had not even completed the 6th grade. But beyond years of schooling lies the very different context of schooling with which these students are familiar.

It turns out that the limited experience that most of these students have had in school has been in what they refer to as a *"colegio privado"* ["private school"]. But private schools in Latin America are very different from private schools in New York City. Most described their school as simply *"una casa"* ["a house"]. Many spoke of how they knew the teachers personally. Others described their teachers as relatives. One said, *"Conocíamos a los maestros. Sabíamos donde vivían. Había una que era prima mía. Vivía en el mismo centro y yo iba mucho a su casa."* ["We knew the teachers. We knew where they lived. There was one who was my cousin. She lived right in the middle of town and I used to go a lot to her house."]

Most of these adolescents, even those whose attendance was sporadic or who had been out of school for years, had very fond memories of their past schoolteachers. One young woman told me how her teacher still wrote to her and then showed me the letter she had just received. The letter was wonderfully revealing, for it contained many of the writing errors that these students displayed in their writing. After sending regards from all classmates, the teacher reminded the student to send something for Christmas because they were poor and the student was fortunate to be living in the United States.

As children of the poor in a Latin American society that formally educates only the rich and the middle class, these students have been schooled by teachers with little education and minimal expectations. Many had few opportunities to be schooled. In explaining why he attended school only sporadically, one young man first told me that he had problems with his eyes ("*Sufro de los ojos*"), but then pointed to the real reason for his lack of attendance: "*Allí hay que pagar por los libros y comprar la comida también. Pasaba mucho trabajo.*" ["There I had to pay for my books and also buy food. It was very hard for me."] Many also described their frustrations in a school system that didn't tolerate their differences. Another young man explained: "*Allá es como una cárcel. Le dan con un palo a uno.*" ["There, it's like a jail. They hit you with a stick."] And others spoke about their academic failure and the inability of the school system to help them. A young woman said, "*Fui hasta cuarto porque no pasaba el cuarto. Me quemaba en todo casi siempre.*" ["I went up to fourth grade because I couldn't pass fourth. I used to fail everything most of the time."]

The place of school in these students' lives has changed drastically. Whereas two to three years ago school was a place that they did not have to contend with, now school has become the place they're required to go to every day. A student from Honduras told me how the school system there was different from the one here: "*En Honduras sólo hay seis grados y aquí hay doce.*" ["In Honduras there are only six grades and here there are twelve."] Of course, schooling in Honduras for the elite goes beyond the elementary level, but for this student, elementary school was all that was available. And not only did school mean fewer years for most, it also meant fewer hours. For example, in the Dominican Republic these students went to school only between 8:00 and 12:00.

The differences in the schooling experience of these students and those in the regular bilingual program become evident in the different ways in which students describe their own schooling experience. All students in the regular bilingual class reported that school in their country of origin—even when that country was the Dominican Republic—was harder than school in the United States. Their comments were as follows: *"Allá es más duro el estudio. Allí uno tiene que esforzarse y sacar su nota."* ["Studying is harder there. You have to put a lot of effort and get your grade."] *"Las matemáticas aquí no es tan avanzada. Es muy fácil."* ["Here math is not very advanced. It is very easy."] *"Acá lo veo tan fácil. No me afano porque sé que es por crédito."* ["Here I see it all so easy. I don't put any effort into it because I know that it goes by credit."] *"Aquí no exigen mucho y allá exigían más.* ["They don't demand a lot here and there they used to demand more."] In contrast, the students in the Dual Literacy Program all referred to how much more difficult it is to study in the United States. One said: *"Aquí son más recios que en Santo Domingo. Hay demasiadas leyes."* ["Here they are stricter than in Santo Domingo. There are too many regulations."] Another one said: *"Aquí aprendo más. En Santo Domingo enseñan menos. Conocía a la maestra. Aquí no conozco a los maestros, son más fuertes."* ["Here I learn more. In Santo Domingo they used to teach less. I knew the teacher. Here I don't know the teachers, they're more difficult."]

Besides having very different appreciation of their schooling experience in their old countries, students in the regular bilingual program also seem to have had a very different experience with English than that of students in the Dual Literacy Program. None of the students in the Dual Literacy Program reported having studied English in their countries of origin. In contrast, all but one of the students in the regular bilingual class reported having studied English. Two reasons may account for this difference. First, two-thirds of the students in the regular class had attended secondary schools in their country of origin; a secondary education in Latin America includes English as a subject. Second, it may be possible that students in the regular bilingual program are more middle-class, and we know that studying English is a common endeavor among middle-class Latin Americans. At least three students in the regular bilingual program had attended private English-language schools after their regular school.

It turns out, then, that an important piece of information in selecting the appropriate educational context for recently arrived Latino high school students is a detailed history of their schooling experiences, since going to school in Latin America means very different things for the children of the poor than for the children of the middle class. For the middle class, schooling often means a rigorous academic curriculum with English language lessons. But for the poor, schooling often includes just basic functional literacy and numeracy, with little emphasis placed on cognitive complex tasks or on advanced study. In fact, a secondary education is often beyond the reach of many poor Latin Americans.

WHAT THESE STUDENTS KNOW AND DON'T KNOW

One of the most disturbing aspects surrounding the education of students with little school experience is how differently they evaluate their knowledge and expectations compared with what teachers have to say about them. In the two Dual Literacy Programs I studied, 91% of all students expected to graduate, and 58% had career goals for which a college diploma is necessary. In fact, most students wanted to be either teachers or lawyers.

The teachers, however, tended to evaluate the students very negatively. Students regularly failed courses. One semester, for example, 81% of the students had failed the ESL class, and 74% had failed the Spanish literacy class. The failure rate for the other subjects was 76% for math, 69% for science, and 46% for social studies. This failure rate, which significantly reflects the greater failure of students in language skills areas than in content subject areas, is important because it points precisely to the problem of schooling these students in traditional ways. These students are capable of learning academic subjects, and have the basic background knowledge to make sense of scientific, historical, or social ideas. It is the ability to use their limited literacy and numeracy in complex academic ways that these students need to develop. And it is the knowledge of classroom script, especially the understanding of the roles, responsibilities, and expected behavior of students and teachers, that they lack (for more on scripts for school, see Saville-Troike & Kleifgen, 1986, 1989).

Significantly, then, it is the ESL teacher who has the least understanding of these students. One of the ESL teachers describes her students as "extremely immature. . . . They act like seven years old. They cannot comprehend being quiet. . . . They're uncontrollable. . . . There's hyperactivity and incessant talking." Indeed, students in ESL classes, even with the most gifted teachers, make evident their lack of knowledge of the classroom script. As we will see in the next section, ESL teachers spend most of their time teaching these students how to behave in the classroom, rather than attempting to extend their English-language development.

It is interesting that these students seem to show better understanding of the classroom script with bilingual teachers, especially with those who teach the Spanish literacy classes. The difference may lie in the bilingual teachers' ability to understand and respond to the students' oral outbursts, which often reveal understanding and thinking. For example, when the teacher of the Spanish literacy class asks what a letter of apology is, one student replies in almost one breath:

Maestra, es por ejemplo:
Estimados Profesores Míos,
La presente de esta carta es para comunicarle que mi hija no pudo asistir a la es-
cuela ayer porque está enferma. Por esta razon le suplico que la disculpe por esa
falta. Muy sinceramente,

[Teacher, it is for example:
My Dear Teachers,
This letter is to let you know that my daughter could not attend school yes-
terday because she was sick. For this reason I beg you to excuse her for her
absence. Most sincerely,]

The teacher then reacts not to the student's spontaneous outburst, but to
her ability to instantly compose a letter orally.

Verbally, and in Spanish, these students are articulate and capable of
participating in academic discourse. But because of their limited schooling, they read haltingly and have difficulty constructing the author's
meaning. Yet these same students' writing is often fluid and expressive,
although, as we will see, different from the writing of more schooled adolescents.

Answers to our survey of literacy use in the home confirm the students' greater familiarity with writing their own texts (an index of 2.6 was
obtained for use of writing at home in a scale where 1 = Never and 5 =
Very much) than with reading others' texts (an index of 2.2). Although
answers to what students read at home were vague, writing emerged as a
clear and extensive activity. In most cases, writing occurred when completing homework assignments (50% of the students gave homework as
an answer). However, a significant number of students said they wrote
letters at home (24%). And an even more significant number said they
wrote poems (26%). Clearly, writing, a productive skill able to be used
regardless of the presence of printed texts and outside stimuli, is more
common for these students than reading. It is possible that in the case of
more schooled adolescents who have greater familiarity with printed
texts, the opposite may be true.

This greater and natural use of writing among these students became
obvious on one particular day when, as the Spanish literacy teacher struggled with oral reading, girls passed around hardbound composition
books. Schoolwork was set aside, and many of the girls became engaged
in reading and writing in these notebooks. After weeks of sitting in
classes, the girls started sharing with me these journals, which they significantly call *pensamientos* [thoughts]. Most of these *pensamientos* are love
poems that have been copied from books, but others have been written

by the girls. They spend a lot of time sharing the *pensamientos* with each other. Whereas often the academic writing done in class is sloppy and letters are ill-formed, the pensamientos are written in the best calligraphy, illustrated profusely, and shared only with best friends. I reproduce an example of a *pensamiento* with the writing errors contained in the original.

Soy tu amiga
Tú y yo somos amigas,
puedes contar con migo cundo
quieras porque soy especial
por el simple echo que te
quiero seas rica o podre pero
no vanidosa y tambien que
se guardar un secreto y como
tú y yo sabemos que hay muy
pocas personas que guardan secreto.
Quiero ser tú amiga
dejame abril las puertas
de tú corazon y sabras
como soy.
Me llamo
xxxx
soy tu amiga

[I'm your friend
You and I are friends,
you can count on me whenever
you want because I'm special
because of the simple fact that I
love you whether rich or poor but
not vain and I also
can keep a secret as
you and I know that there are very
few people who keep secrets.
I want to be your friend
let me open the doors
of your heart and you will know
how I am.
My name is
xxx
I'm your friend.]

Little by little, the boys too started sharing their poems. And it became obvious that these students, despite their limitations with academic skills, had an ability for poetic metaphor and written expression that exceeded that of many of their schooled adolescent peers. Their images were complex, their metaphors forceful. Standard language did not constrain them, and students felt free to construct their own language to write poetry.

Yet the students' writing system is unlike that of schooled adolescents. In fact, it often resembles that of first graders experimenting with invented spelling. Just like first graders who are making guesses about how words are written, these adolescents' writing reflects not the printed words that are unfamiliar, but their own inner bright and forceful voices. Just like the young children in Emilia Ferreiro's studies (Ferreiro, 1990), these adolescents have hypothesized relations between writing and language that are different from those held by schooled young people. These hypotheses result in the following common categories of writing errors:[3]

1. Word agglutination
   Ex: *querespetar, miabuela, queno, llavoy*
2. Word separation
   Ex: *en seña, a buela, a tras, a prender, don de, con migo, en contró, se que da, inutil mente*
3. Acoustic equivalency (following phonological patterns in Caribbean; see del Rosario, 1979)
   a. equivalency of r = l
      Ex: *fácir, gorpes, fartavan, aprendel, entendel, demostral*
   b. equivalency of b = d
      Ex: *paladra, anbrajoso*
   c. equivalency of i = e
      Ex: *descutiendo, se era, se intero, peliado, pelio, peliandose*
   d. equivalency of f = s
      Ex: *defilachado*
4. Deletion of unstressed final consonants
   a. Deletion of r, j, d
      Ex: *dolo, relo, necesida*
   b. Deletion of s (in pronunciation, /s/ to /h/)
      Ex: *los cuento, mucho meno, sus ojo, eran bueno en darle lo sesenta peso*
5. Metathesis
   Ex: *repestar*
6. Dissimilation
   Ex: *enforsándose*

7. Equivalency of two or more graphemes when they represent one phoneme
   a. b, v = /b/
      Ex: *havía, estava, iva, vuscar, save, conbiértala, trabiesa, bamos, volbia, bez, probocaron, boy, llebaron, a berla, bacaciones, atrebo, ba*
   b. h, 0 = /0/
      Ex: *ija, avia, ombre, ablo, ay, asta, onor, abra*
   c. y, ll = /y/
      Ex: *la lello, calleron, lla, llo, alludar*
   d. s, c, z = /s/
      Ex: *ansiano, fásil, cresía, ensusiaron, antesedente, enceña, divercion, ece, en vos alta, hiso, eforsándose*
8. Hypercorrection
   a. h for 0
      Ex: *habes, haberla, habuela, hera*
   b. s for 0
      Ex: *el días siguiente, de la escuelas, lo siento muchos*
9. Lack of accents
10. Wrong words
    Ex: *la dejaron por un trato en la oficina, dentadura paliza*

The most prevalent conventional error in the students' writing is the deletion of the "s." Yet, an analysis of when this error occurs gives us some understanding of the coherence of the students' writing system. These students, mostly Dominicans, delete the /s/ in speaking, and therefore do the same when they read and often when they write (for more on Caribbean radical Spanish, see Guitart, 1982). It is interesting to note, however, that all the examples of /s/ deletion that we encountered in the students' writing occur in instances when the /s/ is redundant and when plurality has already been communicated. An example of this is found in example 4b above. "*Eran bueno en darle lo sesenta peso*" contains three instances of /s/ deletion. However, the plurality of *bueno* has been communicated by the verb *eran,* and the plurality of *lo* and *peso* has also been suggested by the number *sesenta.* Only when the /s/ marker is redundant do students tend to delete it.

These students are much more active thinkers than many teachers give them credit for, although their hypotheses often result in different applications of knowledge. Whereas these students still hold on to the immigrant dream of making it through schooling, even the dedicated teachers only want to help them for another year, until the clock runs out, that is, until they turn 17 and can drop out and register with a high school equivalency program.

In the next section we will describe the curriculum and teaching strategies used by the teachers. The gap between the teachers' practices and the students' knowledge is made evident, especially in the ESL classroom.

INSTRUCTIONAL PROGRAMS AND PRACTICES FOR THESE STUDENTS

The Dual Literacy Program: Its Structure

The instructional program recommended for students in Dual Literacy Programs generally consists of a block program of double period classes of native language literacy and ESL, as well as single periods of math, social studies, and occupational education taught in the native language, and a physical education class. Students usually remain in the program for one full semester or one full year.

Despite recommendations for process-oriented and integrative instruction, in practice the curricula in many of these programs remain largely reductionist, except in the Spanish literacy class. We will look first at what happens in the ESL and content classes, and contrast those situations with the more fortunate one surrounding the development of Spanish literacy.

Teaching English as a Second Language

In the two sites observed, the gap between the students and the teachers seems greater in the English as a Second Language classes. In general, the ESL curriculum for these students overcompensates for the limited literacy of the students. That is, the ESL curriculum assumes that students are not capable of handling any academic material. ESL texts are thus either nonexistent or extremely easy and childish.

On a particular day, 2 ESL periods were spent on 13 English words dealing with relatives, which the teacher had written on the blackboard: "mother, father, sister, brother, aunt, uncle, cousin, niece, nephew, grandmother, wife, husband, and cousin." The teacher asked only the same question: "How many brothers/sisters/aunts/uncles/cousins/niece/nephews, etc., do you have?" There was traditional choral repetition, common of the outdated and ineffective audio-lingual method. There was also little comprehensible input in this classroom, since the teacher spent most of her time telling students to be quiet. Students copied words from the blackboard but failed to grasp their meaning. I looked over a student's notebook, where many of the English words were written with Spanish accents: "cousín, neíce, síster." When the class was over, I asked the student if he knew what those words meant. He said: "*Ella no lo ha explicado todavía.*" ["She hasn't explained it yet."]. Only the question about cousin provoked a heated discussion in Spanish about the meaning of the word "cousin." One student argued: "*Allá hay infinidades de cousins. . . . Allá hay cousin primero, cousin segundo y cousin tercero. Pero no hay nada tan bueno como primo hermano.*" ["There, there is an infinity of *primos*[4] . . . There are first *primos*, second *primos* and third *primos*. But there isn't anything as good as first cousins."] And as the students argued in Spanish with each other, the ESL teacher, unaware of what the discussion was about, desperately asked for attention.

During a second visit, the same ESL teacher had the following instructions on the blackboard:

Write a composition using the present continuous and present simple.
Write a composition of two paragraphs:

My Life
Par. 1: Present continuous. Ex: I am studying
Par. 2: Present simple.

At the end of the period only a few students had produced compositions. This is an example of a composition of one of the students. It is reproduced exactly as written, although the reader will have to imagine very childish block letters interspersed with sloppy script:

I an tolking to my Deurys
Now I to toiking to my mother
Now I study in English
My brother is bery tol an fat
he toiking to my Deurys
He do the homework

As one can see, this composition even fails to communicate a message to the reader. The student has been limited in his use of language by a teacher who focuses on the forms of language rather than on the messages that those forms communicate. This vision of language shows a linguistically naive comprehension of how language works, for language forms are simple reflections of differences in meanings (for more on communicative grammar, see Otheguy, 1997). Good language teaching should focus on helping students use the meanings of language in order to communicate messages.

Another ESL class used a text with very controlled vocabulary and mechanical exercises. The lesson observed on one day dealt with food and different food groups. Students were asked to orally categorize certain foods into the main food groups. After this oral exercise, a worksheet was distributed. The worksheet asked to circle the right answer and to unscramble some words. Many students did not understand what they were being asked to do. An example that read "Pineapples are proteins-grains-dairy products-fruits" was answered by one student by circling every choice available. Some other students guessed the right answer, although they didn't know what all the words meant. There was no evidence of the use of actions, gestures, or Spanish to contextualize the meanings of English in this classroom (for more on the importance of comprehensible input and the use of the students' first language in ESL classes, see Auerbach, 1993; Krashen, 1981; Lucas & Katz, 1994).

Students in this class had also been asked to memorize the following dialogue, which they recited by heart in front of the room:

I'm going to the store.
What do you need?
I need bread and eggs.
Do you need milk?
No, I don't. I have milk.
Do you want ice cream?
No, I don't.

Student after student came up to the front of the class and repeated this useless, mechanical exercise. There was no evidence in any of the ESL classes of the use of English language or literacy for meaningful and real communication.

Teaching the Subject Areas

Whereas the ESL class overcompensated for the students' limited literacy, the science curriculum seemed to undercompensate, that is, there had been no change in teaching strategies to meet the needs of these students. A science lesson was observed, the aim of which was to explain the function of electrons. The teacher merely dictated a paragraph about Bohr's atomic model. Needless to say, most students in the Dual Literacy Program did not take down the dictation, and therefore would be unable to study.

The math curriculum undercompensated in one school and overcompensated in the other. In one bilingual math class the teacher used the same ditto sheets written in English that he used with the regular bilingual program. But the teacher had little understanding of bilingualism and the limited literacy of these students. His instructions were: "*Vayan leyendo la hoja esta. Leyéndola, penséndola en español.*" ["Start reading this sheet. Start reading it, thinking about it in Spanish."]

The translation of one such math problem becomes a classic example of the complexity of bilingualism. An example read: "Each pump represents 100,000 liters of crude oil . . ." One student translated it as "*Cada pompa representa 100,000 litros de aceite crudo.*" The teacher corrected the student and said: "*Pompa no. Se dice bomba. Pompa es lo que sale del jabón, la bolita que sale del jabón.*" ["Not *pompa*. It is called *bomba*. *Pompa* is what comes out of the soap, the suds that come from the soap."] At which point, a Puerto Rican student for whom balloons are *bombas*, said: "*Maestro, eso sé que es una* bomba." ["Teacher, that is truly what a *bomba* is."] The same inefficacies of communication that exist in the ESL classroom are prevalent in this bilingual math classroom. This teacher has not even started to solve the problems that come from having to develop numeracy when literacy is also limited and when bilingualism and biliteracy are involved.

The bilingual math teacher in the other school, however, has worked diligently on this problem. He uses computers and very simple language in order to teach the math skills these students need to pass the New York State Math Competency Exam.[5] Although the reductionist approach of this class may also be criticized for its emphasis on arithmetic and its evasion of higher-order thinking skills, the fact is that this class does what it sets out to do. This teacher is effective in getting students who have had very limited schooling experience (and therefore very little exposure to math) to pass the state competency exam. But in so doing, he reduces further the language with which students come into contact. The math examples are written in such a way that literacy does not become the obstacle to understanding the example. And although this method is successful in getting students to understand math, it further reduces their opportunities to interact with written language.

Things seem to have reached a happier medium in the social studies class, where students discuss a historical event, read in silence, and then discuss again. Some of the students who did not participate in the science lesson were able to do so now. In general, the social studies teacher relies less on decontextualized Spanish literacy skills in order to teach his subject. Instruction doesn't stop with historical facts, and students practice getting meaning from actual print, participating in the psycholinguistic guessing game that turns reading into an evolving source of knowledge. (For more on this interpretation of the process of reading, see Goodman,

1970. For more on reading in the bilingual classroom, see Freeman & Freeman, 1997.)

Teaching Spanish Literacy

The core of the Dual Literacy Program is the Spanish literacy class. The teachers have been involved in staff development efforts spearheaded by the NYC Board of Education. And significantly, it is in the Spanish literacy class where the most is being done to use the students' sophisticated oral language to develop age-appropriate literacy.

One Spanish literacy teacher is talented in her use of cooperative learning with small groups. Roles have been previously assigned and students function as secretaries, readers, and animators. They then share their written products with the class. The composition that follows was written by a group and was based on a picture the teacher had given them. Although many mechanical errors are evident in the composition, the flow of language is complex and shows control of the writing process.

> *Abigail Guzmán tiene 10 años, estudia en un colegio de señoritas.*
>
> *Todo el mundo la quiere por la personalidad que la distingue de las demás compañeras. Todas las profesoras la quieren por el entusiasmo que pone al estudio. Algunas compañeras le tienen envidia por su belleza, inteligencia, comportamiento, por su gentileza, inocencia y porque siempre anda arreglada. Una tarde cuando salían del colegio la llamaron varias compañeras y le empezaron a insultar levantándole falsos testimonios. En esos momentos ella perdió todos sus estribos lanzándosele a una de sus compañeras por haber incluido a su madre en sus insultos. Duraron unos instantes dándose golpes cuando el director y varios profesores las separaron y la llevaron a la dirección para averiguar por qué se avian peliado siendo Abigail tan sencilla y buena y no le gusta el chisme.*
>
> *Llamaron a los padres de las compañeras de Abigail porque ya ella tenia antesedente de mala estudiante y Abigail la dejaron por un trato en la oficina asta que la fueron a vuscar.*
>
> *A unque tu seas la mas buena y sencilla no deje que un insulto a tu madre pase por alto pero no te jales de las grenas con la persona que la insulto.*

[Abigail Guzman is 10 years old, she studies in a school for young ladies.

Everyone loves her because of her character which distinguishes her from her other friends. All the teachers love her because of her enthusiasm for her studies. Some of her friends are envious of her because of her beauty, intelligence, behavior, for her gentleness, innocence, and because she's always well dressed. One afternoon when they left school some of her friends called her and started insulting her and accusing her of lies. At that moment she lost her senses, hurling herself at one of her friends because she insulted her mother. They hit each other for a few minutes when the principal and other professors separated them and took them to the principal's office to find out why they had fought, since Abigail was so simple and good and doesn't like to gossip.

They called the parents of Abigail's friend because she already had a reputation of being a bad student, and Abigail they left her for a while in the office until they came for her.

Even if you're the nicest and most simple, don't let anyone insult your mother, but don't pull the hair of the person who insulted her.]

When students are encouraged to write freely and are made to understand that writing is a system of expression of thoughts and feelings, language flows fluidly and communicates appropriately, even if it contains errors. But as we saw previously, when students are allowed only correct form, their writing becomes limited and fails to communicate.

In another Spanish literacy class, students were reading and discussing short stories by Horacio Quiroga, José Luis González, and Gregorio López y Fuentes. The quality and depth of the oral literary discussions that students have in this class are striking. Still, no reading texts are available, and the teacher is left on her own to make xerox copies of appropriate reading material.

Until recently, high schools in the United States taught Spanish only as a foreign language. And although many high schools with large Spanish-speaking populations now offer programs of Spanish for native speakers (see Colombi & Alarcón, 1997), adequate reading material for these Spanish programs is still scant. The focus of most instruction for Spanish-speaking students then is to teach Spanish grammar and Spanish-language skills in isolation. The Spanish literacy teachers in the Dual Literacy Programs have gone significantly beyond this approach. Besides teaching Spanish literacy skills, these teachers understand that they are responsible for most of the Spanish literacy context with which these students will come into contact. And with little support from the administration, teachers have set up their classrooms as a community in which Spanish language and literacy is used and valued, developed and expanded. The Spanish literacy teacher is successful precisely because she defines her role as setting up an enriched literacy context, rather than providing reductionist skill exercises.

It is unfortunate, however, that this context is limited to the Spanish literacy classroom and to one specific instructional year. And it is to these limitations of the Dual Literacy Programs in New York City high schools that we now turn.

HOW EFFECTIVE ARE DUAL LITERACY PROGRAMS AND WHAT SHOULD BE DONE IN THE FUTURE?

We must judge Dual Literacy Programs effective if we take the teachers' and administrators' expectancies as the yardstick with which to evaluate them. But if we look at the students' expectations of the educational program and at American society's expectations for high school completion, the Dual Literacy Programs fail.

Four years after the original visit to these programs, Marcos and Dora had disappeared. Only one of the students at one site, and two students at the other, were still in the school, struggling to complete their high school requirements. The others had all withdrawn within a year of completing the Dual Literacy Program. Yet the bilingual counselor at one site reported that at least three-fourths of those who dropped out had gotten high school equivalency diplomas in Spanish GED (General Equivalency Degree) programs. And most were employed.

The truth is that these Dual Literacy Programs seem to make a difference in the immediate school lives of these students. But as extensions of the remedial bilingual programs from which they have grown, they reflect some limitations, as well as some advantages over the bilingual programs. Ironically, Spanish language and literacy development is an important component of Dual Literacy Programs, although it is not part of the transitional policy of traditional bilingual programs. This deeper understanding that the bilingual students' languages are interdependent and that developed literacy in the first language is conducive to extensive growth in the second language (Cummins, 1979, 1984) is an accepted axiom in the Dual Literacy Programs, yet it remains clearly absent from policy surrounding traditional bilingual programs.

As remedial programs, however, Dual Literacy Programs are also transitional, with specific recommendations that students move to the regular bilingual program after one year of participation. One year of Spanish language literacy development for students with little formal school experience is clearly not enough. And even the most successful student often fails to adapt to the highly departmentalized structure and transitional nature of the regular bilingual program.

IMPLICATIONS FOR CHANGE

The fact that these same students are eventually successful in high school equivalency programs in Spanish holds an important lesson for the educational establishment. It seems useless and economically foolish to establish educational programs that only act as a Band-Aid for a year. Better use of the high school resources would be to establish alternative high school programs for adolescents with limited schooling that have some of the features presently available in GED programs.

Briefly, then, these alternative high schools for Latino adolescents who are English language learners and have had little formal education in their countries of origin would have the following four features:

1. The focus of the educational program would not just be the development of Spanish literacy, but rather using literacy, both in Spanish and English, to gain social and scientific knowledge.

2. Subjects would not be compartmentalized and school would not be departmentalized. A single teacher working with fewer students in small groups would provide most of the instruction.

3. Students would earn high school credit whenever they achieve appropriate competencies and/or pass the required exams. The educational program would not attempt to graduate students in four years, but rather would be available for as long as it takes.

4. School would not follow the conventional time frame of 9:00 to 3:00, but would offer flexible and compact schedules, making it possible for students to work while attending school.

Realistically, we seem to be moving in the opposite direction. New York State has recently adopted stiffer academic requirements for high school graduation. Students will now have to take and pass the Regents Exam in English, as well as Regents Exams in content areas. The requirement that the English Regents Exam be passed will make graduation highly unlikely for the many English language learners in traditional high schools. And translating the content Regents Exams into Spanish, Chinese, Russian, and Haitian Creole, as is now being considered, will be of little help to language-minority adolescents with little formal schooling.

There seems to be a tremendous gap between the traditional departmentalized high school—which is ineffective with most Latino adolescents today and which, given the new requirements, will precipitate even more Latino high school dropouts—and the GED programs in which most of these adolescents eventually enroll. By refusing to change its structure, the U.S. high school is failing miserably in educating language-minority adolescents. And imposing stiffer graduation requirements for students without making the structural and curricular changes needed to educate the large immigrant population is not consistent with our democratic ideal of schooling for all.

As a nation eager to live up to our democratic ideals and provide educational opportunities for students that the high schools fail to educate, the GED diploma acts as a loophole. But certification of what a student knows or doesn't know is not the same as providing an education. By refusing to educate adolescents who don't or can't conform to traditional schooling, the United States has joined most nations of the world in excluding from a secondary education those who are poor or different.

For United States high schools, the challenge of the year 2000 is clear: As more language-minority students, and especially Latino students, enter the nation's secondary schools, the high schools will have to make a determination. Will they extend to the United States the Latin American practices of excluding the poor and different from a secondary education, or will they evolve enough to accommodate them? Will they take up the challenge as schools in the First World, or will they act as those in the Third World? Beyond resources available lies the way in which we as a nation define our educational task at the secondary level for students like Marcos and Dora, who will be the majority in the 21st century.

NOTES

1. Some of the information for this article is based on a study of the Dual Literacy Programs in two New York City high schools commissioned by the New York City Board of Education's Office of High Schools Bilingual/ESL Program in 1990. The final report was titled "*Socio-educational Limitations in the High School: The Case of Hispanic Students with Limited Proficiency in English and Limited Literacy in Spanish.*" I am grateful to Manny Menendez and Laura Rodriguez, who got me involved initially, as well as to Burt Posner for his update. No specific mention is made of the high schools and of the individuals involved in the original study, but I wish to express my gratitude to the many students, teachers, and administrators who gave freely of their time then and now. Marcos and Dora are pseudonyms; to them, and the others like them, I am most grateful. I learned from them about their dreams and expectations, their frustrations and limitations. Most of all, I learned that beyond their tenacity to learn lies the schools' responsibility to teach them, a responsibility that some schools have shunned.

2. The greater number of Dominicans in the two Dual Literacy Programs studied is simply a result of the greater number of recently arrived Dominicans in New York City. It should not be understood as simply a reflection of the schooling situation of Dominicans.

3. All these examples are taken from students' writing.

4. In Spanish the word for cousin *primo* conveys intimacy while expressing the concept of extended family.

5. As of this writing, these minimum New York State competency exams

have been eliminated and replaced by more rigorous New York State Regents exams, which will be required for graduation.

REFERENCES

Auerbach, E. (1993). Reexamining English only in the ESL classroom. *TESOL Quarterly, 27,* 9–32.

Board of Education of the City of New York. (1995–1996). *Facts and figures. 1995–1996.* New York: Office of Bilingual Education.

Colombi, C., & Alarcón, F. (Eds.) (1997). *La enseñanza del español a hispanohablantes. Boston:* Houghton Mifflin.

Cummins, J. (1979). Linguistic interdependence and the development of bilingual children. *Review of Educational Research, 49,* 222–251.

Cummins, J. (1984). Wanted: A theoretical framework for relating language proficiency to academic achievements among bilingual students. In C. Rivera (Ed.), *Language proficiency and academic achievement.* Clevedon, Avon, UK: Multilingual Matters.

Dual Literacy Programs for Limited English Proficient Students in the High Schools. (1993). Office of High School Bilingual/ESL Programs.

Ferreiro, E. (1990). Literacy development: Psychogenesis. In Y. Goodman (Ed.), *How children construct literacy: Piagetian perspectives.* Newark, DE: International Reading Association.

Freeman, Y., & Freeman, D. (1997). *Teaching reading and writing in the bilingual classroom.* Portsmouth, NH: Heinemann.

García, O. (1997). New York's multilingualism: World languages and their role in a U.S. city. In O. García & J. A. Fishman (Eds.), *The Multilingual apple: Languages in New York City* (pp. 3–50). Berlin and New York: Mouton de Gruyter.

García, O., & Otheguy, R. (1997). No sólo de estándar vive el aula: Lo que nos enseñó la educación bilingüe sobre el español de Nueva York. In C. Colombi & F. Alarcón (Eds.), *La enseñanza del español a hispanohablantes.* Boston: Houghton Mifflin.

Goodman, K. (1970). Reading: A psycholinguistic guessing game. In H. Singer and R. Ruddell (Eds.), *Theoretical models and processes of reading.* Newark, DE: International Reading Association.

Guitart, J. (1982). Conservative versus radical dialects in Spanish: Implications for language instruction. In J. Fishman & G. Keller (Eds.), *Bilingual education for Hispanic students in the United States.* New York: Teachers College Press.

Krashen, S. (1981). *Second language acquisition and second language learning.* London: Pergamon Press.

Lucas, T., & Katz, A. (1994). Reframing the debate. The roles of native languages in English-only programs and language minority students. *TESOL Quarterly, 28,* 537–561.

Marsh, L. (1995). A Spanish dual literacy program: Teaching to the whole student. *The Bilingual Research Journal, 19,* 409–428.

Otheguy, R. (1997). *A grammar of rules controls you. A grammar of meaning empowers you.* Lecture given at the Northeast Conference on the Teaching of Foreign Languages, New York, April 1997.

Saville-Troike, M., & Kleifgen, J. A. (1986). Scripts for school: Cross-cultural communication in elementary classrooms. *Text, 6,* 207–221.

Saville-Troike, M., & Kleifgen, J. A. (1989). Culture and language in classroom communication. In O. García and R. Otheguy (Eds.), *English across cultures. Cultures across English* (pp. 83–102). Berlin: Mouton de Gruyter.

Zentella, A. C. (1997). Spanish in New York. In O. García and J. A. Fishman (Eds.), *The Multilingual apple: Languages in New York City* (pp. 167–201). Berlin and New York: Mouton de Gruyter.

CHAPTER 4

GENDER AND IDEOLOGY IN SECONDARY ESL AND BILINGUAL CLASSROOMS

Paula M. Wolfe and Christian J. Faltis

ARIZONA STATE UNIVERSITY

Most native Spanish-speaking students who enter school not knowing English become bilingual by the time they leave school (Bialystok & Hakuta, 1995). Moreover, many of these students become proficient in several varieties of English, ranging from Ebonics and code-switching to conventional and regional speech (Pedrasa, Attinasi, & Hoffman, 1980). English varieties that students hear and emulate may come from bilingual speakers of English, conventional English speakers, or speakers who have limited contact with conventional English speakers. In school and in their communities, students use both English and Spanish for interacting with friends, fellow students, and family members. The role of the high school, however, is to initiate these students into academic English discourse and to expand their proficiency in conventional English. In most high schools with large numbers of Spanish-speaking students, ESL and sheltered content teachers are primarily responsible for achieving these goals.

PERSPECTIVES UNDERLYING RESEARCH ON ACADEMIC DISCOURSE

With respect to the appropriation of students into an academic discourse, three lines of thinking, based on different conceptions of academic language and language acquisition, underlie much of the research on this topic. These perspectives are: two-dimensional models of language proficiency, the mismatch model, and discourse as a community of practice.

Two-Dimensional Models of Language Proficiency

The first perspective draws from a two-dimensional conception of language: basic everyday language, and academic language. Jim Cummins's (1981) BICS (Basic Interpersonal Communication Skills) and CALP (Cognitive Academic Language Proficiency) model is perhaps the most well-known of this ilk in bilingual and ESL education circles. This perspective characterizes students who fail in school as lacking CALP, due primarily to the inaccessibility of academic-oriented language and literacy in their homes and communities and the predominance of oral interaction deeply embedded in shared personal meaning with ties to situational and contextual cues. The focus of research from this perspective is, given the oral interactional abilities that many immigrant students bring to the classroom, what classroom teachers can do to add academic discourse to the students' repertoire of language abilities, preferably in their native language. At the secondary level, researchers have drawn on Cummins's work to construct ways of enabling students who are becoming bilingual to acquire discipline-specific language that is context-reduced and academically challenging (Chamot & O'Malley, 1987; Spanos, Rhodes, Dale, & Crandall, 1988). Other researchers have explored the nature of academic language within different classroom levels, subject matter content, and classroom tasks (Saville-Troike, 1984; Short, 1994; Solomon & Rhodes, 1995). Also included in this perspective, although not directly concerned with students who are becoming bilingual, are researchers such as Lemke (1990) and Christie (1995) who have worked to further distinguish academic from nonacademic language by discussing it as a regulative register (teacher talk about the overall goals and sequence of the lesson) and by identifying specific semantic relations and thematic patterns of disciplines such as science (Lemke, 1990).

The Mismatch Model

The second main perspective on academic language stems from the language-socialization mismatch model. In this model, how students fare in school depends on the extent to which the discourse recognized and reinforced in the school is similar to or differs from the ways that students are socialized to use language for getting things done at home. Research from this perspective draws from Mehan's (1979) seminal work on classroom discourse, in which he described typical turn-taking and participation patterns evident in academic interactions. Mehan showed that most classroom discourse is based on a unique interactional structure he termed Initiation-Response-Evaluation, or IRE. In this pattern the teacher initiates an interaction, usually through a known-answer question or directive, and the student responds. The teacher then judges the acceptability or correctness of the response by saying something back to the student or the class in general. Researchers have used Mehan's work to argue that there is a mismatch between how non-native English speakers participate in discourse and how the school expects them to participate. For example, ethnographic work by Heath (1983) and Philips (1983) illustrated that the participant structures the teacher used and reinforced for interaction purposes in school were qualitatively different from those used or even found in the home. Many studies from this perspective have concluded that language–socialization mismatches negatively influence academic success for language-minority students (Au, 1980; Cazden, 1988; Macías, 1990; Mohatt & Erikson, 1981; Trueba & Delgado-Gaitán, 1988).

The language–socialization mismatch perspective also shows up in research designs for studying gender and language. While there is rarely any cross-reference between the two research foci, the early work done on the role of gender in classroom discourse found that the lion's share of interaction patterns tend to accommodate a predominately male style of exchanging ideas (Ong, 1981) and that the female interaction style is not consistent with success in the classroom (Coates, 1986; Delamont, 1980; Jones, 1989; Losey, 1995; Sadker & Sadker, 1984; Spender, 1982; Stanley, 1986).

Discourse as a Community of Practice

A third group of researchers has advanced a different view of academic language and classroom discourse. In this view, academic language is a social discourse that entails ways of communicating, understanding and acting like an insider (Gee, 1992). Discourse is an essential feature of membership within any community of practice, including academic subject-matter communities such as English literature, math, science, and social studies. Becoming a member of a community of practice requires a neophyte to be acquired into the discourse that is recognized and used by more capable members of the community of practice (Lave & Wenger, 1991). A neophyte can be acquired into any type of discourse, from teacher-centered, transmission-oriented discourse to discourse that counts on the co-participation of the teacher and students for learning to occur. According to Lave and Wenger (1991), discourses range from transparent to oblique, with difference resting in how easily new members gain access to "insidership." When the teacher has prior knowledge of the answers expected of students, access to and participation in the community of practice depends mainly on how well students master the teacher's knowledge, which may or may not enable students to perform as insider members. This discourse-as-providing-known-answers is most often associated with teacher-centered pedagogy. In contrast, teachers who co-construct knowledge with their students offer a different pathway to learning. Rather than insisting that students master known concepts, teachers from this perspective work to move students toward insidership by engaging them in the mutual construction of the discourse that community members recognize and use to discuss and critique their knowledge system. This discourse-as-a-community-of-practice perspective has theoretical ties with whole language researchers (e.g., Graves, 1983; Edelsky, 1991). Whole language and discourse-as-a-community-of-practice assert the need for tasks that require co-participation for increased membership in the community of practice.

The first two research perspectives have in common the assumption of one monolithic event called "classroom discourse," without regard to the nature of curriculum design or classroom organization. The focus is on how the student acquires the classroom discourse. In contrast, the third perspective takes an entirely different theoretical slant about how and why learning occurs: the discourse acquires the student rather than the other way around (Faltis & Hudelson, 1994). This perspective makes it necessary to focus on the nature of classroom learning to uncover the kinds of discourse students are or are not being acquired into, especially in school.

PURPOSE OF THE STUDY

In what ways does academic discourse vary according to how it is enacted in the classroom? How do classrooms in which shared co-participation is valued differ from classrooms organized around a teacher-centered approach to interacting with students? In what ways does gender interact with how students are acquired into academic discourse? The purpose of the study in this chapter is to address these questions by contrasting what happened in four high school classrooms to learn how access to and participation in academic discourse varied according to students' gender, and more importantly, the classroom ideology underlying how knowledge gets constructed.

METHODOLOGY

We followed a group of 14 Spanish-speaking high school students (most of Mexican origin) from January to May 1996 through four of their classes: a traditional English as a second language (ESL) class; a sheltered biology class; a sheltered English literature class; and a bilingual (Spanish and English) world history class. The ESL, biology, and world history classes were teacher-centered; the English literature class was holistic. We took extensive notes and audiotaped teacher/student interactions. We conferred about our notes and discussed what we had written after each observation visit. At the end of data collection, we transcribed the notes and tapes to be used in our analysis.

Two distinct approaches to analyzing the data were taken. First, we did a basic quantitative analysis of gender-specific interaction across the four types of classrooms. This analysis consisted of counting several aspects of interaction, including amount of talk, number and length of turns, and amount of resistance talk. We considered *resistance talk* to be instances when students orally challenged the teacher or classroom peers. Challenges could be in the form of using Spanish when English was expected, ridiculing peers for participating, or calling out answers without having the floor. We also developed a typology of student language production when we analyzed the distribution of language between girls and boys.

The second part of the analysis consisted of an exploration of interactions initiated and sustained by students and directed toward the teacher. Lemke (1990) argues that students become proficient with an academic discourse when they appropriate and use it to their own ends. For students who are becoming bilingual, we considered the appropriation of academic discourse as those instances in which students displayed understanding by negotiating meaning with the teacher for clarification or to extend an idea. Repeating what the teacher said was not considered to be evidence a student had appropriated the discourse. Accordingly, while we paid attention to both types of discourse, we were interested in ascertaining the extent to which teachers provided opportunities for girls and boys to engage in sustained interaction with the teacher using language that moved them toward insider membership of the academic discourse.

RESULTS

Results are presented for each class we studied, with an eye toward understanding the interaction between gender and classroom participation. Using classroom interaction data, we show how language participation patterns were allocated by gender, and how classroom ideology impacts the distribution and quality of interaction according to gender.

Gender in the Teacher-Centered Classes

A central question that emerged for us over the course of our data collection and quantitative analysis was, "How does gender interact with access to and participation in academic discourse in teacher-centered class-

TABLE 4.1. Number of Turns, Talk Time, and Resistance Time for Boys and Girls Across Traditional Classroom Settings.

	ESL		Sheltered Science		Bilingual History	
	Boys (8)	Girls (10)	Boys (3)	Girls (8)	Boys (12)	Girls (1
Mean # of turns	25	22	52	21	27	15
Mean length of turns*	1.3	2.3	1.32	2.24	1.9	.7
Resistance Time	16.3	0	0	0	17.8	1.6
Total Talk Time	32.6	51.3	116.4	27.8	26.4	10.8

*All times are in seconds and are calculated as means

rooms versus classrooms in which students co-participated in the construction of knowledge?" Losey (1995) claims that Mexican American women tend not to speak in whole group situations because they are "shy" or "lack self esteem." Rather than supporting the stereotype of the "quiet Mexican girl," we found that the adolescent girls successfully participated in all three of these classes. In the ESL class, girls on average spoke and took longer turns than the adolescent boys. Moreover, through our interviews, we learned that the girls were highly motivated to learn English and had high expectations of success. Table 4.1 shows the language interaction patterns across the three traditional classrooms distributed for gender.

Upon further analysis of our initial understandings, two interesting patterns of interaction surfaced. First, each of the three teacher-centered classrooms we visited had as a defining feature the use of triadic dialogue or IRE (Mehan, 1979). According to Mehan (1979), IRE structure consists of two adjacency pairs, the first being the completion of an initiation by a response, the second, an evaluation of the initiation-response pair. Girls and boys interactional exchanges typically followed this pattern across the three teacher-centered classrooms. Girls were more adept than boys at classroom discourse that entailed completing the first adjacency pair for the teacher. Accordingly, girls had access to and chose to participate in known-information exchanges with the teacher, who then would consummate the second pair, typically with a trite evaluation statement. In other words, girls did much of the basic language work (DeFrancisco, 1991) in these teacher-centered classes. Boys, on the other hand, engaged in more resistance talk, and had more turns at talk than girls in the sheltered and bilingual classes.

Although girls participated more frequently in the ESL class than the other two traditionally structured classes, the type of language they used was essentially simple definitions, recall, and answers to yes–no questions.

TABLE 4.2. Type of Student Language Production in ESL.*

	Boys	_Girls_
Student Generated:		
Clarify Directions	4	0
Ask for Information		
(not related to lesson)	0	1
Teacher Generated:		
Define	6	12
If/Then	1	0
Recall	2	9
Report	2	0
Resistance	12	0
Yes/No	0	2

*Numbers represent averages

In other words, girls participated in exchanges that contributed very little to either their English or their membership to the academic discourse of the class. When boys did engage in IRE sequences with the teacher, it tended to occur in instances when their responses required sustained academic language. Boys, however, were also notable for overtly flouting traditional triadic dialogue either by refusing openly to complete the first adjacency pair, or by violating other traditional discourse interactional maxims (e.g., don't answer when another is nominated, don't offer irrelevant information, and—specifically for ESL classes—don't speak Spanish in a monolingual English classroom). This was especially evident in the ESL class, somewhat evident in the world history class, but was totally absent in the sheltered science class.

To get a sense of the boys' interactional patterns as compared to the girls', we tabulated the types of language production used by boys and girls across the three traditional classrooms, ESL, science, and world history classrooms. These are shown in Tables 4.2, 4.3, and 4.4.

These tables show an inverse relationship between quality of discourse and the differential participation between boys and girls. As the need for student language production increased in length and complexity, boys increased their participation within this discourse, and consequently tended to dominate the classroom talk. Likewise, girls decreased their participation as the requirement for sustained and more academic discourse increased. Walkerdine (1991) found similar results in her study of boys and girls in mainstream classes.

TABLE 4.3. Type of Student Language Production in Sheltered Science.*

	Boys	*Girls*
Student Generated:		
Clarify Directions	0	5
Challenge Teacher Interpretation	3	0
Hypothesis	3	0
Teacher Generated:		
Define	4	1
Explain	4	1
Hypothesis	11	4
If/Then	5	1
Label	7	2
Predict	1	0
Recall	8	7
Report	5	0
Resistance	0	0
Temporal	1	0
Yes/No	9	6

*Numbers represent averages

TABLE 4.4. Type of Student Language Production in Bilingual History.*

	Boys	*Girls*
Student Generated:		
Clarify Directions	2	4
Request for Attention	3	1
Recall (Unsolicited)	10	9
Teacher Generated:		
Hypothesis	2	0
Label	2	2
Recall (Nominated)	2	4
Report	2	0
Resistance	12	4
Yes/No	0	2

*Numbers represent averages

TABLE 4.5. Number of Turns, Talk Time and Resistance Time for Boys and Girls in Sheltered English Literature Class.*

	Boys	*Girls*
(Avg. 10 girls, 8 boys)		
Avg. Number of Turns	79	84
Avg. Length of Turns	10.1	12.2
Response to Teacher's		
Direct Questions	5	
Avg. Resistance Time	2.7	0
Avg. Total Talk Time	797.9	1024.8

*All times and numbers represent averages

Gender in the Sheltered English Literature Class

It was clear from our quantitative analysis that the range of options for girls was much more restricted than for boys, except in the ESL class, where the discourse was highly controlled. The question that interested us then became: Are there certain discourse structures that enable girls and boys to participate more equitably, and at the same time have similar opportunties to appropriate academic discourse? Because it appeared that the girls in the study were more likely to follow than break classroom discourse rules, we hypothesized that a classroom structure in which student-initiated language was a necessary part of classroom interaction would foster a more equitable distribution of classroom language and therefore more equitable participation of girls and boys. The first data we examined were those having to do with student language production. These are presented in Table 4.5.

Table 4.5 shows that students in the sheltered English literature class produced substantially greater amounts of language than were found in the three traditional classes (see Table 4.1). It also shows that acts of resistance were virtually nonexistent.

Table 4.6 presents a distribution of the types of language boys and girls used for classroom interaction. Many of the language production types were also found in Lemke's (1990) study on the discourse of science in mainstream high school science classes. This table shows that students in this class were using language for a wide variety of purposes, and that the language they used was appropriate for gaining insider membership into the academic discourse of English literacy.

In contrast to the teacher-centered classes, where girls were more likely than boys to accommodate the teacher's requests for known-

TABLE 4.6. Type of Student Language Production in Sheltered English Literature Class.*

	Boys	Girls
Teacher Generated:		
Define	3	4
Recall	2	4
Elaboration	1	4
Clarification	3	5
Student Generated:		
Clarify Directions	1	1
Challenge Teacher Interpretation	2	2
Ask for Information		
(not related to lesson)	3	5
Recall(Unsolicited)	1	3
Request for Attention	3	0
Metaphor/Analogy	1	2
Adversative Addition	0	1
Cause/Consequence	7	5
Problem/Solution	3	3
Temporal Sequence	6	3
Identification	7	10
Meronym	10	8
Location	5	7
Comparative	4	7
Narrative	2	6
If/Then	7	2
Label	9	8

Numbers represent averages

information, and where boys were willing to participate when the discourse was less restricted, this class achieved an equitable distribution of all types of language between girls and boys as well as expanded possibilities for the production of sustained language.

It is not enough, however, for students simply to produce more language. Likewise, it is not enough that girls and boys have more equitable access to exchanges with the teacher. These results, though positive, do not necessarily ensure that students who are becoming bilingual are appropriating academic discourse. In fact, many of the exchanges of information and strategies teachers used for developing themes of particular importance were remarkably similar across all four classrooms. There was a striking difference, however, in the way students were acquired into the classroom discourse. To learn about different pathways into classroom discourse, we conducted a qualitative analysis of discourse between the teacher and students in two classrooms.

The Teacher-Student Debate

In the following sections, we examine in some detail two instances of a discourse event that Lemke (1990) has referred to as the teacher-student debate. In this kind of discourse event, a student challenges the teacher's interpretation or thesis. The challenge is then followed by an exchange that moves to resolve the conflict.

An Example for Sheltered Science. The first debate occurred in the sheltered biology classroom introduced earlier. The debate centers around the lesson's primary objective, which is to answer the question, "Where do seeds get the energy to grow?"

To address this question, the teacher first engages the students in a brief experiment to test for starch in seeds. The teacher works with students to establish that part of the seed is starchy while a small part (the nonstarchy part) is the embryo that will grow into the plant. We pick up the interaction where he is now attempting to get students to understand that the starchy part of the seed is energy and why a seed would need that energy. Each of the teacher's turns are marked with a *T*. Ricardo, who challenges the teacher's thesis, is marked with an *R*, and other students who participate in this exchange are simply marked *M* if they are male and *F* if they are female.

T: Okay now, we just talked about light being necessary for plants for their energy, why would we need energy in the seed? If we are going to say that the nonstarchy part is for energy for the, actually for the embryo, why would the embryo need seed, ahh, need energy? Why can't it just get energy from the light?

*F*1: It has to grow.

*F*2: It has to grow.

T: It has to grow first? Uh okay, and where does it grow, where does the seed grow?

R: The part of . . .

T: Where do seeds grow?

M: Underground.

T: In the ground?

R: Yes.

T: Now can seeds get energy from the light when they are in the ground?

Chorus: Nooo.
T: Why not?
R: Yes.
T: Yes?
R: Um in the spaces, in the, in the dirt.

Ricardo has directly contradicted the teacher's expected chorus answer. The teacher's inflection implied that the answer to his question, "Can seeds get energy from the light when they are in the ground?" is obvious, and in fact earlier in the lesson he engaged in a shorter debate to demonstrate (by way of showing students seeds that had germinated in the dark) that seeds do not get their energy from the light. Ricardo, however, contradicts this by answering a yes–no question in a way that the teacher was not expecting, and his answer serves here to challenge the teacher.

The teacher then turns Ricardo's answer back on to him as if to challenge him to defend his point. Ricardo then answers "in the spaces, in the, in the dirt," which is a restatement of an earlier challenge made by Ricardo when he said, "Maybe a little bit of light got into the ground." The debate then continues:

T: Have you ever planted seeds?
R: Uh.
T: Sure you have, I know 'cause you do work that sometimes you must plant seeds, okay? How much light is in on the seed when you plant them?
R: Uh.
T: Hector, how much light is on the seeds when you plant the seeds?
M: None, 'cause it's too far.
T: 'Cause it's underneath.

At this point, the teacher tries to change the tenor of the debate by relating it to Ricardo's personal experience. Ricardo appears to sense that this is a trap and refuses to answer. So the teacher nominates another student to give the answer he is looking for. Only then does Ricardo offer alternative evidence, albeit evidence that seems to point to a different conclusion: "But the seed can get energy 'cause the sun will make the ground get hot."

As Lemke (1990) suggests, Ricardo is articulating his "commonsense" understanding, which is easier to see if we turn his sentence around: The ground gets hot, therefore, the seed can get energy. Since Ricardo has now articulated his assumption about how the seed receives energy, one could expect the teacher to contradict it with his own or at least offer evidence to illuminate Ricardo's erroneous assumption. However, the teacher here responds quite differently: "Well, maybe the ground will get hot and maybe it won't. I can take you some places where I was just last week where the ground wasn't very hot but there was sunlight."

Rather than dealing with Ricardo's main argument that there is energy in the soil (in the form of heat), the teacher contradicts Ricardo's evidence, saying, "Maybe the ground will get hot and maybe it won't," and then offers anecdotal evidence to support his own position. This is commonly called a "straw man" argument—to attack something that is not essential to the conclusion or argument.

Ricardo responds by refining his original argument to respond to the teacher's "straw man" argument: "But I thought, I thought the sun in the spaces in the ground gets down there." Ricardo is also backing off his position, which is shown by the use of "I thought," which makes it clear this is his opinion rather than something he considers to be a scientific fact.

Even though the debate ostensibly continues for several more turns, the rest of the episode is essentially an extended joke by the teacher to *maintain control of the class* and at the same time force Ricardo to give up his alternate thesis:

T: You think the sunlight gets into the [ground]? All right, I'll let you do an experiment, you have a little brother?

R: I have a kid, I have one.

T: Well, I was just going to ask you to dig a hole and you get in the hole and ask your little brother to cover you.

R: Ahh.

T: Now leave your eyes open and . . .

R: I don't think so. (*girls laugh*)

T: and I want to see how much light you can see.

T: Maybe you can wear some goggles over it.

R: You can't get me in a hole.

T: There, you can take these with you and you can use these. (*holds up a pair of goggles*) I want you to go in and have your little brother bury you under the ground and you get a straw so you can breathe, okay? And I want you to tell me how much light is down there. (*all laugh*) Ricardo? How much light is down there?

R: None.

T: None, huh, can seeds get energy from the light?

R: No, but for . . .

T: Can seeds get energy from the light?

R: No, not that way . . .

T: Do seeds need energy for that first growth?

R: Yes.

T: Ahh, okay we need to test these ideas and that's what we are going to do tomorrow . . .

The teacher uses several control tactics (Getting Personal, Being Funny, Interrupting Students, noted by Lemke, 1990). The most effective one was when Ricardo refuses to give up his point; the teacher simply interrupts and repeats his question, intimidating Ricardo into accepting his Teacher Thesis. In the end, neither Ricardo nor the teacher has confronted the other's basic assumptions about how seeds get energy in the absence of light. Ricardo and the teacher leave the debate holding onto different conceptions of the answer to this question.

An Example from Sheltered English Literature. The following teacher–student debate occurred as part of a one-on-one editing conference after the student approached the teacher at her desk and told her that the teacher aide had indicated there was a problem with the tense of her narrative.

S: Mrs. Aimes says that there's some editing.

T: Okay, like what?

S: Here [points].

T: Okay, [reads] "Just then she sees the bird and knew it is a sign for her." Tell me what's going on, what you're trying to do.

S: It's my story? Well, the girl . . . ran away, away from home? . . . But then she saw a bird and like thought it was like her grandma Miss or whatever to say, to tell her to go home.

T: Uh-huh, I, you said *saw a bird,* right? I think the, your story switches tense a few times, like this needs to be in past tense. I think it should be, "She *saw* the bird and *knew* it was a sign. . . ."

S: Yeah but, yeah but I thought that 'cause it's happening, now to her, not before we use different tense, like the bird *is* there now.

From the outset, this debate is quite different from the one that occurred in the science class. Before the teacher asserts her Teacher Thesis, she tries to get a sense of the student's intention or goal. This has the effect of acknowledging that the student has a worthy point of view. The student then explains her goal and the teacher goes on to assert her thesis that, "I think your story needs to be in past tense." It is important that this thesis is not asserted as a fact, but rather as an opinion.

The debate then continues:

T: It is . . . I don't know if I can even explain it to you, let me see a minute . . . Okay, I know it is happening to the character right now but you have to keep the same tense all the way through. Authors usually use the past tense to tell stories.

S: Uh-huh, but for her it's not past [points to character's line in the story].

T: Well, that's true, just, what book are you reading right now?

S: That one [points].

The teacher tries to convince the student that narratives must be written in the past tense and offers her a rule or principle to support this—"Authors use past tense." Native English speakers who have been acquired into writing conventions know that authors do not generally jump from tense to tense within one piece of discourse. Having learned the English tense system bit by bit at the sentence level, this student may not have learned how the bits interact in longer pieces of discourse (Celce-Murcia & Larsen-Freeman, 1983).

The teacher and student next embark on a lengthy exchange with the teacher using several thematic development strategies (see Lemke, 1990, for a detailed discussion of the strategies) to invite the student into the discourse:

T: Go get it and let's see how the author does it. [Student gets book.]

T: Okay, see, but all the way through she uses past tense "Sarah *walked* toward the window, she *marveled.*"

S: Yeah, for the . . . for the author it's past but for her, for her it's not . . . so when, last year in Mrs. Sawyer's class, she said like, to show that it happened in the past use the ending . . . the past tense and then to say it is happening in the, happening now, use the, you know, so why is, why wouldn't it be for . . . for her the bird is there?

T: This is confusing, I know. Try it this way: When you tell a story think of it as something that you saw happen last week and you are sharing it with your, with us, with your readers, right? It's you, the author, who decides the tense, the character . . . what's happening to the character doesn't matter.

Because this classroom is designed to have students "do what writers do," the teacher refers to how actual authors write rather than give the student discrete grammatical information. Initially this move may seem unimportant; however, this particular exchange more than any other distinguishes the discourse in this class from that of the more traditional classes. The teacher's initial move establishes that both she and the student are involved in activities that place them (as legitimate participants) in a wider (in this case, literary) community that has certain rules, patterns, and so forth that make up its discourse. For the teacher as well as the student, these tasks are authentic (other writers really do them) and are meaningful (they enable you to achieve your goals).

In the final section of the debate, the teacher and student come to understand each other's perspectives and then work to establish a new, mutually constructed understanding:

S: So, but then when do you use?

T: Present tense?

S: Uh-huh, like Mrs. Sawyer always showed [points to board]. He walked. He walks. So . . .

T: Yeah, but tense works differently in stories . . . but I don't think present tense is used that often in stories but I'll look for it, you look to.

S: Where, like?

T: Oh, wait a minute, let's look at this book [teacher's novel she had been reading]. Look here, the author writes "I hear a bell ding." That's in present, so how come, why is it?

S: Maybe, the, it's . . . the . . . he uses I, he's in the story.

T: But he could have said, "I heard a bell ding," couldn't he?

S: Yeah.

T: You know what I think it is? I think it is we're talking about two different things here. Things happen to characters over time in both of these stories, right? [Holds up books] You don't change the overall tense of the story to show what's happening to the character, you use one tense and then you use words like you used here, "Just then" or "after that" to show what's happening to the character. It's the author's decision about do you want your audience to feel like the story is being told to them [holds up student book] or do you want them to feel like they are watching it happen right now [holds up her book], past or present, but either way you have to keep one tense all the way through.

S: So if I did, if I was going, if I wanted . . . If I was using present tense I would write, "She sees a bird and know, knows it's a . . . ?" and not care what she is, what the character? . . . Aye, Miss, just say like, "*first* she *does* this and *then* she *does* that," like that?

T: Exactly, but your story is . . .

S: Can I switch tense ever?

T: Yeah, you can but, well . . . go back and use these novels as a guide and decide which tense you want and then try to make it the same all the way through, I think.

S: Use this?

T: Uh-huh, I think past tense might be easier, but use one and then we'll work out the details when I come see what you've done later, okay?

Again, the teacher refers the student to the community of practice, what authors actually do: "Let's look at this book. . . . That's in present, so how come, why is it?" At this point, the exchange is no longer a debate where the teacher tries to get the student to support or accept the Teacher Thesis. Rather, the exchange has become a mutual exploration or quest by both teacher and student to adapt their thematic perspectives to the one(s) held by "insiders" in the literary community of practice. Moreover, the teacher uses meta-discourse (or talking about talking) when she says, "You know . . . I think we are talking about two different things here." In this way she not only recognizes the legitimacy of both thematic perspectives, she also signals the new thematic understanding as a different way of talking about the topic at hand.

In this classroom, even though the event is the same, the outcomes are very different in two senses. First, the participants are positioned in the dialogue quite differently. Both teacher and student are willing to admit the possibility of the other's position: "Yeah, for the author it's past" and "Well, you're right." Because of this, the student is positioned as having a valid thesis and therefore a legitimate claim to participation in the community of practice. Also, when the teacher defers to a more expert member of the community—"Go get it [your book] and let's see how the author does it"—she positions herself not as the expert holder of knowledge but as a fellow participant with the student. Both teacher and student are involved in activities that place them, as legitimate participants, in a wider community of practice that has certain rules and patterns that make up its discourse.

The second way in which this debate differs has to do with the outcome. While in the first debate the student's thematic perspective does not change, in the second debate, both teacher and student change their perspectives and generate a new, mutually constructed one.

Accordingly, we contend that within this particular classroom there are multiple opportunities for students to engage in the language (albeit imprecisely at first) of the discourse community. In this kind of formal environment for students who are becoming bilingual, not only are both boys and girls using more language, they are also being invited equitably into academic English discourse.

CONCLUSION

While this research was initially framed as an exploration of student language production and gender, it became clear that a more important question than who talks and who doesn't was how gender roles interact with classroom discourse. That is, which discourse structures provide not only more equitable roles for boys and girls, but also expand possibilities for acquisition into an academic discourse?

Based upon the analysis of classroom discourse across the four classroom settings, including differences between the ways boys and girls participated, we draw the conclusion that the decision to organize classroom discourse is politically or ideologically driven. In other words, when two similar events happen in two classrooms containing similar students but result in divergent patterns of exchange, the reason for the difference stems from political and ideological bases about classroom discourse: not only who gets to talk and when, but also what gets accepted as evidence for academic discourse.

Accordingly, we believe that it is important to declare candidly that

1. bilingual, sheltered, and ESL teachers come from and represent diverse communities of practice;
2. there is not one "academic language" for all students;
3. classroom discourse is a matter of the way communities of practice acquire new members; and
4. participation in communities of practice that involve academic discourse varies according to the political and ideological perspective that predominates in the classroom.

How diverse communities of practice enact classroom discourse remains unclear. There have been very few studies of holistic classroom discourse in bilingual and ESL secondary classes. Likewise, the influences of culture, gender, and subject area on discourse in secondary-level bilingual and ESL classes needs additional study. Further work on classroom communities of practice will likely entail the use of discourse analysis approaches that examine what happens in certain classrooms of a particular ideological perspective without necessarily making a comparison with other perspectives on discourse. What is clear to us from this study is that the discourse enacted in the ESL literature classroom was qualitatively different from that of the three other classrooms the students attended. As this may be one of the first studies of this type at the secondary level and with bilingual students, we know that more research is required to further understand how and why classroom discourse enacts and is enacted by the theoretical and ideological bases of teachers who work with adolescent students who are becoming bilingual in school.

REFERENCES

Au, K. H. (1980). Participant structures in a reading lesson with Hawaiian children: Analysis of a culturally appropriate event. *Anthropology and Education Quarterly, 11,* 91–115.

Bialystok, E., & Hakuta, K. (1995). *In other words*. New York: Basic Books.

Cazden, C. (1988). *Classroom discourse*. Portsmouth, NH: Heinemann.

Celce-Murcia, M., & Larsen-Freeman, D. (1983). *The grammar book: An ESL/EFL teachers course*. Rowley, MA: Newbury House.

Chamot, A., & O'Malley, M. J. (1987). The cognitive academic language learning approach: A bridge to the mainstream. *TESOL Quarterly, 21,* 227–249.

Christie, F. (1995). Pedagogic discourse in the primary school. *Linguistics and Education, 7,* 221–242.

Coates, J. (1986). *Women, men, and language: A sociolinguistic account of sex differences in language*. London: Longman.

Cummins, J. (1981). The role of primary language development in promoting educational success for language minority students. In California State Department of Education Office of Bilingual Education (Ed.), *Schooling and language-minority students: A theoretical framework* (pp. 3–48). EDAC, California State University, Los Angeles.

DeFrancisco, V. L. (1991). The sounds of silence: How men silence women in marital relations. *Discourse and Society, 2*(4), 413–429.

Delamont, S. (1980). *Sex roles and the school*. Methuen: London.

Edelsky, C. (1991). *With literacy and justice for all*. London: Falmer Press.

Faltis, C., & Hudelson, S. (1994). Learning English as an additional language in K–12 schools. *TESOL Quarterly, 18,* 457–468.

Gee, J. (1992). *The social mind: Language, ideology, and social practice*. New York: Bergin & Garvey.

Graves, D. (1983). *Writing: Teachers and children at work*. Portsmouth, NH: Heinemann Educational Books.

Heath, S. B. (1983). *Ways with words*. New York: Cambridge University Press.

Jones, M. G. (1989). Gender bias in classroom interactions. *Contemporary Education, 60,* 218–222.

Lave, J., & Wenger, E. (1991). *Situated learning: Legitimate peripheral participation*. Cambridge, UK: Cambridge University Press.

Lemke, J. (1990). *Talking science: Language, learning and values*. Norwood, NJ: Ablex.

Losey, K. M. (1995). Gender and ethnicity as factors in the development of verbal skills in bilingual Mexican American women. *TESOL Quarterly, 29*(4), 635–661.

Macías, J. (1990). Scholastic antecedents of immigrant students: Schooling in a

Mexican immigrant-sending community. *Anthropology and Education Quarterly, 21,* 291–318.

Mehan, H. (1979). *Learning lessons.* Cambridge, MA: Harvard University Press.

Mohatt, G., & Erikson, F. (1981). Cultural differences in teaching styles in a Odawa school: A sociolinguistic approach. In H. Trueba (Ed.), *Culture and the bilingual classroom.* New York: Newberry.

Moll, L. C. (1988). Some key issues in teaching Latino students. *Language Arts, 65,* 465–472.

Nieto-Gomez, A. (1973). The Chicana—Perspectives for education. *Encuentro Femenil, 1,* 34–61.

Ong, W. (1981). *Fighting for life.* Ithaca, NY: Cornell University Press.

Pedrasa, P., Attinasi, J., & Hoffman, G. (1980). Rethinking diaglossia. In R. Padilla (Ed.), *Theory in bilingual education* (pp. 75–97). Ypsilanti, MI: Eastern Michigan University.

Philips, S. (1983). *The invisible culture: Communication in classroom and community on the Warm Springs Indian reservations.* Prospect Heights, NJ: Waveland.

Rosebery, A. S., Warren, B., & Conant, F. R. (1992). *Appropriating scientific discourse: Findings from language minority classrooms.* The National Center for Research on Cultural Diversity and Second Language Learning. Santa Cruz, CA: University of California, National Center.

Sadker, M., & Sadker, D. (1984). *Failing at fairness: How American schools cheat girls.* New York: Charles Scribner's Sons.

Saville-Troike, M. (1984). What *really* matters in second language learning for academic achievement? *TESOL Quarterly, 18,* 199–219.

Short, D. (1994). Expanding middle school horizons: Integrating language, culture, and social studies . *TESOL Quarterly, 28,* 589–608.

Solomon, J., & Rhodes, N. (1995). *Conceptualizing academic language.* National Center for Research on Cultural Diversity and Second Language Learning. Santa Cruz, CA: University of California, National Center.

Spanos, G., Rhodes, N., Dale, T., & Crandall, J. (1988). Linguistic features of mathematical problem solving: Insights and Applications. In R. R. Cocking & J. P. Mestre (Eds.), *Linguistic and cultural influences on mathematics learning* (pp. 26–61). Hillsdale, NJ: Lawrence Erlbaum.

Spender, D. (1982). *Invisible women: The schooling scandal.* London: Writers and Readers Publishing Cooperative Society.

Stanley, J. (1986). Sex and the quiet schoolgirl. *British Journal of Sociology of Education, 7,* 275–286.

Trueba, J., & Delgado-Gaitán, C. (1988). *Minority achievement and parental support: Academic resocialization through mentoring.* Unpublished manuscript. (ERIC Document Reproduction Service No. ED 299 339)

Walkerdine, V. (1991). *Schoolgirl fictions.* London: Methuen.

PART II

The Curricula

CHAPTER 5

INTEGRATING LANGUAGE AND CONTENT FOR EFFECTIVE SHELTERED INSTRUCTION PROGRAMS

Deborah J. Short

CENTER FOR APPLIED LINGUISTICS

I told them last week they were going to do a poster. I have the posters in the back. On Wednesday or Thursday. When they have the knowledge. They're going to bring in crayons. And you know, this is something I would not have thought of doing years back, because I'd feel, well the elementary teachers have the time to do this. But I find, I'm teaching, they're learning, and I can justify doing these activities which cause better crystallization. I think the knowledge will stick better.

—Mr. Connor, 7th grade social studies teacher

Mr. Connor[1] is a dedicated teacher, and perhaps a rare teacher as well. He had taught for 34 years at the time of this interview, the last 26 in the same district. He was old enough and had enough years in the system to retire, but chose not to. Most teachers at that stage of their careers are not interested in new methodologies or changes of routine. Many bide their time until they can leave the profession with their maximum retirement benefits. Mr. Connor was unusual in this regard. Eight years earlier he had changed his routine and volunteered to teach social studies to English language learners, mostly Haitian refugees. He had no previous training in ESL methodology or second-language acquisition theory, nor did he receive any once he took on his new assignment. But he did have a great affection for the students and a willingness to modify his instruction to address their learning needs. As he stated, "I've been doing this for eight years, and I'm still working on it. It's an ongoing process."

There are many teachers across the United States who are being asked to teach content to English language learners (ELLs) without training. Sometimes they are ESL and bilingual teachers who have to teach mathematics or science or another subject for which they do not have specific certification. They may be very comfortable with the methodologies for developing their students' language skills, but not with strategies for demonstrating geometric proofs or conducting scientific inquiry-based activities. Others, like Mr. Connor, are certified to teach the subject area but have had no training for making that content comprehensible to students with limited proficiency in English. The notion of using demonstrations to convey meaning of key vocabulary words, for example, was not second nature to Mr. Connor. Up until this particular school year, he would have asked students to read the definitions of key words in the text glossary and encouraged them to look at their bilingual dictionaries at home.

Ms. North, another social studies teacher who, like Mr. Connor, sought to improve her instruction to ELLs, also did not previously focus on language development in class:

> And I still remember it last year when you came in for that Martin Luther lesson, and I was doing the Who, What, When, Where, Why, and they had not a clue, and you said, "You know, if you would tell them exactly what a 'who' is, they would have a much easier time telling you." And I'm going, "Oh, yeah, okay, that would work!" And, you know, it was so much easier because I did that in the beginning of this year and at that time it had to do with—. And that seemed so simple, but that's not a content social studies thing, it's an English, this is what the word is, and I just, for several years, I guess assumed they got it somewhere. It's just not in my curriculum guide to do vocabulary.

Both language and subject area teachers are being asked to integrate language development with content learning. This instructional approach is increasingly found in elementary and secondary schools and may be manifested in various program types—bilingual, ESL, sheltered, and regular mainstream programs. A recent study (Sheppard, 1995) showed that approximately 15% of the school systems in the United States offer at least one course that integrates language and content instruction. This research revealed, however, that great variety exists in these courses in terms of type of program, teacher, and learner; subject area(s) addressed; use of native language; and more. Nonetheless, a hallmark of the approach is the development of techniques, lessons, and curricula that teach students academic skills and content knowledge while they are in the process of mastering English. When done correctly, students systematically develop English language skills while they deepen and expand their understanding of the subject matter.

BACKGROUND

The year 2000 has been heralded as a turning point, not only for the century calendar, but also for changes in the U.S. educational system. Although school reform ideas from the 1980s, like the national education goals, have been recast in the mid-1990s, the highest motives for reform—improved delivery of educational services, enhanced student achievement, and preparation of students for the world of work—remain steadfast. Federal education legislation, state and local education initiatives, and business interests (Johnston & Packer, 1987; U.S. Department of Labor, 1992) have presented a powerful call to change the way our school systems educate children. As educators associated with linguistically and culturally diverse students, we know that change in educational programs for these students is of critical importance.

Educational change as envisioned, though, will not come easily or quickly. Nor will it endure without fundamental shifts in the behaviors and attitudes of the educators and the students. The challenge in the change process stems from the economic pressure of tightened school budgets and limited resources; social tensions and natural resistance to change; and the increasing diversity within the schools' student population, which will rise steadily through the year 2000 and beyond (Cummins, 1994; Waggoner, 1988), yet for which teacher education, school-based programs, curricula and materials, and instructional practice have not shifted accordingly.

Among the diverse students present in our schools are those for whom English is not their first language. The number of these language-minority students continues to grow exponentially, but their level of academic achievement lags significantly behind that of their language-majority peers and appears to be worsening (Council of Chief State School Officers, 1991). One study concluded that Hispanics are the most undereducated major segment of the U.S. population—they tend to enter school later, leave school earlier, and are less likely to complete high school or participate in postsecondary education (National Council of La Raza, 1991). Cummins (1994) found that language-minority students have higher dropout rates and are more frequently placed in lower ability groups and academic tracks than language-majority students. Moreover, a longitudinal study by the National Center for Education Statistics (1988) showed that while Asian students as a group had higher levels of achievement in reading and math than other minority groups, Southeast Asians were well below average, and Pacific Islanders had the greatest academic needs of all.

INFLUENCES ON SCHOOL SUCCESS

These demographic and test score findings are cause for serious concern, since there is growing evidence that most schools are not meeting the challenge of educating linguistically and culturally diverse students well. Even with programs designed for English language learners, staffing and funding sources have not been able to keep pace with the demand. Shortages of teachers qualified to teach students with limited English proficiency or to teach bilingual courses, limited fiscal resources due to the weak economies in areas with high demand for bilingual programs, and reduced funding from the federal government contribute to the problem (McDonnell & Hill, 1993; Zelasko, 1995).

English and native language support programs are also not sufficient. For school success, ELLs must have opportunities to learn academic content while studying English so they do not fall behind native English-speaking peers (Council of Chief State School Officers, 1992). However, in many schools, LEP students do not have access to content instruction in core curriculum areas, as a study by Minicucci and Olsen (1992) revealed, in which only 6 of 27 secondary schools in California provided full coverage of content courses through the native language or sheltered instruction.

As work by Collier (1987, 1989, 1995) and others has shown, programs that delay English language learners' access to content classes severely retard their proficiency in academic language and negatively affect their cognitive development, unless students are receiving content instruction in their native language. While most students show sufficient growth in acquiring social language skills (e.g., reading and conversational skills geared to nonacademic and survival interactions) in a few years, they less successfully acquire the language needed to fulfill school tasks such as reading textbooks, participating in content-related classroom discourse, and writing reports in that time frame. Educational change is needed to counter this tide of poor practice.

Sociocultural factors also influence the provision of equitable education to ELLs. Immigrant students often feel isolated by language and cultural barriers. In many school districts, students from non-Euro-American backgrounds are expected to assimilate quickly, yet in so doing, they may leave their cultural heritages behind. For adolescents who have already developed their cultural identity, this implicit policy is not only unacceptable but also difficult to accomplish.

The students must adjust to U.S. schools in which curricula and materials, placement and testing practices, and school policies are often too Euro-centered to serve the needs of diverse learners adequately (Banks & Banks, 1989; Crawford, 1993). Most instruction in U.S. schools remains traditional in nature, with teachers as transmitters of information and students as receivers (Goodlad, 1984; Tharp & Gallimore, 1988), yet this traditional style does not benefit culturally diverse students (Banks & Banks, 1989; Crawford, 1993; Faltis, 1993a). Unfortunately, most school systems have not adopted a new perspective, namely to value and respect the students' cultural heritages and make them part of the educational process.

In the classroom, teacher background is a significant factor that affects student success. Most teachers are from Euro-American, middle-class backgrounds with cultures that differ from those of most English language learners, yet teacher preparation institutions rarely train teacher candidates in strategies for teaching linguistically and culturally diverse students (Zeichner, 1993; Crawford, 1993). Mr. Connor's experience supports these research findings:

> I had absolutely no formal training at the time the district decided to set up an ESL program. I was asked, and there was no formal training. But I think they were relying on my experience as a teacher. And I was groping for various techniques, and these were not available at the time.

When teachers are unfamiliar with their students' cultures—which can influence learning styles, communication patterns, and involvement in class—they hold negative expectations for students or inaccurately interpret their interaction patterns, such as eye contact, self-nomination to talk, and small-group behavior (García, 1994; Nieto, 1992; Zeichner, 1993). Students who are unfamiliar with the teacher's or school's culture are at a clear disadvantage when it comes to participating in class and learning.

Furthermore, school systems can hinder the success of ELLs when inappropriate curricula, assessments, and instructional materials are used. Without sequenced curricula for language and content learning, and corresponding materials, students may not systematically develop their language skills and subject area knowledge. Developing such curricula is not a simple task, however. The Teachers of English to Speakers of Other Languages (TESOL) organization recently produced ESL standards for pre-K–12 students that call for students to use English to achieve academically, but the translation of these standards into curricula has only just begun in some states and districts, and actual implementation in the classroom is even farther away (TESOL, 1997). Appropriate instructional materials that match state content-area curriculum guidelines, for native language or sheltered approaches, are very difficult to find (Crandall, 1993), as are resources that make connections to the students' cultures. Moreover, the assessment of content learning for ELLs is an area of intense debate. What language to test students in, whether to provide accommodations or modifications, whether to exclude some students from testing, and how to measure content knowledge while not penalizing students for weak language skills are among the issues (Gottlieb, Chapter 7).

THE SHELTERED INSTRUCTION APPROACH

Despite the bleak picture regarding language education programs and policy in the United States, we have accumulated a great deal of knowledge and experience about what works for educating language-minority students. In small, concentrated efforts, individual school sites across the United States have begun to make a difference as they strive to improve the academic track record of language-minority students. Educators in these schools, who are dedicated to serving these students, have designed and refined administrative and pedagogical innovations that successfully include language-minority students in schoolwide reform. These educators have collected what we know about effective practice for English language learners and have experimented with recommendations for school change that the general education literature espouses.[2]

Most traditional programs are founded on the belief that students should move into English-only (i.e., mainstream) classrooms as soon as possible. This has been a political decision in many cases, federally supported through the grant-making process. However, researchers have examined the length of time needed to develop appropriate academic language skills and concluded that ELLs in the models most commonly found in schools (i.e., transitional bilingual education, where students exit in 2–3 years, or pullout ESL classes) require 4 to 7 (or more) years for students to achieve a level of proficiency in academic English comparable to the average, mainstreamed, English-speaking student (Collier, 1987, 1989, 1995; Cummins, 1980). Unfortunately, most traditional programs do not allow for students to spend this much time learning English. Nor do most secondary students have the time before graduation. From a cognitive development stance, such short time frames for language support programs render a disservice to English language learners.

The focus of this chapter, however, is on an alternative approach to the traditional program model, specifically sheltered instruction. It is an approach that can extend the time students have for getting language support services while giving them a jump-start on the required subject matter they will need for graduation. A sheltered program must not be viewed as simply a set of additional or replacement instructional techniques that teachers implement in their classroom. To really make a difference for English language learners, a sheltered program must be a broader, school-based initiative that takes into account the total schooling ELLs need.

As noted earlier, an increasing number of schools are creating courses where language development is a goal alongside content learning. In some cases, the course may be known as content-based ESL. It is taught by a language educator whose main goal is English language skill development but whose secondary goal is preparing students for the mainstream, English-medium classroom (Cantoni-Harvey, 1987; Crandall, 1993; Mohan, 1986; Short, 1991). This course may, in fact, be the first in a series of courses offered to students.

In content-based ESL, content from multiple subject areas is often presented through thematic instruction. Teachers seeking to develop the students' English language proficiency incorporate information from the types of courses ELLs are likely to enter and/or courses they may have missed if they are new to the school system. For secondary adolescent students, a theme, such as the preservation of the rain forest, might be selected and lessons could include objectives drawn from biology, social studies, economics, and algebra. Whatever the subject matter, for effective content-based ESL instruction to occur, teachers need to provide practice in academic skills and tasks common to mainstream classes (Adamson, 1990; Chamot & O'Malley, 1991; Mohan, 1990; Short, 1994).

Another way that schools and programs integrate language and content instruction is through a sheltered approach where language and content objectives are systematically woven into the curriculum of one particular subject area, such as algebra, biology, or American history. The regular subject curriculum is presented to the students through modified instruction in English. Developing the students' academic language proficiency is often a less explicit goal. Yet it must be a *daily* goal that effective teachers attend to as they plan and deliver their lessons (Crandall, 1993; Faltis, 1993b; Short, 1994).

In some schools, sheltered instruction is provided to classes composed entirely of English language learners. In others, a heterogeneous mix of native English speakers and ELLs may be present. Bilingual, ESL, and content teachers may be the instructors for these classes (Sheppard, 1995). The training of these teachers is especially critical at the high school level. In many states, for ELLs to receive core credit for the sheltered classes (as opposed to elective credit), which is necessary for high school graduation, the instructor must be certified in the subject area. The teachers are often trained in ESL methods as well, to make their instruction more accessible to those students learning English. Ironically, however, as Mr. Connor's testimony reveals, despite the readily apparent value of such training, it does not always take place.

The rest of this chapter will describe some of the key features that research and practice have indicated make sheltered instruction work well for English language learners. These include:

- A schoolwide vision of education that places the responsibility for the education of ELLs on all personnel, holds high standards for student achievement, and embraces and builds on diversity within the school population.
- An articulated and flexible program that provides ELLs with access to content early on in their schooling, moves them through language support services into English-medium (mainstream) classrooms, offers multiple pathways for exiting the program, and supports the students during the transition.
- Organization of the learning environment structure that facilitates language and content learning, as well as extension of instructional time to help adolescent ELLs catch up to the native English-speaking peers.
- Appropriate professional development to ensure that shared responsibility for ELLs is understood and instructional delivery is methodologically sound.
- Curricula and materials that promote language development in conjunction with the acquisition of content knowledge.
- Instructional practice that is grounded in research and prepares students for the rigors of mainstream courses.
- Assessment tools that systematically measure growth in student knowledge.

School Vision

Sheltered instruction should not be something that happens in one or two classrooms in a school. It should be integrated into the school's vision that considers the total education of the English language learners. The importance of a school's vision is noted repeatedly in literature on school reform (National Center for Restructuring Education, Schools and

Teaching, 1994) and in research done at schools with large numbers of language-minority students (August & Pease-Alvarez, 1996; Berman et al., 1995; Lucas, Henze, & Donato, 1990). The language support program is a temporary placement for ELLs; the ultimate goal of the program is to prepare them for successful work in mainstream classes. To move the students through the language support program and into the English-medium settings, several elements must be in place.

First, all faculty must assume responsibility for the students (TESOL, 1996). English language learners are not the ESL or bilingual teacher's "problem." They are students whom the entire school staff must be committed to helping achieve. Some faculty might interact with ELLs more than others, but all faculty need to hold high expectations for those students and be, at least, conversant about their cultural backgrounds and language learning needs. For this perspective to take hold in some schools, certain faculty members might need to shift their attitudes and beliefs. One of the more effective ways to have teachers confront their beliefs is through a vision-setting exercise where the stakeholders would develop a vision statement that explicitly includes ELLs.

Second, a school should hold high standards of achievement for the English language learners, both in and out of the language support program, and provide the resources to meet the standards. The language support program should be rigorous. The sheltered curricula should not be watered down, and the instructional materials should be appropriate to the cognitive levels of the students. Further, key aspects of a curriculum should not be eliminated. For instance, ELLs should not be denied opportunities to participate in laboratory science experiments or use equipment in industrial technology classes. At a high school for ELLs in New York City, for example, the students not only use computers with access to the Internet in the classrooms for research purposes, but also have a computer lab where they create World Wide Web pages for themselves and for their school. This lab is the envy of a technical community college down the street. Professors at that college have expressed interest in sharing the facility and teaching joint classes with the secondary and college students.

Third, the school must recognize the importance of helping the students maintain and continue their cognitive development in their native languages and include the students' cultures in curricular and extracurricular activities. Some schools may not have the resources to provide native language instruction for their ELLs, but they can stress the importance to students that they continue to use their native language in their homes and communities. As noted earlier, when students have the opportunities to develop their native language proficiency, their acquisition of

English is usually more robust (Collier, 1995; García, 1994; Genesee, 1987; Hakuta, 1986). Similarly, most students learn best in an environment where they are comfortable. A school that embraces the ELLs' cultures along with the cultures of all members of the education community creates such an environment (Kauffman et al., 1994).

Other elements should be included in the school vision so ELLs and their families feel they are part of the educational community. The presence of bilingual counselors, the availability of interpreters for parents, school documents translated into the languages of the families, policies that respect cultural diversity, bilingual books in the libraries, and the like send an important message to the ELLs that they are welcome and the staff is concerned about their education.

Program Design

For sheltered instruction to work effectively, it needs to be part of a comprehensive, articulated program. The program should include educational goals that adolescent ELLs will attain as part of the sheltered program as well as goals for their overall secondary education experience, whether they be directed toward a post-secondary academic path or a career-oriented one that may or may not require post-secondary education. All programs for adolescent ELLs should afford them the choice between these two directions.

Sheltered instruction can be found in numerous language program settings: English as a second language programs; transitional, maintenance, and developmental bilingual education; two-way immersion; newcomer programs; and alternative high schools (Faltis, 1993b; Kauffman et al., 1994; Sheppard, 1995). It may be offered to a wide range of students, from those with low literacy and/or limited formal schooling to those students with high academic credentials from their native countries.

Some school systems with ELLs from multiple language backgrounds have implemented an ESL, rather than bilingual, program. Many of them have instituted a sheltered approach such as a High Intensity Language Training (HILT) program. The program goal is to teach students English and provide access to content. Core curriculum courses, such as mathematics, science, and social studies, are sheltered. Depending on the design, students may have a sheltered English language arts class or an ESL class. All participating teachers would have ESL or bilingual training. At the middle school level, they may or may not be certified in the content area where they teach. At the high school level, they usually are.

Many HILT programs have several levels for student placement, as

TABLE 5.1 Placement Levels for HILT Programs

HILT—A	HILT—B	HILT—C
content-based ESL (two periods)	content-based ESL (two periods)	math (pre-algebra)
sheltered math (6th grade math)	sheltered math (7th grade math)	transitional English language arts
sheltered science (6th grade science)	sheltered science (life science)	science (physical science)
sheltered social studies (6th grade social studies)	sheltered social studies (American history)	sheltered social studies (world studies)
physical education	physical education	sheltered health/sheltered technology
elective	elective	physical education
		elective

shown in the middle school example. Table 5.1 is an example of a 3-year schedule for students beginning at level A in 6th grade. The school day has seven periods.

Students at the HILT levels A and B receive two periods of content-based ESL. Within these periods, students learn about study skills and academic tasks (e.g., note-taking, doing library research) and study inter-disciplinary thematic units to provide background information and experiences for different subject areas. Level A students have to learn social language skills and information about schooling and the American cultural heritage as well. Level B students do more sophisticated work on expository text and writing styles associated with different subjects, such as laboratory reports for science and cause–effect essays for social studies. Literature is incorporated into all levels. In HILT-C, students have made the transition to mainstream math and science and have a transitional English language arts class as a bridging and support course.

Variations of this example are many, depending on the resources available at the school and the needs of the students. In some cases, a course like sheltered American history might be taught over a two-year period in order to complete the full curriculum. Students begin it in HILT level A and continue in level B. This model is similar to the way foreign languages have traditionally been studied in the middle school. Another modification, especially if the ELLs have had interrupted schooling in the past, is to design the sheltered math and science courses as opportunities to teach the grades 1–5 math and/or science curricula of the elementary schools. Or, if the students are well versed in either subject from prior schooling in the native language, they could spend only one semester learning the technical vocabulary, how to use the textbook, and how they are expected to participate in the math or science discourse of the class, and possibly develop problem-solving, inquiry and application skills if those were not stressed in earlier courses.

The key to a sheltered program like this is flexibility to move in and out. Some students may not need sheltered instruction in all subject areas. For example, one student might need sheltered social studies in HILT B, but no longer need sheltered science. A schedule that allows them to spend some time in the sheltered program and some time out would be suitable. As will be discussed below, the team/house/academy design is one structure that offers some of the flexibility needed.

A school with a transitional bilingual education (TBE) program, which only serves students for 2 or 3 years, might place the ELLs into sheltered courses upon exit (Faltis, 1993b). While students in TBE programs have been receiving content instruction in their native language, due to the brief nature of the design, the students may not have the time to learn the corresponding aspects of academic English—the technical vocabulary of the subject areas, the text structures of written text, the ways of talking about the subject in English. Therefore, a year with sheltered courses may be the appropriate bridging mechanism for these bilingual students.

When a school offers a late-exit bilingual program, one that serves students for 5 or 6 years, sheltered instruction should be part of the design. As the English language learners approach the later years of the program, instruction in English should increase. The bilingual teachers may chose to provide part of the instruction in English, with some native language support to teach the content. For some courses, such as mathematics, the amount of English to learn to facilitate the transition to an English-medium course may be much less than the amount needed for social studies, which is much more literacy-dependent (Short, 1994).

In both types of bilingual programs, it is important to continue to develop the cognitive skills in the native language even as instruction in English might increase. Many researchers argue that having native language support in ESL programs is also beneficial to the students because academic skills they learn in their first language transfer to their second, and because to become fully bilingual one must have cognitive competency in both languages (Collier, 1995, García, 1994; Genesee, 1987). Indeed, ESL programs, too, should encourage the students to maintain their native language skills and, where possible, support further development of that language, either through the presence of bilingual professionals, home language clubs, or community initiatives (Lucas & Katz, 1994).

Two-way bilingual immersion programs do develop such bilingual competency, and sheltered instruction is an integral feature of the design. In a two-way class, where approximately half of the class are native speakers of English and the other half are native speakers of the target language, teachers shelter their instruction all the time because second language learners are always present (Christian, 1994; Christian, Montone, Lindholm & Carranza, 1997; Genesee, 1987). The successful academic achievement of students in these programs provides some evidence of the merits of sheltered instruction (Lindholm & Gavlek, 1994). The need for sheltered instruction diminishes, however, as the two-way students reach the secondary school level. By the end of the middle school grades, most students (unless the program permits newcomers to enter) have already developed the grade-appropriate academic skills they will need, in both languages.

No matter what the language support program type, a variation on the self-contained sheltered classroom is the "push-in" model. In some schools, when the ELLs reach a certain level of proficiency, they might be placed in all-English-medium classes and an ESL resource teacher "pushes in" to co-teach with the assigned subject-area teacher. While the push-in model has not yet been well documented, there are suggestions for making the co-teaching effective. First, the ESL resource teacher must be considered an equal partner with the content teacher. All students in the class (ELLs and others) are expected to treat both teachers as teachers, not one as the teacher and the other as an aide. Second, the ESL resource teacher should have specific duties of instruction that are delivered to the whole class. In other words, the ESL resource teacher would not sit in one corner with the ELLs and tutor or provide separate instruction. Third, the duties should relate to the ESL resource teacher's skills and could be characterized as enhancing communication in that subject. For example, the ESL resource teacher might conduct pre-reading activities or lead classroom discussions that are geared toward identifying prior knowledge among the students or toward checking student comprehension of a topic. The ESL resource teacher might be the writing expert in the class, helping all students with writing assignments. In these ways, the ESL teacher can help shelter the lessons for the ELLs in the class.

The final consideration in the program design is the plan for monitoring and supporting the students once they have exited the language services program. Far too many students are inaccurately placed in lower-track classes because a support system, be it tutorial classes, a study buddy, or the like, is not in place to ease the transition process. Sheltered classes help in this area, of course, but the regular mainstream environment can be daunting for ELLs without a transition plan. At a middle school in California, former ESL students are re-evaluated by the mainstream and ESL teachers after 30 days of being placed in mainstream classes and then again after 6 months (Kauffman et al., 1994). A high school in New Jersey offers tutorials and mentoring with teachers during the first semester after the transition, and in a Kansas high school, students spend time observing in regular classes before exiting the language support program (Short & Boyson, 1997).

Learning Environment Scaffolds

Besides planning how to move students along the English language continuum and how to ensure secondary students access to content, programs can also consider how they structure the learning environment and make use of instructional time. Schools with effective programs are creative in their design of the school day for teachers and students. A growing number have reorganized their schools into smaller learning communities, sometimes known as houses, teams, or academies.

These schools are not constrained by the traditional bell schedule of a secondary school (Berman et al., 1995; Minicucci, 1996). They have, for example, instituted block scheduling so teachers in these teams have the flexibility to plan instruction in meaningful chunks of time. As teachers in a team divide up the time in instructionally sound ways, not in a fixed schedule of seven 45-minute periods, students have more time for sustained interaction with the material, and therefore teaching can proceed in such a way that learning can occur. Moreover, interdisciplinary themes can be explored more fully than usually possible in secondary schools, and content as well as instructional activities (e.g., journal writing, peer conferencing, literature across the content areas) can be linked.

Academies, such as a law enforcement or health and dental careers academy, move interdisciplinary curricula to a higher level and in many instances offer students work force preparation as well as language and content learning. A high school in Northern California, for instance, offers all students a common core curriculum in 9th grade (ELLs take ESL and English language arts classes), and then students select an academy (health, graphic arts, business, or career exploration) for grades 10–12. They take core courses along with vocational courses geared to the academy, and they participate in internships outside of the school. The ELLs have an extra bilingual support class while in the academy.

These types of smaller learning communities, where a limited number of teachers share and are responsible for the same students, benefit secondary English language learners, especially when content teachers and language specialists are placed on teams together. In the academy high school described above, all teachers in one academy have common planning periods. Colleagues can share information about individual students' language development as well as strategies and techniques for enhancing instruction. Team and academy groupings also facilitate the implementation of interdisciplinary curricula. Sheltered classes fit easily into this design, and when sheltered and nonsheltered courses are available, students can exit the language support program according to their capabilities in different subjects, yet remain on the team.

Another structural design that can maximize the contact ELLs have with instructors who develop their academic language skills is time extension. In schools committed to smoothing the transition to the English-medium setting for their ELLs, before- and afterschool tutoring has been instituted. These tutorial classes (or homework clubs or study groups), which use sheltered instruction, become a regular feature of the school day. Trained educators work with the ELLs in a variety of ways. The time slot may be utilized as a study skill opportunity, a homework coaching time, an ongoing process writing workshop, or an orientation to computer technology (e.g., how to conduct Internet research in the computer lab). In schools with a year-round schedule, these time extension courses occur during the intersessions. That academy high school not only has block scheduling and the bilingual support classes for students, but also several afterschool programs and two Saturday programs that sponsor native-language literacy for the Spanish-speaking, Ukrainian, and Russian students and their parents. There is an afterschool tutorial and homework center equipped with computers for the ELLs.

Another variation to the school structure is the establishment of semester-long courses to serve students who have had grade-level–equivalent instruction in their home countries, yet need to acquire the English associated with the subjects before moving on to higher-level coursework. As mentioned earlier, a student who has already completed a life science class in his or her home country may only need a semester of sheltered life science to learn the technical language, the expectations for participation in science class in the U.S., how to follow directions for laboratory experiments and write lab reports, and so on.

Semester-long classes have also been successful with secondary students who have low literacy skills in their native language and English. In a Virginia district, a high school math course that teaches the basic objectives from the K–8 math curricula was developed and effectively implemented with low-literacy students through sheltering techniques, with heavy emphasis on hands-on activities, concentrated math language development, and connections to the students' life experiences in using math outside the classroom (Buchanan & Helman, 1993). Students could move into a semester of sheltered pre-algebra before taking mainstream algebra the following year.

A final example of time extension is sometimes informal policy and sometimes explicit, namely, allowing ELLs more time to graduate from high school. Some school districts plan an English language learner's schedule so a 5-year or even a 6-year program is delineated. For adolescent students who enter secondary schools with very low levels of proficiency in English, the pressure of completing high school in 4 years is eased.

Professional Development

Developing a cadre of professional teachers who can integrate language and content instruction is essential for the effective education of ELLs. Teacher education institutions must start training their undergraduate students in the theory and practice related to educating culturally and linguistically diverse learners. This charge must target all departments that grant teaching degrees. Given the demographic projections for the student population, it is likely that all current teacher candidates will encounter some culturally and linguistically diverse students during their teaching careers. In order to serve all their students well, these candidates must be prepared from the start of their careers, before they begin student teaching. All undergraduate teaching programs should at a minimum require coursework in second language acquisition, cross-cultural or multicultural awareness, English as a second language methodologies, and the development of sheltered curricula. These teachers-to-be should have opportunities to observe diverse classrooms with master teachers and work in diverse settings as they train (Sleeter & Grant, 1987).

Because such coursework and training have not regularly occurred in most teacher education programs to date, professional development for practicing teachers is needed. As Zeichner (1993) and Crawford (1993) have reported, most practicing teachers have not had courses in these areas, nor do they come from backgrounds similar to the English language learners. As a result, these teachers need support. This support can come through multiple avenues, of which three will be discussed here: collaboration with more skilled colleagues at the school, a carefully designed series of in-service workshops, and professional development lab schools.

In some instances, professional development occurs at the school level when one teacher realizes that he or she could be teaching ELLs better. Without district-level support, that teacher might turn to a colleague who has the interest and is willing to collaborate. Often this collaboration occurs between a content teacher and an ESL or bilingual teacher. They each have a specialized set of skills and knowledge to bring to the dialogue and work jointly to improve one another's teaching. They may take turns observing one another's classes to learn more about the curriculum, materials, course objectives, and students. The language partner may help the content teacher become more aware of the type of academic discourse he or she is using in class and may give suggestions for making the presentation of content more comprehensible. The content partner might suggest reading passages for the language teacher to use or skills-based activities to implement. They might generate some strategies for assessing the English language learners in the content area. They may begin to prepare lessons together, eventually leading to a sheltered curriculum for one course.

The two teachers below, Ms. North and Mr. Ferguson, taught middle school social studies in classes where ELLs were integrated with native English speakers. Ms. North began participating in professional development activities to help her integrate language and social studies about 3 years earlier. She was, at this point, considered a leader in her middle school:

> A lot of times, they [other teachers] come to me: "What are you doing?" I go, "Come and see what's up on my wall." "What is that? Where can I get that? I'm working on this. Where can I find this?" Or we'll talk and I'll say, "You know, I'm working on Asia, and—what can I get for this?" "Wow, have I got something for you!" A lot of times, if I see someone who needs help . . . and . . . a lot of time like, if I'm talking to the new teachers, you know people . . . "Oh, well, after you've learned to sort out discipline, how about cooperative learning?" And, "Here's some good cooperative learning ideas." We helped some teachers last year—

During his second year of teaching, Mr. Ferguson started taking courses in ESL methodologies. He was to shift to ESL teaching in his third year. His enthusiasm for this shift was evident in his following comment, which reflects the in-school professional development that he and Ms. North had initiated.

> What's great about that is, if we get what we've asked for this year, I'll be able to work more with those teachers who have just ESOL kids for those classes, and we'll be able to really do some serious thematic units. . . . I think that will work out better for us . . . to go ahead and just get those five teachers to start doing some serious thematic units, and then saying, "Hey,

this is what's working for us," and then pushing and seeing how far we can get other people to go along with it.

In other cases, the professional development is conceptualized at the district level. Recognizing that the old style of teacher training—one-shot (in the dark) workshops on a few selected days throughout the year— has not been effective (González & Darling-Hammond, 1998), program coordinators and principals have initiated more long-term designs. Often working with outside consultants or in-house resource specialists, a series of workshops on the sheltered approach are planned for a certain group of teachers. Both language and content teachers attend these sessions jointly, which helps crystallize the philosophy that all teachers share re- sponsibility for the English language learners. Over a period of several months, the teachers can concentrate on a specific area or goal, such as learning about sheltered instruction practices, developing sheltered cur- ricula, writing interdisciplinary units, analyzing individual content areas to identify specific features of their academic discourse, or generating assessment tools for sheltered classes. A workshop series provides time for teachers to reflect on their own practice, try new techniques and re- port on them, receive feedback on instructional practice, and, as is often important at the secondary level, where many teachers work in semi- isolation, work as part of a larger team.

A third alternative is the professional development lab school. While this has been written about in more detail elsewhere (cf. González & Dar- ling-Hammond, 1998), it is an effective means to train sheltered teachers. When a school district and a teacher education institution pair up, the lab school can become the site for preservice and in-service professional development. With master teachers teaching in the lab school, both un- dergraduate and practicing teachers would have classrooms in which to observe exemplary practice. The school would also provide a venue for research, so, for instance, schools that want to pilot new program models or assessment systems could do so while the university personnel provide technical assistance and conduct formative evaluations.

Curriculum and Materials

Teachers who teach content to English language learners frequently voice concern over "covering the curriculum," which may include state man- dates. As Ms. North explained, "I used to feel very constrained, because I was obsessed with getting to the end of the curriculum." In some cases, a teacher must also contend with a department chair or a middle school team that seeks adherence to a schedule allocated for each section of the syllabus. The controversy most often happens when there is no sheltered curriculum in place; rather, the teacher is trying to adapt an existing curriculum, usually day by day. A solution is to develop a specific sheltered curriculum that covers the core objectives of the course yet delivers instruction to ELLs in comprehensible ways.

Developing such curricula and materials for sheltered instruction is a time-consuming process, because both language and content objectives must be carefully planned so sequential and complementary learning occurs. This means the language objectives must be carefully aligned with the content topics so the structures and functions being taught emerge from the subject matter. This process requires curriculum developers to look at two sets of frameworks, those for the content area being sheltered and those for English as a second language. Developers might want to consult their local and state frameworks as well as national standards. Sheltered courses that have thematically linked and project-driven lesson units are particularly successful. A theme allows for natural language development in the course of the content topics; academic language (e.g., vocabulary, functions) can be introduced and reinforced throughout the thematic lessons. Projects are not only useful assessment tools, but also anchors for students to confirm and apply their new knowledge.

While a curriculum development process can occur in many ways, a recent research study, "Integrating Language and Culture in the Social Studies," provides one model (see Short, 1993a, 1994). One component involved developing sheltered social studies curriculum units. All lessons in the units were designed to incorporate content, language, and thinking/study skill objectives with student-centered activities in order to make social studies more accessible for English language learners. The lessons were planned to give students a chance to acquire and enrich knowledge individually and cooperatively through reading tasks with authentic and adapted texts, role-plays and interviews, physical movement and drama, art projects, process writing, and library research.

The content objectives were drawn from the national social studies and history standards (National Center for History in the Schools, n.d. a&b; National Council for the Social Studies, 1992, 1994), commercial textbooks, curricula, and other documents (cf. California State Dept. of Education, 1987; Crabtree, Nash, Gagnon, & Waugh, 1992). The language objectives were selected to be compatible with the content and to promote development in listening, speaking, reading, and writing skills, with specific attention to language tasks required in a social studies class, such as reading for specific information, taking notes, listening for details, generating outlines and timelines, presenting an oral report, and writing a comparison essay.

Thinking and study skill objectives also matched the content objectives and led teachers to pose more higher-order questions and require more integrated tasks. In some lessons, activities were designed to encourage students to consider multiple points of view, those of the participants and observers in certain historical events. In others, students had to determine cause–effect relationships, both as a means of understanding the escalation of conflict and of considering alternative conflict resolutions. In addition, many lessons helped students prepare and interpret timelines, maps, graphs and outlines; summarize information; use authentic source material; and make decisions—all skills determined critical for middle school students by the National Council for the Social Studies task force on scope and sequence (Jarolimek, 1989).

The lessons included a mix of authentic and adapted materials. Authentic materials helped prepare students to read mainstream textbooks; teachers supported the students as they worked on comprehension skills and directed their attention to key points in the text. Students worked with original source documents, reference and biographical material, and authentic poems, letters, songs, maps, and political cartoons, as they would in a mainstream course. Adapted materials were written to bridge gaps found in the textbooks, specifically to provide information about the different gender, ethnic, racial, and socioeconomic status of peoples who lived in the historical periods being studied and around the world. In order to write these passages, trade and reference books, museum materials, and ethnic and cultural resource organizations were consulted.

Graphic organizers were part of each lesson to assist student comprehension of the content objectives and reading passages and to familiarize them with the more popular text structures. Some of the organizers were intended to help students categorize and systematize the information they gathered. Some lessons used flow charts to organize information presented in a cause–effect manner; others used timelines to show chronological progression. Venn diagrams helped students become aware of comparisons, and tree diagrams helped the students understand enumeration. Coupled with these structural organizers, teachers were encouraged to explore and directly teach the rhetorical markers with the students—words signaling comparison, sequence, and so forth.

Instructional Practices

How sheltered instruction is implemented in a classroom varies widely. While many characteristics of sheltered lessons have been identified, it is not yet known which of the elements are critical components for the instruction to work and which provide added value. Further research in this area is in progress, but at present we can describe a number of successful practices for teaching and learning in a sheltered class. The sheltered approach is not a new set of skills that teachers must acquire at the expense of their current practice. Indeed, the sheltered approach draws from and complements methods and strategies advocated for both language (e.g., ESL, bilingual, foreign language) and mainstream classrooms. This fact is beneficial to English language learners because the more familiar they are with the activity structure, the easier it will be for them to focus on the new content once they are in a mainstream classroom. Not all of the recommendations enumerated below, however, must be implemented in every lesson. Some may work more successfully with advanced students, others, with beginners. Those interested in pursuing this topic further should consult the books that have been written specifically on strategies and techniques.[3]

1. *Make connections between the content being taught and students' real-life experiences and prior knowledge.* Learning most often involves hooking new information onto prior knowledge. Besides their limited English proficiency, many ELLs are at a disadvantage with the content curriculum because they lack background knowledge of the topic at hand or have gaps in the information they do know. Teachers must plan instruction to provide some background schema for these students and activate what prior knowledge exists. Thematic units are one means of accommodation because the linked lessons provide needed time to develop some foundational knowledge. Looking for connections to students' personal experiences and generating analogies is another way to bridge the gaps and help students learn the content being taught.

2. *Pay attention to language issues and employ strategies that will help students learn the language of the content area.* Effective sheltered teachers know the academic language associated with the content area they are teaching. They are aware of the semantic, syntactic, and pragmatic aspects of the language as well as the more holistic expressions of the discourse, such as how one asks questions like a scientist or reports on past events like a historian. They use this knowledge to tailor their teacher talk, to generate language objectives, to capitalize on language learning opportunities in the course of a lesson, and to create events and activities in their classrooms that promote student communication about the content, in oral and written form.

To help students with vocabulary development, which is important to academic learning, teachers must select and implement instructional techniques suited to the content of the lesson. They cannot rely on textbook glossaries to identify the key words and teach their meanings to students, because glossaries do not identify most of the words that ELLs need help in understanding. Rather, textbooks assume a certain body of knowledge is already known (because all students presumably took courses at earlier grade levels), so the books only highlight new technical terms. While ELLs need to know these new terms, they also need to learn much more. Vocabulary techniques used by sheltered teachers include explicit instruction, dictionary practice, defining vocabulary through context, demonstrations, illustrations, impromptu role plays, and connecting words to the students' personal experiences or current events. Some sheltered teachers also reinforce vocabulary through artwork and writing projects.

Teachers must also train students in using a textbook and understanding academic text structures. Textbooks play a large role in most secondary mainstream courses, so students need to be familiar with not only the basics, such as the difference between an index and a glossary, but also how to skim through a chapter using headings and when to interrupt the reading of the main narrative to read sidebars or look at figures and illustrations. One excellent strategy is to teach ELLs to identify the linguistic cues of text structure (e.g., discourse markers that indicate comparisons are being made). Teachers can also make the textbook reading process more comprehensible through vocabulary previews, pre-reading oral discussions, prediction activities, note-taking practice, and so forth.

3. *Promote critical thinking and study skill development.* ELLs must be prepared for the academic demands of mainstream courses so they will succeed once they make the transition out of the language support program. One way to facilitate the transition is to teach higher-order thinking and study skills explicitly. Teachers can weave activities requiring these skills into any sheltered lesson, even with beginning-level students, although the level of complexity will vary accordingly. Beginning-level students can look at pictures in a book and predict what the corresponding reading passage will be about. They can participate in a science experiment and draw conclusions about the results they observe. They can sequence pictures or statements about the events in the experiment. More advanced students can formulate a scientific hypothesis and then plan ways to test it out. They can learn to think critically about information they receive, comparing, for example, multiple accounts of a historic event to determine, if possible, what is fact and what is opinion or conjecture.

Questions and activities that encourage students' reasoning ability, such as forming hypotheses, making inferences, analyzing situations, justifying opinions, and predicting future events, are the backbone to later student success in mainstream classes. The language used by the teacher or students need not be complex for thinking skills to be exercised, but asking higher-order questions must become part of the daily routine. It is easy to ask simple recall and comprehension questions, and teachers sometimes fall into that trap because they believe that is the degree of difficulty their English language learners can handle. To the contrary, it is critical to ask the more difficult questions—the whys, the hows, and the how do you knows. Although limited English skills may restrict students' abilities to articulate their responses, they can still think about these questions and how they would answer, even in their native language. To help students find the words to respond, teachers can model critical thinking skills, in a step-by-step approach to reasoning, through "think-alouds."

4. *Use graphic organizers to help students represent information and identify relationships.* Graphic organizers are very useful tools in sheltered instruction. They can be used in motivation tasks to activate student background knowledge and personal experience. Semantic webbing, for instance, allows students to organize their thoughts by contributing and categorizing information. Graphic organizers also help students comprehend text—through pre-, concurrent, and post-reading activities—by separating important information from extraneous details and reducing dependence on written words to understand meaning. Graphic organizers similarly provide a means to familiarize students with the structures of text and rhetorical styles. Venn diagrams can help students understand comparison, while flow charts explain cause and effect. Such organizers therefore act as bridges between reading and writing, especially as students learn to use organizers as pre-writing tools. Furthermore, graphic organizers can serve as study frameworks. English language learners can take notes in the form of an outline, timeline, grid, chart, or another suitable format. Because such organizers play major roles in academic subjects, the more practice ELLs have with them in a sheltered course, the better.

5. *Be process-oriented and provide modeling to help students make the transition to academic tasks.* Learning is rarely about the end product. Students in sheltered classes may need guidance in how to learn or accomplish a particular task. Effective sheltered teachers model both appropriate language and activities for the students. Functional language, for example, can be modeled in the context of a dialogue, as between a scientist and a reporter regarding the results of an experiment. Demonstrations or other actions can not only show the meaning of new words, but also the expected procedures to be used in completing an assignment. Teachers can model an activity with a small group of students while the ELLs and others look on and comment afterwards as one technique for helping students understand what is expected of them. The writer's workshop, a process writing approach used in mainstream classrooms, is also ideal for English language learners who would benefit from writing drafts, getting input, and revising their work.

6. *Tap the students as resources for information.* Sheltered teachers realize the ELLs have a great deal to contribute to the classroom interaction. English language learners may have different world views, perspectives, and opinions that add richness to the discussion. They have most likely lived in different ways from their classmates, and their personal experiences and funds of knowledge can shed light on certain applications of the information being addressed in class. Furthermore, the students' knowledge of their native countries' histories and cultures can be

mined for making comparisons or adding detail to what is being studied. By focusing on ELLs as resources, teachers validate the students' knowledge and experiences and make them part of the educational process.

7. *Incorporate cooperative learning activities and seek peer tutors among classmates.* With cooperative learning, ELLs support one another as they learn, practice, and apply the subject matter, perhaps drawing on knowledge of the topic that one of the students may already have. They also interact verbally, practicing their oral academic language and social skills. Teachers may allow students in some cooperative groups to discuss the assignment in their native language. This is a way to reinforce the content being studied and accomplish a task. The reporting of the assignment, though, would be in English so that academic language learning occurs.

Sheltered teachers may rely on the English-speaking students or more advanced ELLs as tutors and partners. Some students may have a skill to share, such as being able to conduct research online. Others may have more facility with English, such as stronger literacy skills, so they could assist classmates in reading and writing activities. Still others might have the content knowledge from schooling in their home countries and could teach their classmates through English or the native language.

8. *Allow some use of the native language.* Sometimes students process and understand content information better when they have opportunities to discuss it in their native language. In cases where students from the same language group are in a class, encouraging some communication in the native language when they work in pairs or small groups can be beneficial. Similarly, suggesting students discuss the content at home in their native language is another means of reinforcing the information. In these ways, as ELLs learn the concepts, teachers can focus on teaching them the appropriate language to discuss and apply academic concepts in English. Furthermore, students benefit cognitively if they continue to develop their native language proficiency.

9. *Increase multicultural content in teaching.* Most textbooks and curricula do a poor job of including multicultural content (Banks & Banks, 1989; Beck & McKeown, 1991), yet such content should be included in sheltered courses to increase the relevance of the subject and to mediate the cultural discontinuity ELLs might feel. However, rather than relying on a "foods, festivals, and famous people" approach—a random sampling of cross-cultural information disconnected from the curriculum (e.g., discussing the life of a famous Mexican artist during Hispanic Heritage Week or reading a legend about Chinese New Year in February)—it is preferable to infuse multiple perspectives and multicultural content systematically and substantively throughout the curriculum. Multicultural content can be added in several ways. Teachers may use students as cultural informants as discussed above. They may seek out supplemental reading material to add to the lessons or write their own. They may invite community resources into

the course as guest lecturers. They may establish "cultural application days" where once every two weeks the class discusses what they have been learning and how it might apply to different cultures and countries.

Moreover, where possible, the multicultural strategies, materials, and discussion topics should be used in mainstream classes, so native English speakers would also participate. Since it is important for all students to learn about minority cultures and their contributions to society, schools can, in this way, help equip all students with the skills needed to function in the culturally diverse world outside the school doors.

10. *Offer students multiple pathways to demonstrate their understanding of the content.* As students are still learning English, they may have difficulty articulating all they know and have learned about a content topic. By planning hands-on and performance-based activities, in addition to oral discussion and written assignments, teachers can check on student comprehension of the subject matter and students can confirm their own understanding of new concepts. These types of activities are less language-dependent and therefore allow students to demonstrate and apply their knowledge without the distraction of remembering subject–verb agreements, choosing transition words, or other stylistic and form-related phrasings associated with speaking or writing. Teachers may also want to create a list of possible unit projects or activities and have students select one (or more) for which they will be graded. For instance, in a unit on medieval Europe, students might be asked to choose among the following: design three stained glass windows, each of which should include the figure of an important person and at least three symbols to represent his or her life; write an essay comparing medieval Europe to feudal Japan; create a diorama of a feudal estate; or prepare and perform a skit between a serf and a craftsman.

11. *Adjust instruction for the different learning styles.* Gardner's work on multiple intelligences (Gardner, 1993) has popularized the concept of learning styles and engendered new teaching approaches in mainstream and sheltered classrooms alike. All students have several learning styles, although often one or two predominate. As teachers get to know their students, they can recognize and build on the students' stronger styles. This may be especially fruitful for classes with ELLs, where, as mentioned earlier, many teachers are less familiar with their cultures and learning styles. In general, students benefit when lesson activities vary; they deepen their understanding when it is stimulated or reinforced through different modes, such as visual representations, discussions, physical movement, and so forth.

12. *Develop a student-centered curriculum.* Secondary students, as they progress up grade and proficiency levels, are able to assume more and more responsibility for their learning. Therefore, teachers need to become guides and information resources while students select the topics and activities they wish to pursue. Activities that hold students' interest will help improve their academic perfor-

mance in class, because when students are actively involved, they can better process the material and acquire the language.

When teachers use student-centered activities, they reduce the amount of teacher talk and decrease reliance on textbooks and workbooks. They expose students to more opportunities for using language in creative, meaningful, and motivating ways. A student-centered curriculum can create a supportive environment that capitalizes on opportunities for language practice, accepts the students' learning errors as they occur naturally, and encourages their learning achievements. Sheltered lessons lend themselves to projects and journal writing, for instance, where students have voice in the selection of topics and thus are more invested in the outcomes.

Assessment

Assessment is addressed more fully in Chapter 7, but several points related to assessing sheltered instruction will be mentioned here. Assessment is often a gatekeeper for secondary students; therefore, care must be taken to give ELLs all the opportunities possible to demonstrate their understanding of the core content.

Although the main goal of sheltered instruction is teaching the subject area's curriculum, teachers cannot always assess content knowledge with ELLs in the same way they do with native English speakers. Most assessment instruments actually test both content concepts and language ability, particularly reading comprehension and writing. Because language and content are woven together in the sheltered approach, it is difficult to isolate one feature from the other in the assessment process. Thus, when reviewing a student error on an assessment measure, a teacher may not be sure whether the student was unable to demonstrate knowledge because of a language barrier or whether the student did not know the content material being assessed (Short, 1993b). This distinction needs to be made clear, however.

First, assessment should match instruction. The type of assessment activities students are asked to do must be similar to learning activities they have experienced in class. It is unfair to ask students to perform a new task in an assessment situation. The resulting scores will be much less valid; they will not demonstrate what a student knows and does not know. Furthermore, if students receive some accommodations during instruction, such as extra time to process both the language and content information embedded in an assignment, the same accommodations should be present in assessment situations, especially during high-stakes tests.

One recommendation is to check student knowledge of the content through a familiar structure. For example, if the class has been working on writing comparative essays and students are comfortable with the process, then the teacher may select a topic studied but not yet written about for an assessment measure. Suppose the science class has written essays describing animal classification and recently has been studying plant classification. Asking the students to perform a similar writing task on the new topic (plants) is a reasonable way to assess their knowledge.

Second, before any assessment procedure is designed, teachers must define their objectives and inform the students in advance. Although it is not uncommon to find teachers assigning two grades to a writing sample, like an essay—one for form (e.g., grammar, spelling, use of topic sentences) and one for content (e.g., topical, accurate, use of supporting evidence)—this practice does not work for all subject areas or testing situations. Instead, it is more advisable to focus on a single objective, be it content- or language-specific. Some assessment tools could be used exclusively for checking content comprehension, while others could be designated as language-development measures. When students know in advance what they will be tested on, they can make more informed choices while studying.

Third, assessment in sheltered classes should incorporate variety. Teachers need to include both formal and informal measures in their overall assessment plan and should develop and implement a diversified portfolio of assessment tools. Having the students perform a test on one particular day provides only limited information that must be interpreted in light of the setting. Alternative assessment techniques balance the norm- and criterion-referenced tests teachers are required to give. These alternatives include performance-based tasks, portfolios, journals, projects, interviews with students, anecdotal records of student achievements, and observation checklists. Although all students can benefit from a wide range of assessment procedures, variety is particularly important for ELLs because they 1) are often unfamiliar with the type of standardized tests usually required in American schools, and 2) may have different learning and testing styles.

Finally, students should be given frequent opportunities to demonstrate growth in their knowledge base and should be evaluated on their personal progress. Assessment is not a foot race in which individual students should be pitted against one another. Instead, a new paradigm for assessment is needed, in which each student is measured against himself or herself to determine if learning has taken place. In sheltered classes in particular, where students may have different levels of language proficiency, the value of this shift in focus becomes apparent. If teachers gather baseline data on what their students know and can do with the content information before instruction occurs and then what they know and can do afterwards, teachers can identify student growth.

CONCLUSION

This chapter has tried to suggest some parameters and recommendations for integrating language and content in effective sheltered programs. Demographic shifts in the K–12 student population indicate that more and more teachers will be called upon to provide sheltered instruction. In order to implement an effective program, several elements need to be part of a comprehensive school- or district-wide plan. These include a vision for the success of all students, including ELLs; a well-articulated program design that focuses on the development of both language skills and content knowledge; an organizational structure where learning is reinforced through multiple venues and extended time; adequate professional development for faculty so they can implement the sheltered approach; curricula specifically written for sheltered courses, along with appropriate materials; delivery of instruction through successfully identified strategies and techniques; and assessments designed for sheltered courses.

The three social studies teachers who were assigned sheltered classes at their schools without background or training, Mr. Connor, Ms. North, and Mr. Ferguson, all sought to improve their teaching. They found that with support, professional development, and curricular materials, sheltered instruction could be done. They built on skills they already possessed and added more. They formed coalitions with other teachers and took leadership roles in their schools. And they continued to reflect on their practice.

Connor: I find I'm teaching, they're learning, and I can justify doing
   these activities which cause better crystallization. I think the knowledge will stick better. I find an improvement in the unit tests, the quizzes of the year. I have to look at the final exams. We're gonna analyze each item and see if there's been improvement as a result of this year. This year's more intense in terms of applying these various techniques, so I have to evaluate them myself at the end of the year . . .
North: Oh, I'm such a good teacher now! I, and I vow I'm going to be Teacher-of-the-Year yet. I think I've got it nailed down . . . Now, I can identify where I'm weak. . . . I am so much more sensitive to the

type of student that I'm teaching. . . . I've completely changed my teaching strategy.

Ferguson: I think for me, one of the good things that I got out of it . . . I was more of a, "Here's a reading. You read it. You get the vocabulary, and then you answer questions" type of person. Now I find myself—which I really felt uncomfortable doing at the beginning—which was doing different things like role-playing, actually getting kids to debate in class. I think one of my problems was, to me was, I had just never done it before and I wasn't sure how well it was going to be received and how well I could do it, so I was kind of a little shy, a little scared of doing it. . . . I needed a little nudge, and that nudge really helped me, I think. My kids enjoyed a lot of the lessons. They got sick of . . . especially my first year, it was, "Okay, here's what we're reading today." I got caught in that rut. Now my strategies . . . my repertoire has grown considerably and I use a lot of different strategies.

NOTES

1. "Mr. Connor" and the other teacher names are pseudonyms.

2. A National Academy of Sciences report (August & Hakuta, 1997) summarizes and analyzes major research studies conducted over the past 20 years and identifies positive ways of educating these children. The report points out, however, that much more research is needed on, among other topics, scaling up—i.e., converting good isolated programs into widespread practice.

3. See, for instance, Brinton, Snow, & Wesche, 1989; Cantoni-Harvey, 1987; Chamot & O'Malley, 1991; Crandall, 1987; Enright & McClosky, 1988; Faltis, 1993a; Mohan, 1986; and Short, 1991.

REFERENCES

Adamson, H. D. (1990). ESL students' use of academic skills in content courses. *English for Specific Purposes, 9*(1), 67–87.

August, D., & Hakuta, K. (Eds.). (1997). *Improving schooling for language minority children: A research agenda.* Washington, D.C.: National Academy Press.

August, D., & Pease-Alvarez, L. (1996). *Attributes of effective programs and classrooms serving English language learners.* Santa Cruz, CA, and Washington, D.C.: National Center for Research on Cultural Diversity and Second Language Learning.

Banks, J., & Banks, C. A. M. (Eds.). (1989). *Multicultural education: Issues and perspectives.* Boston: Allyn and Bacon.

Beck, I. L., & McKeown, M. G. (1991). Social studies texts are hard to understand: Mediating some of the difficulties. *Language Arts, 68,* 482–490.

Berman, P., McLaughlin, B., Minicucci, C., Nelson, B., & Woodworth, K. (1995). *School reform and student diversity: Case studies of exemplary practices for LEP students.* Washington, D.C.: National Clearinghouse for Bilingual Education.

Brinton, D. M., Snow, M. A., & Wesche, M. B. (1989). *Content-based second language instruction.* New York: Newbury House.

Buchanan, K., & Helman, M. (1993). *Reforming mathematics instruction for ESL literacy students* (Program Information Guide No. 15). Washington, D.C.: National Clearinghouse for Bilingual Education.

California State Department of Education. (1987). *History-Social Science framework.* Sacramento: California State Department of Education.

Cantoni-Harvey, G. (1987). *Content-area language instruction: Approaches and strategies.* Reading, MA: Addison-Wesley.

Chamot, A. U., & O'Malley, J. M. (1991). *The CALLA handbook.* Reading, MA: Addison-Wesley.

Christian, D. (1994). *Two-way bilingual education: Students learning through two languages* (Educational practice report No. 12). Santa Cruz, CA, and Washington, D.C.: National Center for Research on Cultural Diversity and Second Language Learning.

Christian, D., Montone, C., Lindholm, K., & Carranza, I. (1997). *Profiles in two-way immersion education.* McHenry, IL: Delta Systems.

Collier, V. (1987). The age and rate of acquisition of second language for academic purposes. *TESOL Quarterly, 21,* 617–641.

Collier, V. (1989). How long? A synthesis of research on academic achievement in a second language. *TESOL Quarterly, 23,* 509–532.

Collier, V. (1995) *Promoting academic success for ESL students: Understanding second language acquisition for school.* Elizabeth, NJ: New Jersey Teachers of English to Speakers of Other Languages–Bilingual Educators.

Council of Chief State School Officers. (1991). A concern about . . . multicultural education. *Concerns, Issue XXXIII,* October 1991, 1–9.

Council of Chief State School Officers. (1992). *Summary of recommendations and policy implications for improving the assessment and monitoring of students with limited English proficiency.* Washington, DC: Author.

Crabtree, C., Nash, G., Gagnon, P., & Waugh, S. (Eds.) (1992). *Lessons from history: Essential understandings and historical perspectives students should acquire.* Los Angeles: University of California, Los Angeles/National Center for History in the Schools.

Crandall, J. A. (Ed.). (1987). *ESL in content-area instruction.* Englewood Cliffs, NJ: Prentice Hall Regents.

Crandall, J. A. (1993). Content-centered learning in the United States. *Annual Review of Applied Linguistics, 13,* 111–126.

Crawford, L. W. (1993). *Language and literacy learning in multicultural classrooms.* Boston: Allyn and Bacon.

Cummins, J. (1980). The cross-lingual dimensions of language proficiency: Implications for bilingual education and the optimal age issue. *TESOL Quarterly,* *14,* 175–187.

Cummins, J. (1994). Knowledge, power and identity in teaching English as a second language. In F. Genesse (Ed.), *Educating second language children: The whole child, the whole curriculum, the whole community* (pp. 33–58). Cambridge, UK: Cambridge University Press.

Enright, D. S., & McClosky, M. L. (1988). *Integrating English: Developing English language and literacy in the multilingual classroom.* Reading, MA: Addison-Wesley.

Faltis, C. (1993a). Critical issues in the use of sheltered content teaching in high school bilingual programs. *Peabody Journal of Education, 69,* 136–151.

Faltis, C. (1993b). *Joinfostering: Adapting teaching strategies for the multilingual classroom.* New York: Macmillan.

García, E. (1994). *Understanding and meeting the challenge of student cultural diversity.* Boston: Houghton Mifflin.

Gardner, H. (1993). *Multiple intelligences.* New York: Basic Books.

Genesee, F. (1987). *Learning through two languages: Studies of immersion and bilingual education.* Cambridge, MA: Newbury House.

González, J., & Darling-Hammond, L. (1998). *New concepts for new challenges: Professional development for teachers of immigrant youth.* McHenry, IL: Delta.

Goodlad, J. I. (1984). *A place called school.* New York: McGraw-Hill.

Hakuta, K. (1986). *Mirror of language: The debate on bilingualism.* New York: Basic Books.

Jarolimek, J. (1989). In search of a scope and sequence for social studies. *Social Education, 53*(6), 376–385.

Johnston, W., & Packer, A. (1987). *Workforce 2000: Work and workers for the 21st century.* Indianapolis, IN: Hudson Institute.

Kauffman, D., Burkart, G., Crandall, J., Johnson, D., Peyton, J., Sheppard, K., & Short, D. (1994). *Content—ESL across the USA.* Washington, D.C.: ERIC Clearinghouse on Languages and Linguistics.

Lindholm, K., & Gavlek, K. (1994). *California DBE projects: Project-wide evaluation report, 1992–1993.* San Jose, CA: Author.

Lucas, T., Henze, R., & Donato, R. (1990). Promoting the success of Latino language minority students: An exploratory study of six high schools. *Harvard Educational Review, 60*(3), 1–26.

Lucas, T., & Katz, A. (1994). Reframing the debate: The roles of native languages in English-only programs for language minority students. *TESOL Quarterly, 28,* 537–561.

McDonnell, L. M., & Hill, P. (1993). *Newcomers in American schools: Meeting the educational needs of immigrant youth.* Santa Monica, CA: Rand.

Minicucci, C. (1996). *Learning science and English: How school reform advances scientific learning for limited English proficient middle school students* (Educational Practice Report No. 17). Santa Cruz, CA, and Washington, D.C.: National Center for Research on Cultural Diversity and Second Language Learning and the Center for Applied Linguistics.

Minicucci, C., & Olsen, L. (1992). *Programs for secondary limited English proficient* students: A California study. Washington, D.C.: National Clearinghouse for Bilingual Education.

Mohan, B. (1986). *Language and content*. Reading, MA: Addison-Wesley.

Mohan, B. (1990). Integration of language and content. In *Proceedings of the first research symposium on limited English proficient students' issues* (pp. 113–160). Washington, D.C.: U.S. Department of Education, Office of Bilingual Education and Minority Languages Affairs.

National Center for Education Statistics. (1988). *National Educational Longitudinal Study*. Washington, D.C.: U.S. Department of Education.

National Center for History in the Schools. (n.d.a). *National standards for U.S. history*. Los Angeles: Author.

National Center for History in the Schools. (n.d.b). *National standards for world history*. Los Angeles: Author.

National Center for Restructuring Education, Schools and Teaching. (1994). *Building blocks and stumbling blocks: Three case studies of shared decision-making and school restructuring*. New York: NCREST, Teachers College, Columbia University.

National Council of La Raza. (1991). *Hispanic education: A statistical portrait 1990*. Washington, D.C.: Author.

National Council for the Social Studies. (1992). Curriculum guidelines for multicultural education. *Social Education, 56,* 274–294.

National Council for the Social Studies. (1994). *Curriculum standards for social studies*. Washington, D.C.: Author.

Nieto, S. (1992). *Affirming diversity: The sociopolitical context of multicultural education*. White Plains, NY: Longman.

Sheppard, K. (1995). *Content—ESL across the USA: Volume 1. Technical Report*. Washington, D.C.: National Clearinghouse for Bilingual Education.

Short, D. (1991). *How to integrate language and content instruction: A training manual*. Washington, D.C.: Center for Applied Linguistics.

Short, D. (1993a). *Integrating language and culture in middle school American history classes* (Educational Practice Report No. 8). Washington, D.C.: Center for Applied Linguistics and the National Center for Research on Cultural Diversity and Second Language Learning.

Short, D. (1993b). Assessing integrated language and content instruction. *TESOL Quarterly, 27,* 627–656.

Short, D. (1994). Expanding middle school horizons: Integrating language, culture and social studies. *TESOL Quarterly, 28,* 581–608.

Short, D., & Boyson, B. (1997). *Secondary newcomer programs in the United States, 1996–97 directory*. Santa Cruz, CA, and Washington, D.C.: Center for Research on Education, Diversity & Excellence and Center for Applied Linguistics.

Sleeter, C., & Grant, C. (1987). An analysis of multicultural education in the United States. *Harvard Educational Review, 57,* 421–444.

Teachers of English to Speakers of Other Languages. (1996). *Promising futures* (Professional Papers Series No. 1). Alexandria, VA: Author.

Teachers of English to Speakers of Other Languages. (1997). *ESL standards for pre-K–12 students*. Alexandria, VA: Author.

Tharp, R., & Gallimore, R. (1988). *Rousing minds to life: Teaching, learning, and schooling in social context*. New York: Cambridge University Press.

U.S. Department of Labor, Secretary's Commission for Achieving Necessary Skills. (1992). *Learning a living: A blueprint for high performance*. Washington, D.C.: U.S. Department of Labor.

Waggoner, D. (1988). Language minorities in the United States in the 1980's: The evidence from the 1908 census. In S. McKay & S. C. Wong (Eds.), *Language diversity: Problem or resource?* (pp. 69–108). Boston: Heinle & Heinle.

Zeichner, K. (1993). *Educating teachers for cultural diversity* (NCRTL Special Report). East Lansing, MI: Michigan State University, National Center for Research on Teacher Learning.

Zelasko, N. (1995). National standards and language minority students. *NABE News, 18* (7), 1, 28, 36.

CHAPTER 6

INCIPIENT BILINGUALISM AND THE DEVELOPMENT OF ENGLISH LANGUAGE WRITING ABILITIES IN THE SECONDARY SCHOOL

Guadalupe Valdés

STANFORD UNIVERSITY

Elisa, Bernardo, and Manolo, the students whose texts I present in this chapter, are young people of Latino background who arrived in this country speaking only Spanish. They enrolled in a middle school in California in the greater San Francisco Bay Area, and they bravely began their struggle to learn English in order to acquire an education. All three of these children were, and are, at-risk. Indeed, as is the case in countries all over the world, children who do not speak the language in which schooling is conducted face grave difficulties in obtaining an education. In the United States, even though there is a commitment to educating all children, newly arrived immigrants from non-English-speaking countries encounter serious problems within the educational system.

Currently, newly arrived immigrant Latino students who enter American schools at the middle school and secondary levels face particularly difficult circumstances (LaFontaine, 1987; Davis & McDaid, 1992; Minicucci & Olsen, 1992; Chamot, 1992; Rumbaut, 1990; Lucas, 1992; Portes & Gran, 1991). Schools, especially those that until recently served mainstream English-speaking populations, are unprepared to work with large numbers of very different students who often have had little access to quality education in their own countries.

For the most part, schools have dealt with "the problem" in similar ways. They have expanded their ESL programs; they have instituted "sheltered" instruction[1] in some subjects; and in some cases they have even provided instruction in non-English languages in a limited number of subject areas. New teachers (ESL specialists, language development specialists) are being hired to teach these "different" students, while established existing faculty concentrate on the often dwindling number of "mainstream" students.

The dilemma facing schools is a difficult one. Students who arrive in this country must learn English. They cannot be truly accommodated by the schools until they are able to profit from instruction conducted solely in English. At the same time, existing faculty have had little exposure to limited-English-speaking students. There is much that teachers do not know about how English language develops in second-language learners, and there is little information available to guide them in determining when ESL students at different levels can "compete" with mainstream students. Many of them, therefore, elect to have very little to do with students who speak and write the very "imperfect" English found in the texts produced by students such as those whom I will describe here.

Given such responses by teachers, in many schools there are currently two separate worlds: the world of ESL and the mainstream world in which "real" American schooling takes place. ESL students become locked into a holding pattern in which they enroll in three periods of ESL and in "accessible" subjects such as art, cooking, and PE. As a result, students who enter school in the middle school years leave middle school still as part of the ESL track. Moreover, they generally remain in this same separate world during their entire 4 years of high school (Harklau, 1994 and Chapter 2, this volume). Even when they are "mainstreamed" in other subject-matter classes, few non-native-English-language background students ever manage to enroll in the *regular* (non ESL) English class; this has proved a persistent barrier to college preparatory study for immigrant students.

PURPOSE OF THE STUDY

The purpose of this chapter is to examine the problems currently faced by newly arrived immigrants as they struggle to acquire academic writing skills in secondary schools in this country. I will focus on three Latino middle school students who arrived in this country with what I term "zero" English.[2] Through a description of the instruction they received and of the stages of development through which they went as writers of English, I hope to present a vivid picture of both the needs and competencies of ESL students in general and to suggest how "mainstream" non-ESL teachers of composition can work successfully with these apparently "different" students.

THE STUDY

My research involved a total of three middle schools, four focal students who were studied in depth over that two-year period, four different ESL teachers, and numerous subject-matter teachers who had the focal children in class. It also involved interviews with school personnel, the subjects themselves, and their parents.

Observations were carried out in classrooms at all three schools in order to collect information about the ESL instructional program(s) in which the students were enrolled. These observations focused on what ESL instruction was and did in a particular school, what students did in class as they studied English, and how much access they had to English both in and out of class. By comparison, observations and tape recordings of the subject-matter (sheltered) courses focused on the demands made by these classes on the oral and written English language skills of both the focal students and other immigrant students in the school.

During the period of the study, the students' productive and receptive skills in spoken and written English were assessed with specially designed procedures in order to record growth in speaking, listening to, reading, and writing English. A total of four English language proficiency assessments were made during the 2 years of the study. Because of the emphasis on writing development, written products produced at school and by both the focal students and other students in the same classes were also collected. Such products included worksheets, written assignments, projects, tests, and other miscellaneous materials.

THE STUDENTS

I will discuss the progress made by Manolo Fuentes, Elisa Lara, and Bernardo Salas,[3] three of the four students who were part of the study. Elisa and Bernardo were followed at Garden School during the entire 2-year period. Manolo was followed at Garden School during the first year and at J.F.K. School (the school to which he transferred) during the second year.

Manolo

Manolo was a tall, good-looking youngster who towered over most of his classmates. He had a pleasant baby face and a serious and respectful demeanor that made most teachers like him. He was both a large child who enjoyed riding his bicycle with his cousin and playing with tiny cars, and an adolescent who was quite aware of the girls around him.

When the study began, Manolo was only 12 years old and was about 5 feet 10 inches tall. He had arrived from Mexico City during the summer of 1991. He, his mother, Rita, and his older sister, Estela (16), had moved to California to be with his father, who had been working here for 2 years. Manolo's brother Anselmo (18) had followed his father a year previously.

In Mexico, Manolo had completed 6th grade. He could describe his classes in some detail and was happy to talk about his plans for the future. In love with planes, he wanted to become an Air Force pilot and to fly very large planes. He seemed confident and articulate. We were thus somewhat surprised at the level of his ability to write in Spanish. Manolo's composition was surprisingly unsophisticated compared with the writing produced by Elisa and Bernardo:

Spanish Composition: Manolo Fuentes

Manolo Fuentes bino a los Estados Unidos en 1991. En pese a benir a la escuela alprinsipio sentia mal porque cuando salia a la calle ablavan muchas personas en ingles y llono en ten dia lo que desian le echeganas al ingles y aora en tiendo se pedircosa en ingles y mesiento vien pienso esforsarme en el ingles y la escuela y rregresar a Mexico cuando sea grande por a ora seguir en la escuela y estudiar mucho

Manolo Fuentes came to the United States in 1991. I began to come to school at first I felt bad because when I went out in the street many people spoke English and I didn't understand what they said I put effort into English and now I understand I know how to ask for things in English and I feel good I plan to work hard at English and at school and to return to Mexico when I'm older for now stay in school and study a lot

Manolo makes no attempt to use the written accent, and he produces a very large number of incorrectly segmented words, for example *llono* (for *yo no*), *en pese* (for *empecé*), *en ten dia* (for *entendía*), *echeganas* (for *eché ganas*), *en tiendo* (for *entiendo*), *mesiento* (for *me siento*), and *a ora* (for *ahora*). Word segmentation errors such as these are generally typical of first and second graders and not of students of *primero de secundaria* (seventh grade) like Manolo. Other errors, however, involving confusion between *b* and *v* *(benir, bine, ablavan, vien)*, confusion between *s*, *c*, and *z* *(em pese, prinsipio, desian, esforsarme)*, confusion between *ll* and *y (llono)*, and misuse of *h* (*a ora*) are quite typical of persons who have completed elementary school (1st through 6th grades) and even *secundaria* (7th and 8th grades). The use of double *rr* (*rregresar*) in word initial position is not as common.

Considering the fact that Manolo attended school in Mexico City (a large metropolitan area), it is interesting that his written Spanish is much more flawed than that produced by Elisa, who came from a very rural community school in Honduras.

Elisa

Twelve-year-old Elisa was small and dark-complected. Her high cheekbones and very straight black hair reflected her Indian heritage. She and her sister Elvia (12) had been living with their grandmother, in a small village, for the past 8 years. Their mother, Magda, had finally been able to send for the two girls.

Elisa was homesick. She missed her grandmother, her school, and the places that they went to in Honduras. Elisa was not aware that she was an emergent teen in Honduras. She was a child and treated like a child by her grandmother and the rest of the family as well as by teachers at school. Elisa recalled that she liked school in Honduras and that what she missed most was not being able to go home at noon, have lunch, and then return at 2:00 P.M. the afternoon session that ended at 5:00 P.M. In her new American school, the days seemed incredibly short. When school ended, both Elisa and her sister walked home, where they would spend the rest of the afternoon and evening alone, waiting for their mother, who worked a late-night shift. Both girls were very lonely, and often days would pass before they really saw their mother.

In response to our request that she write in Spanish about herself under the general title *Yo*, Elisa produced the following text:

Spanish Composition: Elisa Lara

Conposición a Elisa Lara
Yo soy Elisa Lara soy muy buena para cocinar y mi abi favorito es cantar soy tri-gueña de pelo negro y indio soy de ojos cafe oscuros y tengo 12 años cuando este grande me gustaria peinar y pintar a las artistas yo respeto a mi mamá y a toda, mi familia Mi abuelita me enseño a respetar y amar a mi familia y me gusta de y me respetarlos heso es muy bueno niños que no respetan a sus padres no ses lo respeta a es que no se le a respetado a el yo respetó porque me respetan Yo soy Elisa Lara y me gusta de el ingles y yo voy a aprender ingles para poderme superar en esté paiz.

I am Elisa Lara I am very good at cooking and my favorite hobby is singing I'm dark-skinned with black and Indian hair I have dark brown eyes and I am twelve years old when I grow up I would like to comb and paint actresses I respect my mother and all, my family My grandmother taught me to respect and love my family and I like to respect them that is very good children that don't respect their parents is that he had not been respected I respect because I am respected I am Elisa Lara and I like English and I am going to learn English so I can get ahead in this country.

In writing a personal description of herself, Elisa wrote a total of 12 sentences. In terms of form, Elisa's writing reflected minimal attention to capitalization and punctuation. She did not use capitals, periods, and commas conventionally. Overall, however, her spelling is quite normative, and except for *paiz* (país), *heso* (eso), and *a* (ha), her only other misspellings involve the use of the written accent. Elisa used accent marks appropriately on her own last name, on *conposición* (sic) and on the word *mamá*. She used these marks inappropriately in *respetó* and in *esté*. She also failed to use accent marks in *café, esté, gustaría, enseñó,* and *inglés*.

At several levels, Elisa did indeed fulfill the assignment. She did write about herself, and she did provide details about her physical appearance, her interests, and her future plans. Relationships, however, between ideas and information are not well established. Connections and transitions are lacking, and some information is incomplete or undeveloped.

Overall, however—especially given the fact that writing or *redacción* was not taught in Elisa's school—she did quite well. Mechanically (except for punctuation), Elisa's writing is quite competent. In terms of content, Elisa's text reflects a view about what a good piece of writing should include that is quite common among Hispanophones. This view holds that writing is not trivial and that it should attempt to address philosophical and moral issues. In Elisa's composition, her embedded discussion about *respeto* is a manifestation of this tendency.

Bernardo

Bernardo was a very serious and quiet youngster of 13 who appeared to be an almost full-blooded Mexican Indian youth. He had very dark skin, high cheekbones, and slightly slanted eyes. He and his sister Marica entered Garden School in January. They had been in Mission Vista for a number of months but had not attended school because their mother could not produce a birth certificate for them. When certificates were finally sent from Mexico, their father, Arnoldo Salas, enrolled them in school.

In Mexico, Bernardo had followed the normal demanding curriculum of a federal *secundaria* (middle school). He had been required to take the following subjects: Spanish (language arts), math, natural sciences, physical sciences, English, physical education, and art. His study of English appears to have been typical of foreign language classes, where the primary focus is grammar and vocabulary. Bernardo commented that he had learned little.

By comparsion, Bernardo's writing in Spanish was quite sophisticated. Bernardo's response to our assignment, which he completed a few days after he arrived at Garden School, was also quite sophisticated in many ways. He wrote the following text:

Spanish Composition—Bernardo Salas

1. Yo naci en el Hospital De Cuernavaca
2. fui creciendo cunpliendo los 6 años me metieron a la Escula de Cuau-chilés La escuela era muy bonita cegido ponian Árbolitos ponian plantas de fruta pero Los niños les decian alas Maestras que no pusieran por que los niños que estudian en la tarde en la escuela los maltratan los quitan. Los maestros hacen grupos paraque un dia los riege uno cada quien tiene su dia para regalos. Mi pápa ce hiva a venir para a ca pero yo no queria y siempre ce vino des pues pasaron los 9 meces y mi máma ce alivio de mihermanita y yo estaba en la escuela Despues mi hermanina pa-saron 8 meses y mi pápa ce trajo a mi máma y pasando los meses Al Año con 7 meses nos mando atraer mi pápa y mi máma a mi hermana y ami

I was born in the Hospital in Cuernavaca. I grew and when I turned six they put me in the Cuauchilés School. The school was very pretty often they put little trees they planted fruit plants but the children would tell the teachers not to plant them because the children that went to school in the after-noon damaged them and pulled them out. The teachers form groups so that one waters them one day each one has a day to water them. My father was going to come here but I did not want him to and he came anyway after that 9 months went by and my mother had my little sister and I was in school After my little sister 8 months went by and my father brought my mother over and as the months passes At a year and 7 months my father sent for my mother, my sister and me

In comparison to Elisa's text, Bernardo wrote a slightly less well orga-nized piece. Also in comparison to Elisa, Bernardo's writing was charac-terized by a number of spelling confusions that are quite typical of Spanish-speaking individuals who have not received much education. These confusions include the use of the grapheme *c* to spell the sound [s] (e.g., *ce vino* for *se vino*); the overuse of the grapheme *h*, which is silent in Spanish (as in *hiva* for *iba*); and the use of the grapheme *v* for *b*. For native Spanish speakers, spelling confusions such as these arise in those instances in which the same sound can be spelled with different symbols. Among highly educated Spanish speakers, these spelling confusions are highly stigmatized, although they are quite common. The presence of such features in Bernardo's text reflects the fact that his experience in writing original texts was probably limited. According to Bernardo, "writing" assignments at his school mainly involved copying texts verbatim.

In comparison to Elisa, Bernardo had many more misspellings in addition to the spelling confusions mentioned above. A total of 13 such misspellings included incorrect uses of accent marks (*árbolitos* for *arbolitos*, *máma* for *mamá*) and incorrect word segmentation (*alas* for *a las*, *mihermanita* for *mi hermanita*, *paraque* for *para que*).

In terms of content, Bernardo did indeed provide some of the information expected in a piece of writing focusing on himself. However, the text appears, at first glance, to deal with two completely different topics: (1) a description of his school and the trees planted at the school, and (2) a narrative about when the family came to the U.S. A more detailed examination of the piece produced by Bernardo suggests that he may have attempted to write an account of his coming to the United States. The structure of the piece suggests that Bernardo wanted to describe the setting for his narrative (his school in Mexico) and move from there to describe the events that led to the family's migration. His attempt was unsuccessful in that it lacks cohesion. Transitions are missing between events, and the ending is undeveloped. The attempt itself is revealing, however. Bernardo tried to write more than a simple description of himself. By describing his school, he attempted to provide a frame of reference within which his experience and his feelings about moving to a new country might be understood. In comparison to the papers produced by the other focal students, Bernardo's piece was the most ambitious.

ON ANY GIVEN DAY, observations of Elisa, Bernardo, and Manolo in their classes revealed three very different ways of responding to school and to the classroom experience. Elisa, for example, sat quietly in her place, and occasionally looked up shyly at the teacher. During the first year of the study, she would rarely raise her hand or volunteer an answer. In the ESL teacher's class, she seldom talked to the other students at her table, but worked carefully and deliberately on her assignments. Inevitably, she would be the last in the class to turn in her maps, her copied sentences, and her other work.

Like Elisa, Bernardo sat quietly and attended to his own work. When in doubt he would look up at his sister Marica for a confirming nod or shake of the head. During most of the first year, he worked on an endless number of worksheets. He was never called on during whole class by the teacher, and he was seldom called on in small group work with the teacher's aide. The ESL teacher had little to say about Bernardo. Since he had entered in January, she expected that he would be in NEP (Non-English Proficient class) again the following year.

Manolo, on the other hand, was very well liked by both the ESL teacher and the aide. He constantly raised his hand and called out answers. He was self-assured and saw himself as knowing just a bit more than his peers. Often he would look around to see if anyone else had raised his/her hand to respond to a question, and upon determining that no one had, he would quickly respond. He smiled broadly when the teacher praised him. Reluctant to help other students, during group work he read other materials, drew and colored pictures, and did not engage in interactions with his less proficient classmates. In part because he did not do group work at the right time, he was often late in handing in assignments. The teacher's appraisal of Manolo was that he was bright but lazy. My appraisal was that he was bright and bored.

THREE APPROACHES TO TEACHING
WRITING IN ESL PROGRAMS

As I have pointed out recently (Valdés, 1992), the English composition/ writing profession is currently divided into two very distinct areas of interest and expertise. These two areas are the teaching of English to mainstream American students and the teaching of English to speakers of other languages. At the secondary school level, most "mainstream" English teachers have little to do with students who have not been exited from the ESL sequence. They consider such English-learning students to be the responsibility of their ESL-teaching colleagues.

For those of us concerned with the ghettoization of non-English-language-background students, however, the question is: can advanced ESL-background students profit from mainstream writing instruction? Should they be allowed to enroll in regular English and even honors English courses? What level of development should they have reached before such enrollments are beneficial?

Teachers of writing who find themselves needing to make decisions about whether or not to admit ESL-background students into their regular courses face a complex set of issues. The fact is that in many cases, as Hornberger (1989) has pointed out, it is not easy to decide whether a perceived problem is a language problem or a problem of limited background in writing and composition. Many students who wish to enter mainstream courses and who have been exited from both limited and extensive ESL programs often have had little exposure to writing. Because ESL instruction frequently focuses primarily on language structure, they know little about key aspects of mechanics (e.g., punctuation) and have little experience in text organization. Not only is their English still "faulty," but their texts appear infantile compared to the writing produced by English-speaking students at the same age and grade level.

Ideally, both ESL teachers and regular teachers would struggle to determine the type of instruction that would most benefit particular students rather than rely on general guidelines or formulas or labels. ESL teachers would work closely with regular (non-ESL) teachers to make judgments about how soon to allow their protégés to leave the nest. Non-ESL teachers, on the other hand, would gather information about the typical stages of development in writing English as a second language before refusing these young people permission to enroll in their classes. They would need to understand how writing is taught to such students and how much these youngsters are able to accomplish in the course of 2 or 3 years of instruction.

The Controlled Composition Approach

The teaching of writing to ESL students using the techniques of controlled composition is quite common in many middle school and high school programs. In the middle school attended by Elisa, Manolo, and Bernardo during the first year of our study, for example, beginning students produced writing by using *guided composition* strategies. Because the teacher (Mrs. Gordon) was concerned about grammatical errors, she tried to guide students into producing sentences that were grammatically correct. In order to do so, she involved students in a very controlled process in which she gave a frame such as:

Capuchin monkeys _____

and a set of elements that could be placed in the blank. For the capuchin monkey piece, for example, the following elements were written on the board.

breaking nuts on branches
live in the jungle in trees
live in South America
medium size monkeys
can jump from one tree to another
black and white monkeys

As will be apparent from the above example, students who could manipulate these basic structures by adding needed elements actually produced grammatically correct sentences. Low-level students, however, simply copied the structures and produced sentences such as:

> Capuchin monkeys breaking nuts on branches.
> Capuchin monkeys black and white monkeys

In general, when students had little interest in the topic on which they were "writing," activities such as this produced little frustration; students simply did as they were told and copied sentences from the board. These activities resulted in almost identical papers written by the different members of the class. These products were not written in paragraph form but consisted of a list of numbered sentences, as in the following writing sample by Bernardo:

1. Koko is a girl gorilla.
2. She likes kittens. She likes to read books about Kittens.
3. She signs words when she reads. She knows 500 words in sign language.

As will be noted, Bernardo's composition follows exactly the same pattern as those of his classmates. All students in the class capitalized the word *kitten*, suggesting that it was probably capitalized on the teacher's list of words. The similarity of the compositions reflects the fact that Mrs. Gordon wrote an entire set of connected sentences on the board, leaving blanks here and there for students to fill in.

Students who did not follow the teacher's directions met with disapproval. When observing such a class it was difficult for us to determine whether students could write more than they were being asked to. We were fortunate, however, in finding that during the second year, Elisa's desire to write independently overshadowed her desire to please the teacher. Angry that she had been placed in the beginning ESL class for a 3-month period at the beginning of her second year in this country, Elisa decided to ignore the teacher's instructions for the Koko assignment, and we had the opportunity of getting a true glimpse of what she could write in English at that point in her language development.

As will be noted from the sample included below, Elisa's text was quite different from those produced by the rest of her classmates. She did not use the stimulus sentences provided by the teacher. Instead, she attempted to communicate her own response to Koko's story. She chose details not selected by the teacher.

The teacher, however, was not pleased with the fact that Elisa was making great progress in finding her own voice. She focused, rather, on the large number of "errors" present in the text, and stated that Elisa needed to control English structure better before she became carried away with content.

Indeed, an examination of the text produced by Elisa on Koko makes evident that there are indeed many spelling errors (leard, awser, littet), a number of syntactic errors (she know what is birthday mean, she don't wanted a cement cat), and an error in numbering text (there is no number 2). However, Elisa was successful in summarizing the presentation about Koko. Her only concession to the teacher's preferences was the numbering of each of her sentences.

Koko's story

1. Koko is a girl gorilla.
3. She leard how to signs words and she know what is birthday mean.
4. I like the part when one of her freinds ask her what did she do on her birthday, and she awser eat, drink and got old.
5. Koko's like's Kittens, she wanten a Kitten for her birthday.
6. But for Christmas she got a cement cat, she got very angry, she don't wanted a cement cat she wanted a real cat.
7. Koko's has a lot of friends, one of her friends take three littet kitten, and she show then to Koko.
8. Koko look at the three Kitten, and there's was two with tail and one with no tail.
9. She select the one did has no tail.
10. And she say she will call the Kitten All ball.

Overall, in this ESL class, as is the case in many others, the development of writing abilities was seen as a very controlled process in which students slowly learned how to write individual sentences using correct grammar and vocabulary. The focus of the activity was both form and correctness. Because, like most ESL teachers, our focal teacher had received no training in the "new" approaches to the teaching of writing, and because she was essentially traditional in orientation, she did not use multiple drafts, free writing, brainstorming, or any other techniques that might have placed the focus on meaning rather than form.

The Process Approach

To be fair, working with the written language with students who are at the initial stages of acquiring a second language is quite challenging. Even for teachers who view limited- and non-English speakers as potential writers of English who can be taught using the same strategies currently popular with native English-speaking students, the questions that arise are many. One teacher whom we observed, for example, taught her beginning ESL class as though it were an accelerated literacy class. She read stories and poetry to students who were just beginning to learn English. She expected them not only to appreciate the writing but also to produce such stories and poems themselves. Instead of worksheets, she gave students time to work on their rough drafts, to talk to each other in Spanish about their writing, to revise their drafts, and finally to enter their final product into the computer. These products varied in sophistication and correctness, but seemed to reflect students' attempts to create real meaning. Samples of such products are included below.

> Is ugly to swiniming. There are many bird different kind a birds. Like eagle and puffins like to see the ocean pacific. The sky and you can heat the echo in the mountains and the birds there noisy and the ocean.
> End

> For the valentine Marivin thick in the money. But Milton said i never have any money, That's because you never said any. Well i think with money or no money i have day for VALENTINE.

Students appeared to enjoy the experience of writing, particularly entering their writing into the computer and pasting into the text illustrations of different types. The teacher posted many of these products on the wall and made many positive comments about how well students were doing.

As will be immediately obvious, there were many differences between the products that students wrote under the traditional teacher's direction and those produced for the more process-oriented teacher. As opposed to the firmly controlled correctness of the guided composition products, the process approach resulted in pieces that were often difficult to understand. Moreover, writing and editing took a very long time.

Process Writing and Direct Instruction

In yet another ESL class, a mainstream English teacher (Mrs. Samuels) who voluntarily took on the task of working with newly arrived immigrant students approached the teaching of writing directly. She stated that her goal in teaching the advanced ESL in middle school was to mainstream students *before* they entered high school. She worked hard to place students in her own regular mainstream English classes so that they might make the transition more easily.

The ESL class itself covered some of the elements of the core curriculum (e.g., reading *Tom Sawyer*), traditional English grammar (e.g., study of time clauses, use of the present progressive, punctuation), and writing. Each class began with a segment of about 10 minutes in which students wrote in their journals in response to a teacher prompt. The teacher generally talked for a few minutes as students prepared to write in their journals and suggested ways in which students might respond.

The teacher gave much attention to the writing of several long papers on various topics. These papers were written over a period of time and went through several drafts, including a draft prepared in response to writing conferences. During the spring of 1992–93, the teacher taught students how to write a paper that would speculate about an effect. This type of paper was one of the writing tasks on which mainstream 8th graders would be tested, and she believed that it was also important for ESL students to learn how to write such a paper.

Mrs. Samuels began work on the speculative paper by explaining what the students would write about and how they would organize their paper. She selected as a title for their papers "A Decade of Difference." She then explained that the paper would have three parts by showing an overhead containing the following segments:

A Decade of Difference

So many things can happen in 10 years. Often ten years can bring positive changes; ten years can also result in differences and negative situations.

 In 1983, I was __ years old and I _____.

 [*Here's where you will use the paragraph you already wrote. Some things may need to be changed.*]

 Today in 1993, I am __ years old and _____.

 (Here's where you'll talk about yourself today and the changes that have occurred to you. You may have had some real family changes, new babies, weddings, divorces.)

 I can only guess what life will be like in ten years, but I do have a dream for 2003. If my dream comes true in 2003, I will _____.

[*There should be some detail here. It should be about what you will do. This is where you will put in your paragraph about what you hope will happen.*]

 If my dream comes true; there will be both positive and negative effects.

 negative effects
 positive effects
Conclusion

Students worked on this paper for about 4 weeks. During that time, journal writing focused them on thinking about the paragraphs they would include in the speculative paper. Many other activities were carried out during the course of writing the speculative paper. These included writing of first drafts, participating in writing conferences with the teacher and other adults, sharing drafts with fellow students, and revising and preparing the final draft that was to be graded by the teacher.

As will be noted, in teaching ESL students to write a challenging paper, this teacher used a combination of strategies. She gave students a general scaffold or structure for the paper as a whole and thereby taught a great deal about organization. She also prompted students to think and to write spontaneously about themselves and their lives, and she showed them how to use initial clustering techniques and note-taking to move to the writing of a first draft. She emphasized the steps in the writing process and used both writing conferences and peer response groups.

As compared to the traditional teacher, this non-ESL professional turned ESL instructor did not believe that teaching ESL primarily involved teaching structures. She pushed students to use their English proficiencies, limited though they might still be, to write about real experiences and to express genuine thoughts. She adapted a process approach to writing so that students who were not totally familiar with the conventions of English writing might learn how to organize their writing in ways in which they would be expected to do so in mainstream classes.

BERNARDO'S WRITING DEVELOPMENT

Overall, Bernardo's writing development moved slowly. At the end of a 2-year period in which he had been enrolled primarily in ESL core (3 periods) and in art, cooking, and PE, Bernardo had reached only a very beginning level of writing proficiency. He could, for example: (1) write simple unconnected sentences that he could produce orally; (2) write very short connected discourse on topics about which he could produce connected oral discourse (e.g., family, self, school); and (3) imitate some elements of models of written language presented to him. He often failed, however, to attend to capitalization and punctuation and other details that were included in the models.

Bernardo's writing abilities in English developed slowly. At the time of the first assessment in May 1992 (after he had been in the United States 5 months) Bernardo produced the following two pieces of writing:

Bernardo—Sample 1 May 1992

pele have friends   played soccer
pele he played for the New York Pele
played his first Pele He became a
millionaire He was the most famous

Sample 2 May 1992

fader   eat   the beibi   have pencil sister

The first sample was produced in response to our request that he write about a reading in English that he read as a part of the language assessment administered to all three focal students who were part of the study. Bernardo was allowed to refer to the reading as he wrote. As will be noted, Bernardo appeared to be copying directly from the text, and in one instance, it is possible that he did not understand exactly what he was copying. This is suggested by the fact that he left the sentence: "Pelé played his first" unfinished.

Bernardo's limitations were far more evident, however, in Sample 2, when he was asked to write about his school or his family. At this point in his English language development, Bernardo was only able to write a list of words across the page. The list includes two verbs (*eat, have*) and several nouns (*fader, beibi, pencil, sister*) as well as an article (*the*). Bernardo made no attempt, however, to construct complete sentences. Bernardo used Spanish spelling conventions to spell English words. He wrote *fader* and *beibi* for *father* and *baby*. However, he also used conventional English spelling.

During the second year of the study, Bernardo spent his time filling in worksheets that accompanied the *New Horizons* series used in the traditional teacher's classes. Frequently, however, he wrote assignments such as the following:

I write a book.	I write a letter.
you write a book.	you write a letter.
He write a book.	He write a letter
She write a book.	She write a letter
They write a book	They write a letter
I write a music	I eat a banana.

What is interesting here is that Bernardo was conjugating English verbs incorrectly, because the teacher has used this procedure to *avoid* errors. Moreover, he was inconsistent in his use of sentence-final punctuation as well as capitalization. And, as was the case when the teacher provided stimulus sentences for controlled composition activities, some of the sentences produced by Bernardo were ungrammatical.

For Assessment III (the second assessment carried out of Bernardo's English language proficiency), Bernardo wrote the following piece:

Bernardo
Mi name is Bernardo Salas have
13 I'm lake play soccer.
Mi love fathe, mothe, sisters
counsin and uncle.

Here Bernardo displays some ability to construct sentences in English and to produce these sentences in writing. He is able to communicate four ideas about himself, which in standard English would read:

My name is Bernardo Salas
I am 13. (Bernardo's *have 13* is a literal translation of the Spanish *tengo 13* [años])
I like to play soccer.
I love my father, mother, sisters, cousin and uncle.

After approximately 1 year of schooling in the United States, Bernardo could provide limited information about himself in English in written form. The information, however, might not be comprehensible to persons not familiar with the writing of non-native speakers of English.

It is important to point out that instruction in Bernardo's ESL class was not directed at helping students to develop specific functional abilities such as requesting information, providing information, recounting an event, summarizing material read, and so on. During the same period Bernardo wrote the previous sample, in class he was normally writing material such as the following:

1. This is my hair.
2. These are my eyes.
3. This is my nose.
4. This is my mouth.
5. This is my foot.

By the second semester of the second year (January to May 1993), however, the teacher began work on a "long" autobiographical piece. For

FIGURE 6.1. Bernardo's Map.

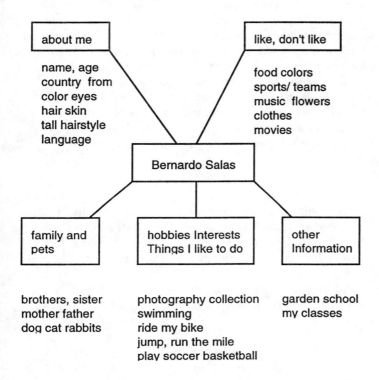

this autobiographical piece, the teacher had introduced a pre-writing activity involving semantic mapping. She handed out blank maps to all students and then proceeded to help them fill out the various categories. Bernardo's map is included below.

Again, the teacher wrote vocabulary words on the board that students could copy to fill in their various categories. As will be apparent, some of the suggested subcategories made assumptions about the students' lives that were somewhat questionable and revealed the teacher's lack of familiarity with the lives of her students. In our experience, new immigrant students who live in poverty do not have either pets or hobbies.

Once again, even when using a process approach to writing, the teacher did not trust her students to create or communicate their own meanings. As will be evident from the final draft of the piece produced by Bernardo, she still controlled the content of the students' papers to a very large degree.

My name is Bernardo Salas. I am 14 year old my color of my eyes are brown my leg is long my skin is brown my hair is black and white my favorite is language I like play soccer my favorite color is green, red, blue I like the jump, run the mile my favorite teams is raiders. Do you like sports What team did you like on football. Do you like raiders. I like chicago bulls on basketball. In Garden middle school we have 36 rooms. We don't cat in the classes I like the movies universal soulder, vethoven, and the movie Delta force I have two I like swimming with my ancles, my father, friends every day my play soccer in the school Cedars with Daniel, Jose.m., Juan. E. Jesus landa and Alfredo my food favorite is pizza of chese I have my bike of color black and white the school garden is big have cafeteria, library
    Sencerely
    Bernardo Salas

At this point in Bernardo's development, he was able to talk about a variety of the categories included on his semantic map. It is evident, however, that he was not writing completely independently. Nevertheless, he was indeed able to include genuine information about himself, his activities, and his friends. Even though he was confused about the format of the assignment and even though he included some letter-like elements, it was Bernardo's first attempt to say something real in writing. With a bit of effort, the reader of this piece is able to learn that Bernardo is a sports enthusiast.

The piece is clearly disorganized. Bernardo has little notion of paragraph development or paragraph unity. This is not surprising, because neither Bernardo nor his classmates received instruction about these matters. Until this assignment was presented, students had been writing lists of numbered sentences on a single topic.

ELISA'S WRITING DEVELOPMENT

Compared to Bernardo, Elisa made an impressive amount of progress in her ability to write in English during the 2 years of the study. As was the case with all focal students, Elisa began by writing what appeared to be a list of single words in English. However, as will be evident from a closer look at her first writing sample, Elisa was really writing a series of sentences: *Thes tha paper; Thes tha father; Thes tha mother.* She is consistent in her use of ditto marks under the original sentence as far as the word *baby.* Elisa also includes another complete sentence: *My mother is Magda.*

Thes	tha	paper	My mother is Magda
"	"	father	
"	"	mother	family
"	"	boy	
"	"	girl	
"	"	baby	
"	"	door	
"	"	window	
"	"	mesuring spoon	
"	"	spatula o turner	
"	"	postre	
"	"	measurins cup	

As was the case with Bernardo, Elisa produced few writing samples during her first semester in the traditional ESL teacher's classroom. Most writing activities involved filling in worksheets or copying vocabulary and very controlled composition. In the spring, Elisa wrote the following piece as part of a class project on national parks.

Social Studies 1°3°
My favorite Park
I like Yellowstone National Park, because in there is a beautiful vision. Yellowstone Park is in three state. They are Wyoming, Montana and Idaho. There is a Interesting thing like, boiling water, Old Faithful, waterful, the blue water in a pool and some animals. The Old Faithful is very Interesting for me because in every hours shoot water. The Yellowstone Park have a river and you can go fishing. I think the Yellowstone National Park was the first Park in America or The United States.

Compared to other students' writing on national parks, Elisa's writing was quite superior. She was not following the teacher's controlled sentence structure, nor was she simply filling in blanks. In this piece, Elisa is displaying information, expressing personal opinion, and giving a reason for her personal opinion.

It is important to note that by the time Elisa wrote her national parks project, she was able to produce oral connected discourse on a variety of familiar topics in English. Our assessment of her oral language made clear that after 9 months of schooling, Elisa was able to provide personal information, to role-play, and to read simple academic materials in English.

Elisa's progress in written English, while dramatic, was less spectacular. For example, her written summary of a reading on Barbra Streisand produced during the second assessment of her English-language abilities did not make evident that Elisa had understood what she read or even that she could discuss the reading orally. Seen by itself, Elisa's summary seems even more problematic than her piece on Yellowstone Park. In her summary, Elisa demonstrates *some* mastery of English structure, but fails to communicate anything beyond the two sentences with which the reading itself began.

> Barbara was a very ugly girl and she wanted to be a actress but her wanted to she need to be a secretary; Barbara wanted to learn dance but her dat don't like to her daughter dace because she think the is going to break.

There is no evidence in this piece of writing that indicates that Elisa has the ability to display information, to express an opinion, or to justify such an opinion. On the basis of this sample, one would be tempted to rate Elisa as a very beginning ESL writer. What needs to be taken into account, however, is that Elisa had had no experience in attempting to produce oral or written summaries. She did not know quite where to begin her summary of the content of what she had read about Barbra Streisand. Another possible factor influencing her performance was the timed nature of the assessment itself. Students were given approximately 10 minutes to write summaries of what they had read.

The second writing sample produced as part of the second assessment revealed much more about Elisa's English language proficiency. Here Elisa responded to our request that she write about herself. She wrote about school and about why she liked going to school. Again, in this piece, Elisa was successful in expressing an opinion and in expressing a justification for her position. In this sample, it is evident that Elisa was writing what she could already say. Moreover, her written English reflects the spoken language directly.

> I like to came to the school because a learn a lot of English. and I learn to do art home a run the mile and a do (esperimin) and I learn. Math. and I learn a lot of things. and I want then when I be big I have a good job. another thing they a like to come to the school is because I have a lot of freinds friends. And because the teaches are very good.

As was pointed out previously, this particular text reflects Elisa's confusion between spoken and written English. The use of *a* for *I*—for example, in "a learn a lot of English" and "a do (esperimin)"—reveals that she produces a schwa-like sound for the pronoun *I* in speaking. She then transcribes this sound both as *a* and *I*. Transfer of native-language syntax is also evident here. Elisa uses an English subjunctive—"and I want then when *I be* big"—to translate the Spanish subjunctive *(cuando sea grande)*.

This text is also characterized by small "errors" that would have passed undetected were one listening to Elisa's rapid speech in English. For example, Elisa wrote:

> another thing *they* a like to do
> the *teaches* are very good

In rapid speech, these small irregularities in Elisa's English would have been insignificant. An interlocutor speaking to Elisa would probably have "heard":

> another thing *that* I like to do
> the *teachers* are very good

Given her growing control of the language and her ability to communicate meaning, elements such as these generally went unnoticed in Elisa's speech. However, when writing in response to a task such as that required by Assessment II, Elisa reflected her oral language patterns and simply transcribed what she could say. This resulted in a set of unique "errors."

During the second year, Elisa's desire to write independently became more evident. The same month she produced the Koko text for her ESL teacher, Elisa wrote the next text included here and turned it in to her science teacher for extra credit. Here Elisa recounts an experience and provides information about a company located in Silicon Valley.

> Silicon Ghaprics it a big company this company has a lot of buildings, we went to two buildings first we went to building sis, and the people who works there, they take us to a room where the presidents of the company has they meatings. And then we divide us in two groups and then my group went to the second building that was building two. They call building two Human Factors Lab, in building two they talk what the company made? The campany made computers, and they also talk about what they do in building two. What they do is to test people to see how they do in computers. And they ask if someone of us wanted to try to do the test. Then we went to a room and there was two big t.v.'s and we was watching at him doing the test. And then we went to building to again and then I have the chance to play with the computer and it's very easy to play in that computer it was a very nice expeirence to meat people, learnd about computers They tell us

some of the activitis they do. Every year competitive of the best video of
the year. They show us the video and there was very good. I like did we
meat some workers, there was the person who made the aplications her
name is Mimi Celis. The secretery's name is Clara Colon. The engineer
name is Pablo Sanches. The manufacturing's name is Velia Rico. The secu-
rity's name is Hank Sisneros. All they tall us something about ther life.
Dwayne Corneleas/ Product Demo.
Hi talk's about the Iris Indigo, and then hi show us a video about
Moviemaking Tirers
T.V   Safety
Medical   Video
There are made it with computers
Hi also talk about his life.
Hi give us a talk on staying in school
the field trip end at
2:02

From one perspective, this text shows Elisa's strong continuing development in written English. This is a far longer text than those she produced previously. There is significant evidence here of increasing fluency.

On the other hand, from the perspective of organization and mechanics, this text appears to be quite flawed. It contains spelling, punctuation, and capitalization errors, and the direct reflection of Elisa's spoken
English is quite evident. Elisa is using a completely oral style to write this
report. Her notion of a written sentence, as opposed to a spoken utter-
ance, is still developing.

For a number of reasons, it could be said that Elisa is writing beyond
her competence. She has not acquired either the structures or the vocabulary essential for writing about this particular subject. More importantly,
perhaps, this text is quite unfocused. The emphasis shifts from a strictly
chronological recounting of the field trip to a number of different details.
As a single paragraph, this long segment of text is incoherent.

However, considering the fact that Elisa had received no instruction
on text organization and that she had been in the United States for only
1 year, this text is quite exceptional in what it reveals about Elisa's potential and about the ways that limited-English-speaking students begin to
write using their growing oral language abilities.

Elisa's growing sense of herself as an English writer became especially
evident when she fell in love for the first time. The object of her affections
was a monolingual English-speaking youngster whom she met at a church
social. Because they lived in different parts of the Bay Area, most of their
relationship was carried out in writing. The next writing sample is a prose

poem (including revisions) that Elisa prepared to send to her friend Joshua. She shared this writing with us because she wanted us to see how well she was beginning to write. We suspected that the text was not entirely original.

> friend is a big gift that life give to people
> And here I got, one of the bigest pressents,
> you has a friend
> If you could see trough my heart you would see a
> light shining every singale minute that I think about you
> this light means our friendship our beautiful
> friend ship. And my heart and me, have decidedo to keep it.
> And you know way? ~~We have dicided to keep it? WELL~~ becouse
> you have been very nice ~~to me and very kind~~ and cool. to me
> ~~has never someone haven do that before~~
> I hope we can be best friends for our whole life
> Please don't let this light inside of me go away.

By the spring of the second year of the study, then, Elisa believed that she could write in English. She sought opportunities to do so, and she produced different kinds of texts for her different classes, including reports, recipes, and recountings of events. She was able to display information, recount events, express opinions, justify opinions, and express feelings. From an ESL perspective, that is, if one compares Elisa to most Latino students who have been here for only 2 years, her performance is exceptional. Nevertheless, some ESL teachers would possibly be concerned about her lack of grammatical accuracy. Others, however, seeing the continued acquisition of English structure without direct instruction, would feel confident that many of her "errors" would disappear over time.

From a mainstream perspective, however, Elisa's writing is quite problematic. Many regular English teachers, especially those who are not used to reading the writing of incipient and developing bilinguals, would perhaps not appreciate what Elisa has accomplished and what she might accomplish with good instruction in writing itself.

Fortunately for Elisa, her first encounter with a mainstream English teacher was a positive one. During the summer of 1993 she enrolled in two summer school sessions of remedial English for native-speaking high school students. The teacher, an experienced professional committed to developing students' writing proficiency, encouraged Elisa's sense of herself as a competent writer while pointing out some patterns and features in her writing that could be improved.

The final writing sample is a rough draft for a longer paper. Here Elisa's growing ability to talk about herself and her family is quite evident. Compared to where she began, a mere 2 years before, in this paper Elisa displays a good control of English syntax and morphology. She also displays an increasing sense of organization. The three paragraphs in the text indicate that Elisa has now acquired a sense of the fact that different paragraphs focus on different topics. Her second paragraph, for example, is limited to discussing the place of origin of members of her family and the length of time that they have been in this country. In the final paragraph, she speaks exclusively about her family background and extended family.

Family Essay   Rough Draft

My family is made by four people, my sister whose name is Evelyn, my mom whose name is Magda and my dad whose name is Roberto and of course me. We all live in an apartment, my sister and I have are our on own room and my mom and dad have own their room too, we also have a little kitty for a pet. My mom and dad are always working so we go to school and most of the time we're busy doing work at home.

Not all the members of my family are from Honduras. My dad is from Guatemala and has lived here for five years already. My mom is from Honduras and she has live here for eight years already. My sister and I have lived here for two years already.

From the background of my dad, I don't know anything but from my mom backgrounds' I do know some. My ~~greatgram~~ great grandma's name is Maria Jesus, and her two son's names are Antonio and Alberto, her daughder's name is Herlinda. Herlinda is my mom's mom, which that means that she's my grandma. Nobody has the same names in the family They all have different names. I don't know why.

(and I can't ask because my mom is in the Hospital)

MANOLO'S WRITING DEVELOPMENT

Like Elisa, Manolo made great progress in learning to speak English and in learning to write in English. Initially, during the first year, Manolo was far superior to Elisa. The first sample, for example, was written by Manolo during the first language assessment. It will be noted that unlike Elisa, who primarily listed words, Manolo attempted to write a paragraph on the topic of Halloween. His choice is not entirely surprising, because the ESL class had just written a controlled composition on the same topic.

As opposed to the guided composition, however, within which students had been expected to choose elements from a list of words and copy sentences, Manolo actually displayed his personal understanding of the event as well as his own opinion of Halloween. The text, however, contains many spelling errors, several attempts to write in English using Spanish spelling conventions, and no concept of sentence structure whatsoever. Nevertheless, considering that Manolo had been in this country only 3 months, this first writing sample is impressive indeed.

In terms of writing process, Manolo appeared to be translating from Spanish as he wrote. He was not, as was the case with Elisa, writing exclusively what he could already say in English.

> This is the naigt the Hallowen much people go to the strets for candies much people have mask the mommy, bat, or dracula ay like mask the bat or much more mask.

As was the case with the other students in the ESL class, Manolo wrote very little in the first year except for controlled compositions. Manolo, however, did attempt several small efforts at writing under a substitute teacher's direction. He produced the next two samples and entered them into the computer using the program *Writing Center*. At the time, Manolo had been identified by both teachers as the classroom computer expert. At the substitute teacher's request, he entered the texts he produced into the computer and helped his classmates to do the same.

> The Kittiwakes
> I like the air smalls fres and I see in the sky so many kittiwakes and the puffin they live in the rocks. The puffin come face to face froom Alaska. I like the puffin is so funny I see when the brid eat fish and play together.

> Valentines Day
> Im in the street by my friend and I tinck about
> Frebrary 14 Valentines Day and I said to my friend
> lets made harts and my friend said but howo in paper
> whe can draw pictures and my friend said whe neet
> draw millions of pictures for evrione I like the idea.

Both samples included above were available to us only in their computer versions. We do not know whether the spelling errors contained in the text are genuine errors or simply the result of faulty data entry. What is evident from both texts, however, is that Manolo is attempting to display information about the kittiwakes and to recount his experiences in making valentines. His writing is perhaps comprehensible only to those individuals familiar with beginning ESL students.

By comparison, the next sample is quite comprehensible. It is taken from Manolo's national parks project and reveals the effects of controlled composition on student writing. Here Manolo produces correct English sentences with identical structures. He does not attempt to communicate his own meanings.

Social Studies
Carlsbad Caverns
1. I saw some stalactite.
2. I saw some stagmite.
3. I saw water color green.
4. The caverns are very big.
5. The caverns are under ground.

By May 1992, however, when the above sample was written, Manolo was quite capable of communicating a number of different meanings in English both orally and in writing. During the second language assessment, for example, he wrote two texts. One text responded to a reading about Michael Jackson, and the other text talked about his early experiences in the United States. In the first of these texts, Manolo expressed his opinion about Michael Jackson and supported this opinion by giving reasons for liking him. He communicated his thoughts quite clearly, although the text contains both spelling and punctuation errors.

I like Michael Jackson because I like ohw he dance he's very good dancing some times I want to dance like him And he's good singing too

The same growing communicative ability is evident in the next writing sample. Here Manolo displays his rapidly developing oral proficiency in English. This text uses a set of learned expressions that Manolo now produces in his spoken language. Like Elisa, his increasing fluency in writing is related to his increasing oral language competency. In this text, as compared to the first three samples, there is no evidence that Manolo is "thinking in Spanish," that is, that he is creating discourse in Spanish and then translating it into English.

There are a number of peculiar elements in this text. The overuse of the phrases *it's going to be fun, it was fun* suggests that either Manolo did not truly understand the meaning of these phrases or that he was using them as fillers when he could not think of anything else to say or when he did not have a way of saying what he really meant. In spoken interaction, the use of such phrases, especially among young people, often suggests fluency and familiarity with English that may not truly be present. In written language the imprecise use of such expressions tends to stand out more clearly

> When I came to the U.S. in the airplane I was skare because I think it's going to be fun. But when you're here it's hard you don't no about. The first day when I come to school was fun because I can't find the rooms it was fun. When I'm in my home it's different I do my homework and I go out with my bysicle I go out I go very far away from by home and I think like a eagle I want to fly because I really want to fly. In the future I want to worck in the airforce.

By the end of the first year, then, Manolo had developed the ability to write what he could already say. In October of the second year of the study, Manolo had transferred to J.F.K. School in a nearby affluent community. He entered the third level of the ESL program, which was designed to quickly mainstream newly arrived foreign youngsters of European or Asian background. (Manolo was one of about 40 Latino students in the school.) Mrs. Samuels, one of two ESL teachers, emphasized writing in her teaching.

At J.F.K., Manolo also enrolled in a creative writing class made up entirely of mainstream students and taught by a teacher who had recently arrived from Montana who had no experience with limited-English-speaking students. In her class, Manolo produced texts such as the following:

"A War"

> The war was between Mexico and France, France was wining they were getting closer to the castle of getting. On the top of the castle the Mexican flag was still flying. If the French soliders pulled the falg down and raise up their own Mexico would be declared a part of France. As the French soldiers got closer to the castle, there were less people protecting the Mexican fort, in the castle were the kid heroes they were cadets from the army of Mexico. The oldest one was 16 the others were from 16 to 10. Most the the kid heroes died protecting the castle.
> "They give their lives for their country."
> The French soliders got in to the castle there were three kid heroes left, and some soldiers still protecting the castle the others got kill, the three kids that were left run to the top of the castle two died right on the top the one who was left got shoot he took the flag down put it around his body

and he jump down the castle when he hit the ground he died. When the
French soldiers found the flag and the kid they could not take over Mexico
because the flag had blood on it Mexico had won the war.

When she shared this text with us, the teacher seemed a bit baffled.
She did not quite understand what Manolo had tried to do. She had,
nevertheless, responded to it and asked questions about meaning. She
had not corrected his grammar or his punctuation. She was aware that
she should not discourage Manolo's early writing attempts.

For us, Manolo's text was full of meaning. In it, he had tried to recount the tale of the *Niños héroes de Chapultepec* (the Boy Heroes of Chapultepec), known to every schoolchild in Mexico. Since, however, Manolo
had little sense of what his readers might need in order to make sense of
his recounting, he provided no explanations that might have helped his
teacher's understanding.

The text does show that Manolo was able to write longer segments of
connected discourse to narrate and recount a historical event. Oral style,
however, is still quite present in this text, as is transfer from Spanish.
Moreover, punctuation is nonexistent.

The creative writing teacher did not give up on Manolo. She encouraged him to find whatever might interest him to write about, and she responded to his writing as a sympathetic and interested reader. She was de-
lighted when Manolo published a "book," which was bound and displayed
in the classroom. Manolo produced other, more "standard" texts as well.

During the year, the ESL teacher required her students to write several long papers: a biographical incident, a report of information, and a
speculation-about-effects paper. Students were expected to engage in
pre-writing, in writing, and in revising and editing. Included below is the
final draft of Manolo's speculation-about-effects paper.

Speculation About Effects

So many things can happen in ten years. Often, ten years can bring positive
changes; Ten years can also provide difficult and negative situations.

In 1983, I was four years old. I was a little chubby. I had black hair and I
was not very tall then, I like to be heald and everybody liked to hold me. I
lived with my parents, one brother and one sister. I'm the youngest one.
I used to move a lot in my country and go on trips with my family. What
I liked to do in those days was play all day, eat, and watch T.V. I didn't care
about anything else.

In 1993 I'm thirteen years old, I have changed a lot in the last ten
years. Now I care about manythings. I care about school, myself, and other

people. Now I just don't like to play all day, there are many other things that I like to do. I like do homework, eat, play, and watch T.V. I might make my bed or cean room and I also care about how I look.

I can only guess what my life will be like in ten years. By 2003 my dream is to became a soldier or a marine, what I want to do there is learn new things and get to see new places. By that time I would have graduated from J.F.K. and and I might have played basketball in the school team, and also I will graduated from GREEN and maybe in that time I would have played some kind of musical intrument in the band, and by that time I will also have graduated from College and there I would have played basketball and music.

If my dream comes through positive things that can happen are that I will have been a good soldier or a good marine. I might have got to see new places and got lots of new frinends, and I would have learned lot's of new things.

If my dream coome through negative things that can happen might be that I might not get to see my family for a long time. and I might not be able to spend time for my self like going on vacations and have lot's of fun just by my self.

When I was a kid I didn't care about many things. There was some body else to take care of porblems and other things. But now, as I grow it seems that is almost my turn to do it. That's why I have to get ready for the future. that's why I get to do more new things, that's why I get more respon-sibilities and tha's why I have to learn lot's of new things for the future Tha's why now I have to choose what I want to be so I can start making my own life. I want to become somebody and to fell, like somebody.

Compared to other ESL students, and even with Elisa, Manolo's writing revealed a growing control of written English style. We conjecture that Mrs. Samuels's focus on the writing of multiple drafts helped Manolo to begin to differentiate between oral and written styles for different purposes. What is evident is that at J.F.K. School, Manolo was treated like an intelligent, college-bound student. He was expected to be interested in and concerned about a number of different topics.

WRITING DEVELOPMENT AND DEVELOPMENTAL LEVELS

The writing abilities of the focal students discussed here, Bernardo, Elisa, and Manolo, developed in both interesting and unexpected ways. In order to depict this development more precisely, I have elaborated in Figure 6.2 a set of descriptions of the abilities revealed by students at different stages, which I have delineated as Levels 1 through 7.

FIGURE 6.2. Description of Levels of Developing Writing Abilities in Secondary ESL Students.

Levels	Communicative Tasks Performed	Organization	Mechanics
Level 1	Displays familiarity with English words.	Writes lists of familiar English words.	Spells some words correctly. Uses Spanish spelling conventions to spell English words.
Level 2	Attempts to display information.	Writes simple unconnected sentences that he/she can produce orally. May also attempt to write by translating from L1 (i.e., Spanish).	Sentences reflect transfer from student's L1. Spelling errors are frequent. Uses Spanish spelling conventions to spell English words. Does not attend to capitalization and punctuation.
Level 3	Provides personal information.	Can write very short connected discourse (two or three sentences) on topics about which he/she can produce connected oral discourse (e.g., family, self, school).	Sentences continue to reflect transfer from student's L1. Does not attend to capitalization and punctuation. Spelling errors are frequent. May still use Spanish spelling conventions to spell English words. Writing may reflect oral language pronunciation resulting in both spelling errors and non-native like features.
Level 4	Displays limited amounts of information. Explains at a very basic level.	Can write short connected discourse (a paragraph) on a limited number of academic topics about which he/she can produce connected oral discourse.	Sentences continue to reflect transfer from student's L1. Begins to attend to capitalization and/or punctuation. Spelling errors are frequent. Writing may still reflect oral language pronunciation resulting in both spelling errors and non-native like features.

FIGURE 6.2. *Continued*

Level 5	Displays larger amounts of information.	Can write longer segments of connected discourse.	Sentences continue to reflect transfer from student's L1.
		Writes single very long paragraphs.	Some basic syntactic patterns are still not mastered.
		Includes many unrelated ideas in the same paragraph.	Begins to write compound sentences.
			Capitalization and punctuation are still not mastered.
			Uses an exclusively oral style.
Level 6	Displays information • to show that she knows • to show that she reads Explains. Expresses personal opinion. Justifies opinion. Recounts experiences in writing.	Demonstrates little or no audience awareness. Has little notion of text organization but begins to use several "paragraphs." Continues to include unrelated ideas in the same paragraph. Uses idiosyncratic, un-conventional criteria for selection of supporting details.	Sentences continue to reflect transfer from student's L1, but basic syntactic patterns have been mastered. Punctuation may still not be mastered. Uses an exclusively oral style.
Level 7	Displays information • to show that she knows • to show that she reads Explains more fully. Expresses personal opinion. Justifies position. Recounts experiences in writing. Expresses feelings in writing. Narrates.	Sense of audience begins to develop Growing sense of text organization emerges.	Growing ability to choose language for its precise meanings begins to emerge. Awareness of variety of styles used in writing for different purposes emerges.

It is important to point out that these descriptive statements are not statements that describe what students should or should not be able to do after 2 years of English language study. They are, rather, simple summaries of the discussion included above. They are intended to describe what three students, Elisa, Manolo, and Bernardo, were able to do and not do at the end of a 2-year period. The descriptions consider students' performance in the areas of communication, organization, and mechanics. They are less concerned with the type of text (cards, lists, letters) produced by students than with the communicative functions they were able to carry out in writing. More importantly, perhaps, these descriptions attempt to offer more detail about the kinds of functions that students were able carry out in attempting to respond to the writing demands made by the school setting.

In presenting these sets of descriptions, it is my purpose to try to capture some of the many features present in the writing of our focal students as well as the abilities and proficiencies reflected in the writing. I must emphasize the fact, however, that these descriptions are based on a study of writing abilities that students developed in instructional programs that were often less than ideal and that were not directly concerned with writing.

What I can say by using the above descriptors is that two of our students (Bernardo and Elisa) initially began as Level 1 writers and that one of our students (Manolo) began at Level 2. In the educational settings I have described in this report, one of our students (Bernardo) developed writing limited abilities characteristic of Level 3 at the end of a 2-year period. The two other students, Elisa and Manolo, both reached Level 7.

The work carried out with Latino ESL students allowed us to begin to describe the levels and stages of development that these students experienced over a 2-year period and to offer to the profession a point of departure for working with limited-English-speaking students. What our descriptions reveal is what is possible in 2 years for *some* students. What they also reveal, however, is that growth takes place slowly and often involves small steps.

INSTRUCTIONAL IMPLICATIONS

Newly arrived immigrant students face a number of difficulties as they struggle to acquire academic skills in English. The three Latino middle school students whom I have described here are typical of thousands of students who begin their academic lives in this country at the secondary level. As this study has sought to point out, these students do make progress. This progress depends, however, on the students' academic and family background, on the instruction they are exposed to, and on their own determination and talent.

Of the three students described here, for example, Bernardo appeared to bring with him well-developed academic skills. He produced the most sophisticated text at the beginning of the study in Spanish. Unfortunately for Bernardo, he was enrolled in an instructional program that did not directly build on his existing strengths. His family situation, moreover, did not provide a context in which he could continue to acquire English outside the classroom.

Elisa, on the other hand, while initially less fluent a writer in Spanish than Bernardo, was incredibly determined both to learn English and to develop the kinds of writing skills that she would need in order to be successful academically. She wrote extensively and creatively in spite of her ESL teacher's focus on controlled composition.

Manolo, the weakest of the three youngsters in terms of his Spanish writing abilities, had access to excellent instruction. His ESL teacher viewed her students (most of whom were children of newly arrived professionals) as capable of writing competently. She pushed them to write and expected that they would attempt the kinds of assignments required of mainstream students.

For Elisa, Bernardo, and Manolo, the question is where should they go next. As I have pointed out recently (Valdés, 1992), the dilemma for English-teaching professionals is how to decide which students belong where. Mainstream teachers, when looking at the texts produced by Bernardo, Elisa, and Manolo, may simply become overwhelmed. They have no idea where to start or how to help. As Figure 6.3 suggests, the same evidence can lead to very different conclusions and instructional recommendations.

To date, because of the lack of information available about the ways in which second language writing develops within the field of mainstream English language writing, many instructors expect that once the ESL or incipient stage of language learning is completed, non-English-background students will be able to write very much like native speakers of English. Since they are now technically outside of the ESL compartment, mainstream standards are applied, and not surprisingly, many such students fail to meet these standards.

If the instructor is tolerant, if she is committed to valuing content and not form, functional bilinguals will not suffer. They will not be penalized for not being native speakers. If the instructor is not tolerant, however, or if she has no knowledge about the nature of bilingualism, students are likely to receive low grades or to be sent back to the ESL compartment, to

FIGURE 6.3. Non-native-like Writing: Possible Diagnoses and Solutions.

Evidence:	Conclusion:	Solution:	Instruction:
English is non-native like. Many grammatical "errors" present	Student is a learner of English	Send to ESL	A. English grammar B. Mechanics
Produces L1-influenced English. "Errors" are systematic but different across students	Student is a fluent bilingual. Production includes fossilized elements.	Treat as mainstream	A. Practice in editing own writing. B. Instruction in identifying "fossilized" usages.
Produces L1-influenced English "Errors" are systematic and similar across students	Student is a fluent bilingual . She is (also) a speaker of a contact variety of English.	Treat as speaker of non-standard variety of English	A. Compare characteristics of contact variety with standard written English. B. Instruction in correcting non-standard features.

classes and instruction that in terms of the development of their English language proficiency can no longer do anything for them. The very same evidence, that is, the obvious non-native quality of students' written production, may lead both practitioners and researchers to very different conclusions. Differences in production between different types of fluent bilinguals are subtle, and pedagogical approaches as well as theories about composition pedagogy for these students are nonexistent.

Indeed, there are many questions that current research on second language writing and literacy have not yet answered; there is much that we do not know about young language learners and their writing. To date, for example, most research on learners schooled initially in their home language has taken the position that their writing will be contaminated by features of their first language. Instruction, then, is directed at getting them to avoid such contamination by either "thinking in English," editing their own writing using key grammar rules, or adapting writing models considered "good" writing for their own use. Very little attention has been given to what students bring with them, to the understandings they already have about the written language, to the skills they may have already developed, and to the ways in which they can be taught to use their first language strategically in learning to write in English.

Additionally, there is little research on the writing of fluent bilinguals. We know little about "expert" bilingual writers. Assuming that there are expert bilingual writers, however, we need to know how these writers go about the process of writing.

It may be bilingualism *per se* that causes problems for students, but it may also be that length of exposure to writing and writing conventions is more closely linked to writing difficulties. Understanding how the processes of revising and editing work for fluent bilinguals is essential. We need investigations of when and how these individuals revise their drafts, how first and second languages are used in revising and/or editing by different types of bilinguals, and how grammatical rules are used in both of these processes. And, in the light of instructional approaches that emphasize writing to learn, we also need studies of the connections between writing and learning for different types of bilinguals. In what ways does writing improve learning for bilingual students? What kinds of writing have what kinds of effects? In what ways and at what levels of proficiency does writing frustrate or interfere with student learning?

The issues facing the English-teaching profession are not simple, and unfortunately practitioners must move forward without all the answers. Indeed, they must be willing to approach the instruction of English language learners as teacher–researchers. I believe strongly that it will be only through efforts of such instructors that we will begin to design and implement the kinds of programs that can serve an increasingly large population of "diverse" students.

If the developmental descriptions I have provided here are useful, it is because they can suggest that in 2 years even students who start at zero can reach the point where they can carry out communicative acts—like explaining, describing, and narrating—in writing. For Latino students, this was possible when these youngsters were able to acquire the ability to carry out these same speech acts in the oral language. When they could display information orally, they were then able to begin to display this information in writing as well. What this might imply is that it is important for teachers to help students to develop functional oral abilities in English. Once these are in place, they may provide—as they did for the students in this study—an important point of departure from which the teaching of writing can proceed.

For ESL teachers, these sets of descriptions can serve as an indication of what is possible. For mainstream English teachers, these descriptors can suggest that in spite of shortcomings in organization and in mechanics, students at Levels 6 and 7 can indeed communicate quite effectively in the written language. In a very direct way, the set of descriptions is also intended to suggest that for ESL students—as is the case for mainstream students—organization and mechanics are quite separate. Students can learn how to structure paragraphs even if they have not yet mastered the niceties of punctuation. More importantly, however, it appears that over time and without direct instruction, many mechanical "errors" tend to work themselves out.

ESL students face many challenges. Even after 2 years, the most motivated and best students in our study were not quite native-like in their writing. There was much that they did not know; there was much that they had never been exposed to. As opposed to English monolingual students who have been surrounded by texts of different kinds all of their lives, ESL students had limited exposure to the traditions of written edited English. What Elisa and Manolo are only now beginning to learn is that in academic writing, it is not enough simply to communicate meaning. Someone needs to teach them, however, what they may never learn by themselves. Someone needs to point out to them—as Manolo's ESL teacher did in her class—the many features that undergird well-written texts. With a bit of attention and good will, mainstream teachers can work well with the Bernardos, Manolos, and Elisas in our secondary schools. They are good and dedicated students, and they have much to offer to all of us.

NOTES

1. Sheltered content courses are classes in which teachers—who may or may not speak the non-English language(s) spoken by their students—present subject-matter instruction using special strategies. They modify their use of English, and they provide many illustrations of the concepts they are presenting. Research conducted in California on such classes (Minicucci & Olson, 1992) has found that in comparison to mainstream classes, sheltered classes provide very sparse coverage of the subject-area content.

2. The description of the writing of these three students has been drawn from research conducted in two middle schools located in California in the greater Bay Area. The research project focused on the writing of non-English-background students and was supported under the Educational Research and Development Center Program (Grant No. R117G10036 for the National Center

for the Study of Writing). The research examined the development of writing abilities in newly arrived Latino students over a 2-year period.

3 All names used in this paper are pseudonyms.

REFERENCES

Chamot, A. U. (1992). Changing instructional needs of language minority students. In *Proceedings of the Third National Research Symposium on Limited English Proficient student issues* (Volume 1). Washington, D.C.: U.S. Department of Education: Office of Bilingual Education and Minority Language Affairs.

Davis, D., & McDaid, J. (1992). Identifying second-language students' needs: A survey of Vietnamese high school students. *Urban Education, 27*(1), 32–40.

Harklau, L. (1994). Tracking and linguistic minority students: Consequences of ability grouping for second language learners. *Linguistics and Education, 6,* 217–244.

Hornberger, N. (1989). Continua of biliteracy. *Review of Educational Research, 59*(3), 271–296.

LaFontaine, H. (1987). At risk children and youth—The extra educational challenges of limited English proficient students. In *Council of Chief State School Officers, 1987 summer institute*. Washington, D.C.

Lucas, T. (1992). What have we learned from research on successful secondary programs for LEP students? A synthesis of findings from three studies. In *Proceedings of the Third National Research Symposium on Limited English Proficient Student Issues, Focus on Middle School and High School Issues,* Volume 1. Washington, D.C.: U.S. Department of Education: Office of Bilingual Education and Minority Language Affairs.

Minicucci, C., & Olsen, L. (1992). *Programs for secondary limited english proficient students: A California study*. Washington, D.C.: National Clearinghouse for Bilingual Education.

Portes, A. et al. (1991). Characteristics and performance of high school students in Dade County (Miami SMSA) Schools. Dept. of Sociology, Johns Hopkins University, Baltimore, MD.

Rumbaut, G. (1990). Immigrant students in California public schools: A summary of current knowledge. Report No. 11. Center for Research on Effective Schooling for Disadvantaged Students, Baltimore, MD.

Valdés, G. (1992). Bilingual minorities and language issues in writing: Toward professionwide responses to a new challenge. *Written Communication, 9*(1), 85–136.

CHAPTER 7

Assessing ESOL Adolescents: Balancing Accessibility to Learn with Accountability for Learning

Margo Gottlieb

Illinois Resource Center

The 1974 U.S. Supreme Court decision *Lau* v. *Nichols* raised the consciousness of America in regard to the equitable instructional treatment of linguistically and culturally diverse students. For over two decades now, advocates of the language-minority community have struggled with ensuring ESOL students' accessibility to the same rich, challenging academic content as their native-English-speaking peers (La Celle-Peterson & Rivera, 1994). The battle for equity has been the most rigorous at the middle and secondary school front, where the prevalence of a compartmentalized and segregated instructional model has all but precluded the full participation of ESOL students (Minicucci, 1993).

With the dawn of the era of educational accountability in the 1980s, school reform initiatives have become centralized around the provision of academic standards that serve as a yardstick for student, school, district, and state performance. The centerpiece of this movement has been student assessment, where efforts have been directed to measure the extent to which specified criteria have been achieved. Again, the battle has been most rigorous in secondary schools, where high-stakes assessment as a graduation requirement has often impeded linguistically and culturally diverse students from equal education opportunity (Vicent & Rivera, 1995).

The assessment paradigm has been shifting at many levels, however, most markedly in classrooms throughout the United States. Understanding the importance and value of assessment, educators have been abandoning their "teach and test" mindset for a more integrated, holistic approach. Classroom-embedded, performance-based assessment has become an expression of the curriculum and a mirror image of instructional practice (Brooks & Brooks, 1993; Pierce & O'Malley, 1992). No where has the battle been more rigorous than at the secondary level, where student achievement has traditionally been equated with paper-and-pencil, literacy-dependent tasks.

This chapter proposes a vision for the assessment of adolescent ESOL students. It is guided by a framework that encompasses the multiple facets of this information-gathering process: student profiles, institutional and stakeholder perspectives, instructional practices, and purposes for assessment. It is prefaced by a review of current research in the assessment of ESOL secondary students. By acknowledging the complexity and comprehensiveness of assessment, it is hoped that in this age of accountability, students from linguistically and culturally diverse backgrounds will become contributing partners in the continuous improvement of the American educational system.

REVIEW OF RESEARCH OF ASSESSMENT OF ESOL SECONDARY STUDENTS

There are two strands of research that generally have been pursued in the assessment of secondary ESOL students. The first, at the classroom level, deals with instructional variation that leads to differences in student performance. The second, at the program level, generally associated with the field of evaluation research, addresses variation in implementation that leads to differences in program effectiveness. This review centers on the classroom; specifically, it explores the strategies that are employed in secondary schools with ESOL students that result in positive learning experiences.

Various instructional approaches have been used for research purposes to ascertain their impact on secondary ESOL students. Correa (1995) documents how cooperative learning in 9th grade physical science classes, coupled with exploratory, investigatory methods and parental awareness of the project, results in students' post-test gains, better grades in the course, and improved attitudes toward science. Peer tutoring is another approach that may hold potential for ESOL students; Torres-Gavilanes's (1993) investigation of eleventh and twelfth graders shows that although the participants' attitudes were favorable, the results did not lead to an increased rate of passing on the high school competency test. In Cross's 1995 whole language immersion study, the experimental group of high-risk eleventh graders was exposed to daily reading, writing, and speaking while the control group was taught grammar for 10 weeks. Analysis of data on four independent measures, including the Alabama High School Basic Skills Exit Exam, points to language growth for both conditions, with no significant differences between the mean gain of groups.

The use of learning and problem-solving strategies of elementary and secondary ESOL students within the context of the Cognitive Academic Learning Approach (Chamot, Dale, O'Malley, & Spanos, 1992) appears to yield positive results. In this approach, academic and learning strategies are explicitly taught to increase students' metacognitive awareness and to facilitate their learning of content and language. Results indicate that significantly more students identified in high-implementation classrooms are able to solve problems correctly using the prescribed sequence of steps than those in low-implementation classrooms. In addition, these students engage in significantly greater use of metacognitive strategies, such as planning, monitoring, and evaluating one's own learning, than their counterparts in the low-implementation condition.

Generally, it appears that those approaches that may be considered internal to the students themselves, as in the use of learner strategies, rather than those externally imposed upon students, seem to hold greater promise. Oscarson (1989), O'Malley and Pierce (1996), and Gardner (1996), among others, advocate for student assessment in the form of self-report or self-assessment. An internal or self-directed activity with self-assessment allows ESOL students to become more engaged in the learning process. In doing so, the students become more independent learners, take on more responsibility for their own learning, enhance their goal orientation, and have shared power to make decisions. When self-assessment has bearing on the learning situation and is conducted for formative purposes, as a self-management strategy, when the reliability of the assessment is not at issue, it is argued to be beneficial for older ESOL students.

An interesting offshoot of this research is the role of culture in the use of strategies for self-regulated learning. In a comparative study of learning strategies by three groups of upper secondary students (Australian students, Japanese students in Australia, and Japanese students in Japan), Purdie and Hattie (1996) find that both context and culture affect student performance. All students seem to employ a similar range of strategies, with cross-cultural similarities in self-checking, but the pattern of strategy use for each cultural group varies. Statistically significant differences emerge in the importance of certain strategies; the Australian students favor goal-setting and planning, while the Japanese students, irrespective of their learning environment, rely on memorization techniques. In all instances, higher achievers demonstrate a greater variety of strategies, regardless of their cultural background. These findings suggest that ESOL teachers should respect and capitalize on those cultural differences of their students that lead to self-regulated learning.

Another strategic variation cited in the literature is teaching ESOL students to become test-wise that independent of their subject-matter knowledge in order to promote their metacognitive success. In an investigation of the effect of teaching test-taking skills, Amer (1993) states that a group of junior high school English as a Foreign Language (EFL) students outperformed their peers. Their success is attributed to being able to elicit one of the explicitly taught strategies; namely, to read instructions carefully, schedule time appropriately, use context clues, delay answering difficult questions, and check answers. Similarly, Nevo (1989) reports the use of the identical test-taking strategies for reading comprehension for secondary bilingual students in their first and second languages; that is, returning to the passage after reading the question in search of the answer and looking for context clues. Additionally, the research reveals that in their second language, students selected more strategies that did not lead to the correct answer than they did in the first language.

Within the last decade, the field of language testing has begun to address more assessment-related issues, dealing with the collection, analysis, and reporting of multiple and varied data sources. Performance assessment, the act of using direct means of gathering information by having students demonstrate firsthand what they know and are able to do, has gained momentum as a valued complement to standardized, norm-referenced testing. Research is beginning to show that performance assessments can be effective instructional tools as well, having a positive effect on the ways teachers teach and the ways students learn (Khattri, Kane, & Reeve, 1995). With the inherent benefits for ESOL students, who need to be able to demonstrate their conceptual understanding through non-print-dependent tasks, the area of performance-based learning and assessment needs to be examined.

In conclusion, empirical research on secondary ESOL student performance due to variation in instructional approaches (not associated with evaluation studies) is scant and the findings are rather inconclusive. What is needed is a series of validation studies and a long-term research agenda for ESOL students in secondary schools. More investigation is necessary to better define the relationship betwen student assessment and learning as well as to clarify the contexts for assessment. The remaining part of the chapter moves away from the literature's microanalysis of assessment toward a more macroconceptual scheme.

THE PROCESS OF GATHERING INFORMATION: A CONTEXTUALIZED FRAMEWORK FOR ASSESSMENT

Assessment is a multidimensional and multifaceted process. The purposes, practices, perspectives, and student profiles together provide the context for assessment. Each dimension is defined by a number of facets or available options to the assessor; the ones depicted in the framework offered here are not inclusive but merely a representative sample of choices. The alignment of facets across dimensions yields a congruent and valid model for assessment.

The contextualized framework for assessment (see Figure 7.1) depicts the relationship among the dimensions and their respective facets through a series of concentric circles. The central purpose of assessment, improved performance of both students and teachers (Wiggins, 1993), can only be achieved by having useful information available for decision-making. The framework also serves as an operational plan for conducting assessment. The assignment of facets within each dimension must be thoughtfully considered to answer the who, what, how, and why for assessment. Each of the following sections of this chapter is devoted to one dimension of the framework, as applied to the secondary school setting. The concluding section offers an integrating perspective for instruction and assessment.

PROFILES OF ADOLESCENT ESOL STUDENTS: DOMAINS OF INFLUENCE

A profile of the students forms the outermost ring of the framework. In actuality, it represents the interaction among factors associated with the home, school, and community that potentially could impact student performance. Figure 7.2 depicts the relationships of these three domains as overarching venn diagrams with ESOL students as the anchor or centerpiece. The variables within these domains contribute to the formation of a composite picture of ESOL students. The unique qualities that embody the students need to be captured and documented as a first step in planning for instruction and assessment.

FIGURE 7.1. A Contextualized Framework for Assessment.

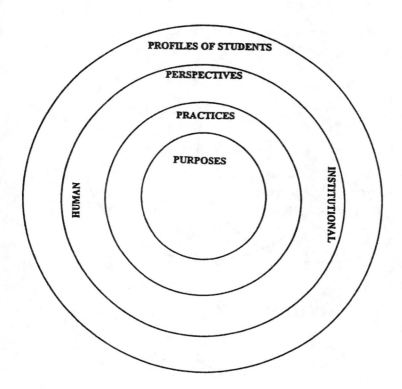

Common across all domains is the facet that acknowledges the amount of support available and provided in the students' native language and culture. The presence of support at home, in school, and in the community acts as a cohesive force in the development of the students and provides stability in their lives. Its absence in any one of the domains is cause for discontinuity that more than likely affects student performance. The interaction patterns that ESOL students develop in L1 (their home language) and in L2 (English) are established and maintained through this support network: in the home, with parents, siblings, and family members; in the school, with peers and teachers; and in the community, with friends, shopkeepers, and workplace personnel. The discussion which follows focuses on the variables associated with each domain identified with adolescent ESOL students.

FIGURE 7.2. A Profile of Adolescent ESOL Students: Domains of Influence.

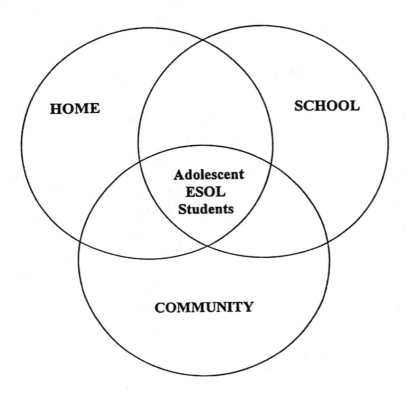

The Home

The richness of linguistic and ethnic traditions resides in the home backgrounds of ESOL students. The home languages and cultures, customs
and values, and experiences of the students need to be acknowledged
and incorporated into instruction and assessment. There should also be
recognition of the circumstances under which the students have immigrated or have migrated within the U.S. International events, economic
stability, and the political situation of the home country often help identify the diversity and complexity of student needs (Lucas, 1993). The status of the students as immigrants or involuntary minorities carries with it
educational implications as well (Ogbu, 1991).

The social context of the home, in particular, has an impact on language learning (Brown, 1987; Spolsky, 1989). Even in learning a first lan-

guage, where there is a biological basis for communication, social interaction is important. In learning a second language, the social situations abound that influence ESOL students in developing a set of attitudes toward the language and culture being acquired. These established social connections in the home environment, in addition to the students' individual personality traits, readily transfer over to a classroom's social environment, where rules or procedures for interaction either facilitate or inhibit learning (Enright & McCloskey, 1988).

The School

The prior educational experiences of ESOL students shape their future performance in school. At the middle and high school level, there is a tremendous academic diversity in the ESOL population, in large part due to the previous 6 years of variable educational exposure. Some students are recent immigrants or refugees, others have transferred from different school systems within the United States, and still others are ESOL students from feeder elementary schools within a district.

Even for those students with quality, continuous schooling (irrespective of the language of instruction), arrival at a new educational environment presents them with challenges due to differences in curricular content, sequencing of courses, teaching methodologies, and home language support (Minicucci, 1993). For underschooled students—who are arriving in growing numbers with minimal literacy skills—and for students whose literacy development is not apace with that of their native English-speaking peers, there simply is not enough time to bridge the educational chasm. The collection of baseline data in the students' home languages and in English is essential to ensure accessibility of an appropriate educational program for these students.

Educational factors are quite easily identifiable. These factors include students':

1. years of continuous education;
2. total years of education outside the U.S.;
3. coursework in L1 and L2;
4. amount of bilingual, ESL, Title 1, special education, or other support services; and
5. continuity of an instructional model throughout the elementary school years.

In order to facilitate instructional and assessment planning, a survey or interview—available in the student's first language and English, and administered upon initial entry into the middle or high school—can readily capture the students' home and educational background information.

The Community

The demographics of the community at large shed light on the resources available to the school in the implementation of its educational program. The density and location of the total population defines the area as urban, suburban, or rural. The density of the community's linguistically and culturally diverse populations is an indicator of the potential availability of services in the home language: social, political, economic, religious, wellness, and educational.

Acceptance of linguistic and cultural diversity and the promotion of bilingualism or multiculturalism in the community influence home and school alike. Oftentimes, the status of the home language and culture plays a role in the formation of community attitudes and beliefs (Ogbu, 1991). When the school, home, and community act in concert, there is a seamless transition for students from domain to domain. When goals and visions are not shared or understood, discord results, and students have to devise strategies to cope with their disjointed worlds.

Adolescent ESOL Students

The home, school, and community frame the life of students; assessment is the mechanism for collecting, analyzing, interpreting, and reporting information from those domains in order to secure the most sound and relevant educational program. For placement purposes or to determine eligibility for support services, it is important for educators to ascertain ESOL students' oral language proficiency, literacy development, and academic achievement in two languages, irrespective of the availability of bilingual services or personnel. To measure what students know only in English, when much of their educational career or life experiences have been in their first language, is not an accurate portrayal of their abilities or accomplishments. (Case in point: if there are Polish students in a school, axiomatically, there are Polish family members at home and a Polish community network to be tapped for instructional and assessment activities, even though there might not be Polish-speaking personnel in the school.)

In recent years, self-assessment has been recognized as a valued contributor to the information-gathering process (Pierce & O'Malley, 1992; Tierney, Carter, & Desai, 1991). Intake information from the students should include relevant demographics as well as the provision for the students' personal goals, their attitudes toward learning English, their

FIGURE 7.3. The Alignment of Some Dimensions of Assessment.

Posture	Accessibility	_____	Accountability
Purpose	Screening for placement	Monitoring progress	Documenting achievement
Proposed Standards	Opportunity to learn	Performance	Content or academic
Perspective	Program	Classroom	School

exposure to English outside of school, and their interaction patterns in various settings, such as the workplace. Collection of these data should provide insight into the students' interests, motivation to learn English, and pattern of acculturation.

To summarize, the home, school, and community are contributing factors in forming profiles of adolescent ESOL students. These domains influence the development of the student and often are predictors of student performance. Assessment across the domains allows educators to obtain a portrait of the students throughout their middle and secondary school years.

PURPOSES FOR ASSESSMENT: SETTING THE GUIDEPOSTS

The ultimate goal of assessment is to improve performance, not only of students, but of teachers, educational programs, and schools. To achieve this long-term goal, assessment needs to be comprehensive, varied, and useful (Wiggins, 1993). Identifying a purpose for assessment often has ties with a set of standards, which, in turn, guide the selection of relevant measures. Overarching the purposes for this process is the general posture or stance that assessment assumes for ESOL students; that is, to promote accessibility to an appropriate and relevant educational program and to demand accountability for learning within that program. The alignment among these assessment dimensions (purpose, proposed standards, and perspective), which forms the basis for validity, is delineated in Figure 7.3.

Assessment for initial screening purposes, conducted at the onset of each academic year for new students, for determination of eligibility for support services, should be addressed from the sources of information derived from the domains of student influence, as mentioned in the previous section. Screening determines the eligibility of students for specified services offered within a school and thus their accessibility to a worthwhile and beneficial educational program. Data obtained through predetermined screening procedures, which may entail student surveys, transcripts, writing samples in English and the native language, interviews, and standardized language proficiency and academic measures, are essential for initial placement decisions for ESOL students.

Once ESOL students are placed in an effective learning environment, there are additional purposes for student assessment that come into play throughout the academic year to make schooling a successful experience. There are basically four other reasons why assessment occurs: namely, to

1. monitor or review the students' academic progress,
2. diagnose student specific strengths and areas of difficulty,
3. reclassify students based on their accomplishments, and
4. mark the students' academic achievement.

Each purpose will now be discussed within the context of secondary schools.

Determination of Academic Progress

Achievement of academic parity with native English speakers is an arduous process that can take up to a decade to accomplish (Collier, 1992); therefore, it is critical to be able to mark continued progress toward that end. Ongoing classroom assessment provides the documentation of that effort. Evidence collected systematically throughout the school year across all learning areas allows ESOL students to determine their movement along the second language acquisition path and provides teachers a barometer of their instructional effectiveness.

As with every purpose, a variety of assessments are a necessary requirement for sound educational decision-making (Bailey & McTighe, 1996; Chamot, 1993, among others). At the secondary level, in general, assessment practices for ESOL students are limited to standardized tests of English oral language proficiency and achievement (Minicucci, 1993). Teachers must realize that the learning that occurs in their classrooms on a daily basis is the most legitimate and valid portrayal of student achievement.

The types of assessment used for monitoring the academic progress of ESOL students, outlined in the section on practices, are largely interwoven into the instructional cycle at the classroom level. Classroom-embedded assessment, conducted throughout the year, should reflect the language(s) of instruction and be anchored in a set of performance standards. That is, the extent of first language and English use within each content area should be mirrored in the assessment of that subject matter. Assessment within the classroom should be guided by standards, a content-rich curriculum, and the knowledge base of its students.

Diagnosis of Strengths and Challenges

In its broadest sense, the diagnosis of student strengths and challenges can result from any assessment; in a narrower interpretation, this purpose is equated with the use of specific instructional skills and strategies. If assessment is to have diagnostic utility, however, the tasks and scoring criteria must support some credible learning theory (Herman, Aschbacher, & Winters, 1992). Information gained from diagnostic assessment should provide direct feedback to students and teachers. Building upon their strengths, students should be guided toward continuous improvement based on their personal developmental level. Building upon their strengths, teachers should refine or revamp instruction based on feedback from assessment.

Diagnosis, being analytic in nature, touches upon individual student skills and learning strategies. Oftentimes it is reserved for students who are not demonstrating substantial progress or for those who are challenged in crossing the threshold to more decontextualized learning situations (Cummins, 1981). As part of monitoring the academic performance of students, assessment conducted for diagnostic purposes needs to be in concert with instructional practices and be representative of the medium(s) of instruction. In fact, when feasible, comparison of student performance in L1 vis-à-vis L2 provides a fuller, more descriptive, and more clear-cut picture of skill attainment by students.

Reclassification of Students

Although summative assessment in the form of standardized tools may have its place at the completion of a course of study, it is formative assessment that reveals how students are performing on an ongoing basis. Decisions related to the reclassification of ESOL students from instructional level to level, including transition from ESL/bilingual services, should be based on an ample set of formative and summative measures that are reflective of the language and cognitive demands of classrooms geared to native English speakers (De George, 1988).

Due to logistical constraints of scheduling large numbers of students, at the secondary level in particular, reclassification decisions often occur around midyear. In general, this practice is detrimental to ESOL students who have not had adequate time to demonstrate substantial growth and, more often than not, does not take into account their potential growth over the upcoming months. Reclassification is a programmatic decision where individual student data are compared to a comparable group of students or to a set of established criteria; it should be a shared responsibility among teachers, students, and parents. Although students lose their ESOL status upon transition, continued collection of assessment data is important to validate the students' academic success.

Measurement of Overall Academic Achievement

With 17 states to date imposing a high school graduation test on their students, assessment for reasons of accountability is rapidly becoming part of the standards-based educational reform movement (Vicent & Rivera, 1995). This gatekeeper to the high school diploma is the ultimate form of high-stakes assessment, and even though several states allow various "accommodations" or "modifications," minority students have tended to show disproportionate failure rates (Jaeger, 1989). There are several reasons for the poor performance by ESOL students on large-scale assessments. First, more often than not, the design or blueprint for the instruments does not take the unique characteristics of this student population into consideration (hence, the extensive need for accommodations). Second, accommodations often tend to mask, not improve, a student's chances for success (case in point, providing more time on a Russian test does not diminish the struggle for a student who is nonproficient in Russian, while it does invalidate the assessment). Third, more than likely, the assessment has not been piloted, field-tested, or normed with or without accommodations on a representative sample of ESOL students.

At a programmatic level, the measure of overall academic achievement of ESOL students is equally as cumbersome. Except for dual language, immersion, or maintenance bilingual education models, where learning two languages is honored and valued, the ultimate goal of ESL and transitional bilingual education is to bridge the gap in English-language proficiency and academic achievement between student groups. Therefore, summative assessment of ESOL secondary students for accountability purposes, usually conducted at the close of the academic year, generally compares the student's performance to that of the school, district, or state average. When ESOL students are transitioning from ESL classes, native English-speaking peers serve as the criterion group, and assessment at that point in time has to replicate what is generally accepted for that content area at that grade level. The considerations that must be taken into account for high-stakes assessment need to be replicated here in order to provide the most reliable, valid, and equitable assessment for these students.

In conclusion, the purposes for assessment help shape the instructional program. At the beginning of the academic year, information from screening sets the stage for teachers to plan and implement appropriate and meaningful instruction. Throughout the year, assessment for monitoring and diagnostic purposes provides ongoing information on the effectiveness of teaching and learning. At the completion of the year, information for accountability can be used to measure overall student achievement and program effectiveness at the school, district, or state level. Overarching the assessment process is its primary purpose; namely, to improve instruction and academic performance of students. All assessment, irrespective of its purpose, should conform to the tenet that no one measure can ever yield a complete profile of student performance.

PERSPECTIVES: DATA SOURCES AND RESOURCES

There are dual perspectives for assessment; one represents the educational institution and corresponds to the level of data aggregation and analysis, while the other recognizes the human players and their roles in the process. This dimension of assessment includes who is collecting information and how the information is to be used. When various persons representing various perspectives are involved in consensual decision-making, the results are more meaningful and useful.

Assessment, as instruction, should begin with the students. Self-assessment assists students to set incremental benchmarks by which they can judge their own achievement, reflect upon the learning process, and develop self-direction for attaining high performance levels (Darling-Hammond, 1994). This notion is especially important for secondary students, who should have input in shaping their learning and assume more responsibility for achieving their personal educational goals. Assessment, as instruction, provides the means for individual students to express their interests as well as their ways of thinking, understanding, and communicating (Neill et al., 1995). In addition, assessment should determine to what extent students have the metacognitive awareness to monitor their own comprehension, use learning strategies, and evaluate the relevance of what they learned.

As social interaction is central to learning, assessment, in its own right, should extend the students' learning experiences by offering these adolescents opportunities to interact. Pairing students for oral language activities is a natural occurrence in ESOL classrooms. The use of a buddy system between ESOL students and their native English-speaking counterparts for peer editing and review of original work provides reciprocal benefits. Adult mentors utilized in the assessment process, whether teachers or other school personnel, community leaders, or family members, expand the audience of assessment.

Self-assessment extends to teachers (Manning, Manning, & Long, 1994) as well. As teaching is a dynamic enterprise, self-reflection or introspection affords teachers the opportunity to continually modify their instruction to accommodate the experiences and learning styles of their students. As a result, there is improvement in teaching in addition to professional and personal growth of teachers.

Collaboration among teachers enhances the chances for students to profit from instruction and assessment. In particular, ESL, bilingual, and content-area teachers should provide a cohesive, unified curriculum, built upon the same standards, to maximize ESOL student chances for success. Selection of topics, themes, problems, or issues should cross teacher boundaries, while their implementation and assessment should directly respond to student needs.

Where responsibility extends beyond students and classrooms, administrators assume a stance on assessment. From their particular vantage points, assessment data contribute to the evaluation of programs, schools, and districts. The effectiveness of ESL/bilingual programs, for example, should be judged on a collection of assessments, documents, surveys, and standard interviews whose results are explained within the context of the demographics of the student population. The insights gained from this perspective are more global and are useful in stimulating schoolwide or systemic change.

From an institutional standpoint, the purpose for assessment has to be synchronized with how the information is to be gathered, analyzed, reported, and used. In ascending the scale of information collection and use from classroom, grade level, program, school, district, and state to the nation, the stakes become higher, time and cost efficiency become paramount, flexibility is diminished, and the authenticity of assessments is forfeited. Measurement to support instruction provides immediate, detailed feedback with direct relevance to teachers and students, while that which serves accountability and policy goals usually entails reducing complexity to a single score (Shepard, 1989). To summarize, why assessment is conducted, who is the intended audience, and how the results are used are questions to be answered when planning for assessment.

A PANORAMA OF ASSESSMENT PRACTICES

An assessment practice, when aligned with a specified purpose, can be a valid indicator of student performance. The purposes for assessment operate on micro and macro levels (Wiggins, 1993). The dichotomous scheme created differentiates those assessments internal to the instructional cycle from those that are externally imposed (Genesee, 1996). This section describes the types on assessments that operate inside and outside the classroom.

Assessment Within the Classroom

The rigid organizational structure of middle and high schools hinders the development and implementation of comprehensive instructional and assessment programs (Minicucci, 1993). In addition, research indicates that teachers at the high school level tend to lecture about 88% of the time (Goodlad, 1984). These problems are exacerbated for ESOL students, who profit from extended, interdisciplinary, concrete activities that require chunks of time for interacting, processing, and reflecting on learning. Performance-based assessment that is integrated into instruction remains a challenge for most secondary teachers.

In tracking the progress of ESOL students over time, a variety of assessment processes, products, and procedures, compatible with defined instructional intents and standards, need to be incorporated into instructional planning and delivery. Instructional strategies that are engaging for students, promote complex thinking, and involve student choice should serve as the basis for assessment. A host of methods and activities can be utilized in the developmental areas touched by instruction and assessment of ESOL students:

1. oral language;
2. literacy;
3. conceptual understanding; and
4. metacognitive awareness.

The daily learning environment of students is the natural hub for assessment. Oral language development of ESOL students in middle and high schools may entail conversations, discussions, debates, interviews, improvisations, brainstorming, retelling tasks, oral reports or presentations, demonstrations, and speeches. Literacy development may center on writing letters, using interactive journals, illustrating literacy events, creating student-authored books, using story maps, maintaining literacy logs or response journals, participating in process writing, and publishing newsletters. Conceptual understanding of ESOL students is promoted through the use of illustrations, learning logs, experiments, research, inventions, investigations, and content-based problem-solving through literature. Metacognitive awareness is heightened in students who engage in self-analysis and reflection of their learning, who are made cognizant of their own learning strategies, and who can critique how they process information through the use of journals and conferences.

In teaching ESOL students, concrete referents for contextual support are necessary to convey meaning. In assessing ESOL students, the amount of contextual support should remain constant with that of instruction. As the middle and secondary school curriculum is largely literacy-dependent, the use of graphic representations across learning areas facilitates the students' ability to grasp the main concepts and to express them in a logical, coherent way. Graphic organizers such as webs, T charts, flow charts, concept maps, and venn diagrams as well as other visuals in the form of tables, charts, maps, graphs, and figures offer a myriad of opportunities for students to demonstrate their understanding of core learning principles.

Instructional and assessment strategies, along with these activities, facilitate student learning. The instructional criteria of the Integrated Language Teaching model proposed by Enright and McCloskey (1988)—which consists of collaboration, purpose, student interest, previous experience, support, variety, and integration—should serve as the backbone for assessment as well. For secondary ESOL students, sheltered instruction in the content areas can be considered a generalized approach for gaining access and understanding to a historically context-reduced, literacy-dependent curriculum. Whatever associated tenets and techniques are incorporated into ESL teaching to foster comprehensible input (such as cooperative group work, language experience, use of manipulatives) should be replicated for assessment.

Instructional and assessment activities or tasks may be amassed to create more extensive, long-term endeavors. Gardner (1991) describes some measures utilized in Arts Propel, an integrated curricular and assessment initiative for middle and high schoolers. Domain projects that are based on concepts central to a discipline last a few days to a few weeks in length. Process folios capture the steps taken by students in the course of designing a product or domain project from initial brainstorming, early drafts, first critiques, journal entries, and interim and final critiques to the final product. An example of a thematic project for secondary ESOL students might surround the investigation of the nature and impact of recycling in their town. Students could tally, measure, and graph; research the environmental effects and debate the issue; conduct a neighborhood survey; interview people in the community; write political/business leaders; wage a schoolwide campaign; and create products from recycled goods. The process and products of instruction and assessment could be captured in an interdisciplinary project and assessed through conferences, journals, or logs, and with a holistic rubric containing descriptive criteria. An example of a four-point, holistic, project-based scale, shared with the students from the onset of instruction, is provided in Figure 7.4.

Assessment is often distinguished from instruction by the requirement to record and interpret information in a systematic, reliable way. Rubrics are the mechanism for recording, documenting, and interpreting performance-based assessment data. These documents, which may appear as inventories, checklists, rating scales, or matrices, serve as the artifacts of assessment and provide the evidence, in the form of specified criteria, of a student's level of attainment. Rubrics offer a focus for instruction; help shape the levels of expected performance for students; define the criteria by which standards are measured; and make assessment data meaningful for students, teachers, parents, and administrators. Ultimately, rubrics should become an expression of instruction and, in doing so, should be as well known to the students as the tasks they undertake (Wiggins, 1992).

Unfortunately, although there are guidelines for the development of performance tasks and accompanying rubrics (Burke, 1994; Herman, Aschbacher, & Winters, 1992; Neill et al., 1995, among others), few consider the linguistic and cultural diversity of ESOL students. In adapting alternative assessments for this population, several strategies might be employed:

1. include multiple indicators and methods by which students can demonstrate their competencies;

2. allow students to use their preferred language to relate conceptual understanding;

3. modify the specifications of the task so they become less language-dependent and more focused on concepts;

4. expand the task so all students, irrespective of their proficiency and experiences, can successfully engage;

5. construct a weighted scale that responds to the students' linguistic and academic range; and

6. redesign the task and scale so they become developmental in nature, moving from concrete, contextualized situations to abstract, decontextualized ones.

FIGURE 7.4. A Holistic Rating Scale for Project-based Instruction and Assessment.

4. Champion

- Develops and implements a logical plan of organization
- Systematically collects, records, and analyzes relevant data
- Uses evidence from multiple sources to justify decisions
- Incorporates extensive support materials and resources
- Expresses complex ideas through visual, graphic, or multimedia representation
- Produces a comprehensive, original project

3. Comprehensive

- Develops and implements a loose plan of organization
- Collects, records, and analyzes relevant data
- Uses evidence to make decisions
- Incorporates varied support materials and resources
- Expresses ideas through visual, graphic, or multimedia representation

2. Competent

- Partially develops and implements a plan of organization
- Collects, records, and analyzes some data
- Uses some evidence to make decisions
- Relies on support materials and resources
- Expresses some ideas through visual or graphic representation
- Produces a complete project

1. Challenged

- Lacks a plan of organization
- Collects some data; draws inappropriate or inaccurate conclusions
- Makes decisions without evidence
- Includes some support materials and resources
- Incorporates some visual and graphic representation
- Produces an incomplete project

In this way, all students will have fair and equitable accessibility to the same promising instructional/assessment practices of the classroom.

Assessment Across Classrooms and Grade Levels

Historically, assessment in middle and high schools has been dependent on forced-choice, paper-and-pencil, discrete-point tests with one correct response that require students to recall or recollect facts. Likewise, the high school diploma has remained tied to credit accrual doled out on a semester basis (Wiggins, 1989). Recently, some interesting options for secondary school students have emerged that rely upon the accumulation and demonstration of comprehensive, in-depth knowledge. Two such innovations will be discussed in this section, the graduation portfolio and graduation by exhibition.

The value of the portfolio as an instructional classroom tool is well documented (see, for example, Arter & Spandel, 1992; Batzke, 1992; Frank, 1994; Gottlieb, 1995; Porter & Cleland, 1995), as are its uses for programmatic and district-level decision-making and, to a limited degree, for state-level accountability. Little attention has been paid, however, to its intrinsic worth for students at the secondary level, where real-life applicability of knowledge gained over a school career is eminent. The graduation portfolio not only is a crossover to the world of work or academia, but serves as individual student accountability for learning. For ESOL students, whose "grades" are not necessarily a register of their capabilities, a portfolio serves a confidence booster in preparing for employment or college, a showcase of their accomplishments, and an opportunity for personal goal-setting.

The Michigan Employability Skills Portfolio (Stemmer, Brown, & Smith, 1992) exemplifies how secondary schools can effectively coordinate efforts and build collaborations with the business community to promote continued success of their students. The employability portfolio, illustrative of authentic assessment by having local businesspeople review the contents and provide feedback to the students, consists of three components or folders: academic skills, personal management skills, and teamwork skills. Preparation for the workplace is a formidable challenge for any student; for ESOL students, who are unaccustomed to the cultural nuances of U.S. business, the demand is even greater. Employability portfolios hold the promise of linking what happens in secondary schools to outside, real-life opportunities.

Exhibition of mastery, proposed by Ted Sizer and a central tenet of the essential school concept, has attempted to assist schools in designing more exciting, engaging, insightful, and relevant assessments that lead students to earning a diploma (Wiggins, 1989). The Crefeld School Exhibitions Portfolio is just one example of how high school students demonstrate their preparation for graduation. Its eight major entries are a compilation of student achievements that include:

1. an artistic exhibition;
2. a literary analysis;
3. a research report;
4. an original experiment;
5. a mathematics application task;
6. an outreach presentation, as part of community work;
7. a final résumé; and
8. a student's postgraduation plan.

Other schools in the coalition use position papers, Socratic seminars, and multimedia presentations to produce students who use their minds well within a high-quality, integrated system of instruction and assessment (McDonald et al., 1993). Irrespective of the entry point of students, by the completion of high school, there is evidence of personal growth across the disciplines.

It would be remiss and irresponsible, in a chapter devoted to assessment, not to acknowledge the testing industry's presence in education and its role in developing and marketing standardized, norm-referenced assessments for ESOL students. Large-scale, standardized assessment remains the primary mechanism to obtain reliable data across student populations, is readily tied to accountability of large school systems, and indicates how students, grade levels, or schools compare across a state or the nation. Therefore, it is incumbent upon educators and advocates of ESOL students to insist that the standardized assessment is a valid indicator of what students know. Ways to increase the validity of these assessments include limiting the amount of test bias, expanding the norming population to encompass multilingual, multicultural students, drawing from ESOL classroom practices and students' educational experiences, making extensive use of graphic representation of concepts, and reporting results in meaningful ways.

Standardized testing more than likely is part of secondary school life. It often serves as the criterion against which the performance of second language learners is measured, and rightfully so when ESOL students approach grade-level norms. It should be one of the variables in the equation of school achievement, along with other forms of assessment, which contributes to a student's overall academic profile.

A POSTURE FOR
INSTRUCTION AND ASSESSMENT

Differentiating between teaching and assessment is both unnecessary and counterproductive. Assessment through teaching . . . tells us more about student learning than externally developed assessment tasks. Working through complex problems requires students to apply a priori knowledge to new situations and to construct new understandings. In the traditional teach-test model, the process of learning all but shuts down while assessment occurs. (Brooks & Brooks, p. 97)

Together, instruction and assessment give more than either gives separately. (Paulson, Paulson, & Meyer, 1991)

Assessment and instruction are intertwined and interdependent, with a shared set of features. These common characteristics could emerge in secondary schools organized around a series of ongoing, multifaceted, multidisciplinary, multicultural, multimedia thematic projects within an integrated model. These comprehensive, student-centered, performance-based projects should spark excitement, enthusiasm, energy, and a thirst for teaching and learning. They should be purposeful and authentic in the truest sense, using the students' life experiences as the foundation for scaffolding or building the knowledge base with transferable connections.

The educational goals set out in Enright and McCloskey's (1988) integrated model for second language learners—joy, community, access, literacy, and power—easily extend to the middle and secondary schools. Students should have opportunities to interact with each other, monitor and reflect upon their own progress, seek business and community support, and exhibit their knowledge. For ESOL students, equity can be achieved by having instruction and assessment contextualized, cognitively complex, conceptually bound, and personally challenging. The results should be meaningful and useful to individual students, teachers, and other educational stakeholders.

Even the constructs of reliability and validity, which have been the traditional cornerstones for assessment, have started to shift their focus toward the classroom. More attention has centered on curricular validity, which focuses on the match between the curriculum and the content of assessment; instructional validity, which addresses the link between instructional practices and assessment material; and ecological validity, which examines the context for assessment or the environment in which it occurs. These forms of validity are especially applicable to ESOL students at the secondary level, who may be tracked based on their English language proficiency and are consequently denied access to the full curriculum, instructional program, and technological opportunities that the school offers (Vicent & Rivera, 1995). As a result, ESOL students are not even exposed to the subject-matter material on which English-proficient students are assessed (U.S. General Accounting Office, 1994).

As the disparity between assessment and instruction lessens, due in part to imposition of educational standards, the goal to have students demonstrate what they know and are able to do becomes centered in the classroom. For ESOL students to attain standards, instruction must address diverse learning styles, educational backgrounds, and language proficiencies of the students; assessment, in turn, must utilize these instructional approaches (Martin, 1995). Exclusion of ESOL students from assessment no longer is a viable alternative; responsibility for learning should rest on student shoulders as well as society at large. Accountability for learning for every student should extend throughout the educational arena, from classrooms to schools, local school boards, and state departments of education.

If schools are to become powerful educational enterprises, assessment needs to focus on the classroom, where, ideally, students benefit from participation and teachers are informed (Perrone, 1991). The dimensions that comprise the framework for assessment—purposes, practices, perspectives, and student profiles—outline the scope of the process. It is necessary for ESOL students to have access to excellence by valuing their backgrounds and experiences within an integrated curricula, capitalizing on material and human resources in the community, and expanding the repertoire of instructional and assessment practices. That is not sufficient. Educators of ESOL students have the dual responsibility of balancing the opportunities for learning with demonstrating in reliable and valid ways how success is met. With the ESOL student population continuing to increase, accountability must also rest with each and every student. Unifying instructional and assessment practices and building collaborations among students, teachers, and community members, as well as encouraging students to fulfill reachable standards in meaningful, productive ways, can lead the transformation of schools and goals into the 21st century.

REFERENCES

Amer, A. A. (1993). Teaching EFL students to use a test-taking strategy. *Language Testing, 10*(1), 71–77.

Arter, J. A., & Spandel, V. (1992, Spring). An NCME instructional module on using portfolios of student work in instruction and assessment. *Educational Measurement: Issues and Practice*, 36–44.

Bailey, J., & McTighe, J. (1996). Reporting achievement at the secondary level: What and how. In T. R. Guskey (Ed.), *Communicating student learning: 1996 ASCD Yearbook* (pp. 119–140). Alexandria, VA: Association for Supervision and Curriculum Development.

Batzke, J. (1992). *Portfolio assessment and evaluation: Developing and using portfolios in the classroom*. Cypress, CA: Creative Teaching.

Brooks, J. G., & Brooks, M. G. (1993). *In search of understanding the case for constructivist classrooms*. Alexandria, VA: Association for Supervision and Curriculum Development.

Brown, H. D. (1987). *Principles of language learning and teaching* (2nd ed.). Englewood Cliffs, NJ: Prentice-Hall.

Burke, K. (1994). *How to assess authentic learning*. Palatine, IL: IRI/Skylight.

Chamot, A. U. (1993). Changing instruction for language minority students to achieve national goals. *Proceedings of the third national research symposium on Limited English Proficient student issues: Focus on middle and high school issues, 1*, 53–80.

Chamot, A. U., Dale, M., O'Malley, J. M., & Spanos, G. (1992). Learning and problem solving strategies of ESL students. *Bilingual Research Journal, 16*(3&4), 1–34.

Collier, V. (1992). A synthesis of studies examining long-term language-minority student data on academic achievement. *Bilingual Research Journal, 16*(1&2), 187–212.

Correa, M. (1995). *Incorporating cooperative learning strategies to improve science achievement scores among ninth grade ESOL I and II physical science students' learning*. (ERIC Document Reproduction Service No. ED 385 154)

Cross, J. B. (1995). *Effects of whole language immersion (WLI) on at-risk secondary students*. (ERIC Document Reproduction Service No. ED 392 027)

Cummins, J. (1981). The role of primary language development in promoting educational success for language minority students. In California State Department of Education, *Schooling and language minority students: A theoretical framework* (pp. 3–49). Los Angeles, CA: California State University.

Darling-Hammond, L. (1994). Performance-based assessment and educational equity. *Harvard Educational Review, 64*(1), 5–30.

De George, G. P. (1988). *Assessment and placement procedures of language minority students: Procedures for mainstreaming. Focus* (Occasional Papers No. 3). Washington, DC: The National Clearinghouse for Bilingual Education.

Enright, D. S., & McCloskey, M. L. (1988). *Integrating English: Developing English language and literacy in the multilingual classroom*. Reading, MA: Addison-Wesley.

Frank, M. (1994). *Using writing portfolios to enhance instruction and assessment*. Nashville, TN: Incentive.

Gardner, D. (1996). Self-assessment for self-access learners. *TESOL Journal, 5*(3), 18–23.

Gardner, H. (1991). *The unschooled mind: How children think and how schools should teach.* New York: Basic Books.

Genesee, F. (1996, personal communication).

Goodlad, J. I. (1984). *A place called school.* New York: McGraw-Hill.

Gottlieb, M. (1995). Nurturing student learning through portfolios. *TESOL Journal, 5*(1), 12–14.

Herman, J. L., Aschbacher, P. R., & Winters, L. (1992). *A practical guide to alternative assessment.* Alexandria, VA: Association for Supervision and Curriculum Development.

Jaeger, R. (1989). Certification of student competence. In R. Linn (Ed.), *Educational measurement* (3rd ed.). New York: American Council on Education and Macmillian.

Khattri, N., Kane, M. B., & Reeve, A. L. (1995). How performance assessments affect teaching and learning. *Educational Leadership, 53*(3), 80–83.

LaCelle-Peterson, M. W., & Rivera, C. (1994). Is it real for all kids? A framework for equitable assessment policies for English language learners. *Harvard Educational Review, 64*(1), 55–75.

Lucas, T. (1993). What have we learned from research on successful secondary programs for LEP students? A synthesis of findings from three studies. *Proceedings of the third national research symposium on Limited English Proficient student issues: Focus on middle and high school issues, 1,* 81–111.

Manning, M., Manning, G., & Long, R. (1994). *Theme immersion: Inquiry-based curriculum in elementary and middle schools.* Portsmouth, NH: Heinemann.

Martin, W. H. (1995, April). *The implications for supporting educational excellence for English Language Learners through statewide assessment policies.* Paper presented at the annual meeting of the American Educational Research Association, San Francisco, CA.

McDonald, J. P., Smithe, S., Turner, D., Finney, M., & Barton, E. (1993). *Graduation by exhibition: Assessing genuine achievement.* Alexandria, VA: Association for Supervision and Curriculum Development.

Minicucci, C. (1993). Gaining access to the core curriculum in intermediate schools: A California study. *Proceedings of the third national research symposium on Limited English Proficient student issues: Focus on middle and high school issues, 1,* 469–505.

Neill, M., Bursh, P., Schaeffer, B., Thall, C., Yohe, M., & Zappardino, P. (1995). *Implementing performance assessments: A guide to classroom, school and system reform.* Cambridge, MA: FairTest.

Nevo, N. (1989). Test taking strategies on a multiple-choice test of reading comprehension. *Language Testing, 6*(2), 199–215.

Ogbu, J. U. (1991). Immigrant and involuntary minorities in comparative perspective. In M. A. Gibson & J. U. Ogbu (Eds.), *Minority status and schooling* (pp. 3–33). New York: Garland.

O'Malley, J. M., & Pierce, L. V. (1996). *Authentic assessment for English Language Learners: Practical approaches for teachers.* U.S.: Addison-Wesley.

Oscarson, M. (1989). Self-assessment of language proficiency: rationale and applications. *Language Testing, 6*(1), 1–13.

Paulson, F. L., Paulson, P. R., & Meyer, C. A. (1991, February). What makes a portfolio a portfolio? *Educational Leadership, 48,* 60–63.

Perrone, V. (Ed.). (1991). *Expanding student assessment.* Alexandria, VA: Association for Supervision and Curriculum Development.

Pierce, L. V., & O'Malley, J. M. (1992). *Performance and portfolio assessment for language minority students.* Washington, DC: National Clearing House for Bilingual Education.

Porter, C., & Cleland, J. (1995). *The portfolio as a learning strategy.* Portsmouth, NH: Heinemann.

Purdie, N., & Hattie, J. (1996). Cultural differences in the use of strategies for self-regulated learning. *American Educational Research Journal, 33*(4), 845–871.

Shepard, L. A. (1989, April). Why we need better assessments. *Educational Leadership, 46,* 4–9.

Spolsky, B. (1989). *Conditions for second language learning.* Oxford: Oxford University.

Stemmer, P., Brown, B., & Smith, C. (1992, March). The employability skills portfolio. *Educational Leadership, 49,* 32–35.

Tierney, R. T., Carter, M. A., & Desai, L. E. (1991). *Portfolio assessment in the reading-writing classroom.* Norwood, MA: Christopher-Gordon.

Torres-Gavilanes, J. (1993). *Improving academic achievement in English as a Second Language students through peer tutoring.* (ERIC Document Reproduction Service No. ED 356 652)

U.S. General Accounting Office. (1994). *Limited English Proficiency: A growing and costly educational challenge facing many school districts.* Washington, DC: Author.

Vicent, C., & Rivera, C. (1995, April). *High stakes for limited English proficient students: Testing for high school graduation.* Paper presented at the annual meeting of the American Educational Research Association, San Francisco, CA.

Wiggins, G. P. (1989, April). Teaching to the (authentic) test. *Educational Leadership, 46,* 41–47.

Wiggins, G. P. (1992, May). Creating tests worth taking. *Educational Leadership, 49,* 26–33.

Wiggins, G. P. (1993). *Assessing student performance: Exploring the purpose and limits of testing.* San Francisco, CA: Jossey-Bass.

PART III

Program Considerations

CHAPTER 8

Enhancing the Education of Immigrant Students in Secondary School: Structural Challenges and Directions

Carolyn Temple Adger and Joy Kreeft Peyton

CENTER FOR APPLIED LINGUISTICS

Education for immigrant students in the United States has been shaped by various dynamics, including the social changes in which immigration is embedded (such as growing industrialization in the 19th century), broad political currents (such as those surrounding the Americanization movement), philosophies and paradigms of professional education, and school ethos. What has remained constant over time is a general goal of acculturating and assimilating immigrants into existing or emerging social structures (Olneck, 1995). Ironically, the very programs organized to assist acculturation—including transitional bilingual education and English as a second language (ESL)—have often been structured as parallel to other school programs rather than integrated with them (Goldstein, 1985 [reported in Olneck, 1995]), and they have been managed by faculty who teach only language-minority students. Such arrangements have contributed to the social marginalization of immigrant students and their teachers and have reinforced a school ethos that casts immigrant education as a separate, specialized school function conducted by an autonomous professional cadre.

Recent innovations at the secondary school level have begun to erode the barriers that set immigrant education apart from other aspects of the mission of schools. For example, with the creation of sheltered content classes, an innovation that aims to support immigrant students' academic progress toward graduation, mainstream content teachers are beginning to work with English language learners and, in ideal circumstances, receive training and support to do so. Thus, in addition to making academic content accessible to English language learners, the creation of these classes expands the circle of educators involved with immigrant students.

However, making secondary schools broadly responsive to immigrant students' needs is likely to require fundamental changes that reach beyond instruction, recruitment, and training of faculty and that challenge well-established practices, patterns, and beliefs. This task has significant implications for the modification of school and district infrastructure. It may call for establishing and empowering multidisciplinary teams of educators, both within and across schools, who are aware of immigrant students' needs and committed to meeting them. The work of these groups may include planning and implementing significant curricular modifications such as aligning the content and requirements of primary language, sheltered, and mainstream content courses so that students taking parallel courses cover the same material and receive the same academic credit; developing academic supports for students who have exited ESL programs but are not succeeding in mainstream classes; and creating programs for students with limited prior schooling and limited or no literacy experiences in their native language ("underschooled students"; see Chapter 3). Making schools responsive to immigrant students may require more equitable relationships between schools and parent groups, and between schools and institutions such as universities and community-based organizations.

This chapter begins by describing structural innovations being implemented by projects in four settings in the United States, as part of the Program in Immigrant Education. The goal of the program is to improve the secondary school opportunities and success of immigrant students, particularly those in the process of learning English. We describe approaches that are being tried to enhance school capacity for working with immigrant students and improve student achievement. We argue that the establishment and maintenance of these structures are central to the creation of responsive schools in which immigrant students achieve at high levels. We conclude with a discussion of the implications of this work for other schools and districts serving immigrant students who are learning English.

THE PROGRAM IN IMMIGRANT EDUCATION

The Program in Immigrant Education was established to address the serious situation facing immigrant students of secondary school age in this country.[1] As Chips (1993) points out, these students face major difficulties in acquiring English and succeeding in school. If they are newcomers to the United States, they have much less time than elementary-age students to learn English and to master the academic content required to graduate from high school. They must pass proficiency tests that require English skills they do not have. They must study academic subjects taught entirely in English and requiring high levels of English academic language, with texts and materials that require high levels of English reading ability. Many schools do not provide native language support or content instruction adapted for these students' English proficiency levels. To attend college or university, these students need to take classes that grant graduation and college preparation credit, and they must navigate the maze of requirements for college application and acceptance. Students with limited literacy skills in their native language and in English face even greater challenges.

The Program consists of four local projects and a coordinating organization. The projects work within their local contexts to address the issues discussed above. Each project consists of a coordinating organization, middle and high schools in one or two school districts, and collaborating organizations—local colleges and universities, businesses, and community-based organizations. The projects have designed innovations that are responsive to the local context and that relate to the following three program goals:

- Improving immigrant students' English language and literacy development;
- Improving their mastery of academic content and skills; and
- Improving their access to postsecondary opportunities, including preparation for higher education and the work force.

California Tomorrow, a research and policy organization in San Francisco, is working with two school districts in northern California. One district is located in an urban, multilanguage, multicultural community where 41% of the secondary school students have a home language other than English. Nearly half are Spanish speakers, but over 50 other languages are represented as well. The other district is in a Central Valley agricultural community where 86% of the students are Spanish-speaking immigrants and migrants, and approximately 60% are still developing their English. The school considers its student body to be almost entirely immigrant.

The Center for Language Minority Education and Research at California State University, Long Beach (CSULB) is working with two school districts in southern California. One district is large and urban, a primary entry point for immigrants. Approximately 75% of the students come from homes where English is not the primary language; 67% of these are from Spanish-speaking backgrounds, and 21% are Khmer-speaking, from Cambodia. The other district is a smaller community that is a secondary receiving area—one to which immigrant families tend to move after they have been in the United States for a year or two. Over 80% of the students are language-minority; 40% are English learners, primarily from Spanish-language backgrounds.

Intercultural Development Research Association (IDRA), located in San Antonio, Texas, is working with two school districts in south Texas. One of the districts is located in a multicultural metropolitan community where 61% of the students are recently arrived immigrants, 72% are Latino, and 43% are learning English. The other district is located in a community on the U.S.–Mexico border. All of the students in the middle schools and high schools involved in the project are Latino; most students are learning English; 18% are recent immigrants; most are poor; all are deemed at risk for school failure.

The University of Maryland Baltimore County (UMBC) is working with a large, diverse school district in Maryland. The student population is primarily African American (ranging from 60 to 70% in project schools), and most of the remainder (roughly 20%) are international students, the majority of whom are immigrants and many of whom are English learners. Students come from over 124 countries and speak 101 different languages. Over 2,000 students speak various West Indian or African varieties of English.

The Center for Applied Linguistics is coordinating the effort, identifying central themes and outcomes across the projects, and making the processes and outcomes of project innovations available widely. During the first 2 years of project implementation, we studied the challenges each project faced in addressing the program's goals, the progress that projects made in promoting quality education for immigrant students, and outcomes of their efforts. We visited project schools; conducted interviews with project, district, and school staff; collected documents developed by school and project staff; and reviewed project reports. Field notes, analytic memos, and project reports were entered into a qualitative data support program and analyzed for recurrent themes. From our analysis of these data, it became clear that a crucial accomplishment during the first 2 years of project implementation was the development of school and school district infrastructure within which specific activities and outcomes could take place.

BUILDING AN INFRASTRUCTURE FOR IMMIGRANT EDUCATION: TEACHER PLANNING AND IMPLEMENTATION TEAMS

In every project, schools and districts had to go well beyond improving instruction to enhance the educational opportunities and achievements of immigrant students. They needed to create new structures and significantly alter traditional arrangements such as school schedules, course sequences, and assessment and placement procedures. The impetus for these important changes and the energy to maintain and refine them came from teams of educators convened especially for project work, organized in various ways, challenged by information about student need, and empowered to sustain change. We describe here two kinds of team arrangements developed (or expanded on) by the projects—school-based teams, created by the projects and expanded to include a focus on immigrant students; and cross-school groups—along with examples of their accomplishments.

School-Based Teams

From research on restructuring schools with high proportions of immigrant students, Minicucci and Olsen (1992) derived principles for helping schools respond to students from diverse cultures, languages, and national backgrounds. Undergirding these principles is the requirement for substantial, broad-based, school-level involvement by teachers and others in identifying needs, conceptualizing responses, and working to actualize those responses. Such involvement is also a central tenet of other current reform initiatives, including the Accelerated Schools Project, where school-based cadres define needs and design improvements to the school's curriculum, instruction, and other areas of school life (Chasin & Levin, 1995).

Involving teachers in reconstructing aspects of their own schools represents a major and essential shift in practice. School-site professional communities bring a practical, realistic view of needs and possibilities in their schools that is crucial to initiating local school reform (Crandall, 1994). Moreover, since maintaining a responsive posture toward student needs over the long term depends heavily on teachers' attitudes, knowledge, and commitment, involving them in reinventing their schools contributes to institutionalizing the capacity for continued renewal (House, 1996). In addition, teachers' sense of responsibility to shared goals and to each other is strengthened (Fullan, 1993; Newmann & Wehlage, 1995).

The projects in the Program in Immigrant Education each organized teams of school-based educators as a central mechanism for reform. For example, the UMBC project created advocacy and research task forces in each project school. Comprised of teachers, administrators, and university faculty, these teams identify challenges facing immigrant students, develop action plans to meet those challenges, and implement and evaluate initiatives. Each task force focuses on a different topic, such as instructional support for mainstreamed ESL students, school-to-work and post-secondary transitions, and developing immigrant student leaders. These task forces, which meet regularly, provide a structure through which groups of ESL and sheltered-content teachers who had been collaborating informally to support immigrant students' learning can work more formally. Official assignment to a task force, a focus on specific goals, regular times to meet, and financial resources from their university partner unify team members, help them maintain their focus on project goals, and provide ongoing support for the implementation and maintenance of innovative structures. The groups' collegiality and sense of identification with a special project, as well as the coherence of their various efforts, has led to a strong sense of community and efficacy that is needed to keep going. The following sections describe some of the issues that these groups (and those created by other projects) have sought to address, and the outcomes of their work.

Promoting Transitions to Postsecondary Education. Members of one UMBC project task force were concerned with improving immigrant students' progress toward high school graduation. One hurdle that Maryland students face is the state Functional Tests in citizenship, math, reading, and writing, which they must pass in order to graduate. Many immigrant students have neither the English proficiency nor the test-taking skills needed to pass these tests. In response to the need they identified, task force members decided that targeted courses would help the students succeed on these critical tests. One such course, taught in the summer, prepares students for the Functional Writing Test. The development of this course inspired task force members to analyze their students' errors on the other tests and to directly teach the skills required for passing them. In the first 2 years of the project, the pass rate for immigrant students in these courses was often as high as the schoolwide average. Task force members also developed a course to help students prepare for the Test of English as a Foreign Language (TOEFL) and the Scholastic Aptitude Test (SAT).

A particularly innovative structure developed by UMBC task force members focusing on post-secondary transitions is the International Honors Council. The Council's primary goal is to encourage college application by high-achieving language-minority students, including immigrant students and English language learners, who might not otherwise go to college, and to help them negotiate the application process. In the first year of this initiative, a group of 30 to 40 high school junior and senior women met weekly before or after school with two female teachers. Their activities helped the students meet application requirements such as filling out applications, developing résumés, writing personal biographies and goal statements, visiting colleges, identifying scholarship opportunities, and applying for admission. The results were impressive: All 27 seniors who participated regularly in Council activities applied and gained acceptance to colleges or universities, and many of them were awarded scholarships. In the second year, the task force expanded this structure to include male high school students, created a Council for freshmen and sophomores, incorporated the Councils into the school schedule as College and Career Preparation courses (the afterschool activity continues), and introduced the Council at a second high school, where it is combined with TOEFL preparation after school. Results in terms of college and university application and acceptance were similar to those of the first year. While the school had not kept track of college applications previously, ESL teachers recalled in interviews that language-minority students from these schools had rarely applied to college, and several students active in the Council said they had never thought of college as an option prior to participation in these programs. Watching students progress through the steps to college enrollment has validated task force members' conviction that immigrant students can achieve this goal with appropriate assistance.

Creating Challenging, Credit-bearing Courses. High schools often find it difficult to place immigrant students in content classes that are appropriate for their English language skills. Students who enter secondary school without advanced English proficiency may be placed in courses in which academic content is not taught and in which no credit toward college admission, or sometimes even toward high school graduation, is granted. Thus, they do not move through school at an appropriate pace to graduate before they are too old to be allowed to continue (Minicucci & Olsen, 1992). Two projects have developed sheltered content courses for math, science, and social studies that help students learning English to progress toward graduation and into post-secondary education. For example, a UMBC project task force member, a chemistry teacher, developed a sheltered English adaptation of the school district's Chemistry in the Community curriculum with authentic applications (Ruddy, 1994). The chemistry classroom simulated a community in which signs were posted informing visitors not to drink the water, fish, or swim because of an unidentified pollutant. Instead of listening to extensive lectures, students were involved in developing safety posters, hypothesizing explanations for the pollution, proposing solutions, and distinguishing fact from opinion (McNab, 1996). On a field trip to a local laboratory farm, students collected and analyzed soil and water samples. Most of the students who took this class, even those with relatively limited English skills, passed the course and gained credit toward high school graduation. Since this course was developed, other sheltered content courses have been added at the two project high schools to increase access of English language learners to appropriately designed, credit-bearing sections of the courses required for graduation.

These initiatives can be traced to groups of individuals who critiqued existing conditions and identified a need, devised a response, and were supported by a structure that allowed them to take action and bring imagined possibilities into being. In a year-end retreat in which team members reflected on their accomplishments, one wrote that the project "has invigorated the school and given focus to students and staff . . . [because the team members are] doing, not discussing." Another mused that "one of the most positive things that can come out of the [UMBC] project is a sense of community" that revitalizes teachers who feel beleaguered by the demands placed on them (Crandall, 1995).

In one project, rather than creating new teams, project staff added to existing school teams advocates for immigrant students. One of the middle schools in the CSULB project was participating in the Accelerated Schools Program (Levin, 1987) before the Program in Immigrant Education was introduced at the school. The Accelerated Schools structure for school reform includes topic-focused cadres of teachers and administrators, including an Academic Cadre; a Parental Involvement Cadre; and a Harmony Cadre, concerned with student relations and multicultural matters. The CSULB project arranged to have project staff members work with these cadres rather than creating new teams to work on project goals. By injecting a focus on immigrant students into the discussions of established, stable groups, project staff members were able to expand the cadres' concerns, influence their activities, and place immigrant students at the center of the school's functioning. For example, the Academic Cadre identified all of the students in the school who were born outside the United States and were not achieving at grade level, and subsequently developed systematic procedures for counseling them and tracking their progress.

Improving Classroom Instruction. Reforms to improve students' school experiences and achievement must reach the classroom and influence the complex ways that teachers and students work and interact with each other. In one California Tomorrow project high school, a schoolwide team, established originally to examine immigrant students' academic progress, evolved into a smaller inquiry group focused specifically on quality of instruction. The schoolwide team had examined achievement data of all students in the school and developed strategies for whole-school change with strong implications for immigrant students. This began with a shift to block scheduling, with three instructional blocks daily of 98 minutes each, a 98-minute tutorial each day, and an "enrichment" period for advising and community-building. With the new schedule, students could spend more time with fewer teachers, concentrate intensively on fewer academic subjects per semester, get individual help, and participate in other activities during the school day, while still maintaining work and family commitments (Olsen & Jaramillo, in press).

Success with altering aspects of the school structure to improve the educational opportunities of immigrant students inspired the smaller group mentioned above of teachers to form the Working Group on Language and Culture to concentrate on instruction in individual teachers' classrooms—promoting literacy development throughout the curriculum, critiquing their teaching practices, and developing plans to improve literacy instruction in all of their classes. The project coordinator, an experienced staff developer, led the group in reading and discussing articles on literacy instruction for English language learners, observed their classes, wrote detailed comments responding to the goals that individuals had set for themselves, and helped the teachers refine their instruction so that their immigrant students would be well served.

The excerpt that follows comes from a reflective memo that the project coordinator wrote to a teacher after visiting the teacher's Transitional Life Science class. Like all of the memos she wrote to the working group members, the coordinator begins this one with positive comments about the teacher's work and the class in general and then states concerns, with reference to concepts and readings the group had been considering in meetings. Finally, she offers to collaborate in seeking solutions.

> Several of your concerns we already talked about, but I would like to reframe some of them in the form of questions so we can tackle what for you are the biggest issues.
>
> What is your normal procedure for beginning class? Is there something for students to do when they enter the classroom so no time is wasted? How about using an overhead projector with some review questions? I could give you some ideas about how to implement this so it would work.

What are the normal standards for asking for attention? In observation, I noted that when you were talking, there were probably 6 or 7 students who were engaged in other activities (drawing, zoning out, reading something else).

How do you check for comprehension when lecturing, talking, or giving information? How do you know if students are getting the smaller pieces of information that lead to the whole? . . .

[*She asked one more question, and then continued.*] I have tons of concerns about literacy issues, since these are transitional students. In general, we might consider using a framework where almost every day students are reading some, writing some, and talking with each other about what they have learned. All of the SDAIE scaffolding strategies are there for us to explore and try with Science, so I'm really looking forward to figuring out some of that with you.

The Working Group on Language and Culture also examined data on immigrant students' school participation and achievement and found that 25% of the immigrant students left school after the 9th grade. To address the students' needs and reduce the school-leaving rate, the group planned, lobbied for, and sought additional funding for an ESL Literacy Project in which a small number of teachers would work with a small group of students, develop curricula, engage in intensive individual coaching and reflection on each other's practice, and track students' achievement. What began as teacher inquiry led to the development of a theoretically sound, clearly articulated, and practical program.

New courses, student organizations such as the International Honors Councils, improved instruction, and other innovations not discussed here (such as student leadership institutes and peer-tutoring arrangements), designed and nurtured by teacher teams in project schools, represent important structural contributions to school-based reform of immigrant education. The teams are the essential structures for engendering change. With support from an outside organization, from district policy and administrators, and from school administrators to ensure regular meetings and resources for translating ideas into school practice, such teams can become the foundation of responsive infrastructural development. Because they are rooted in schools, the teams can identify needs on an ongoing basis, initiate responses, lobby for resources, implement programs, and evaluate and revise them. The teams can also serve a solidarity function for teachers and other school staff who need each other's encouragement and support, as well as a political function, ensuring that immigrant students remain a priority in school change efforts.

Cross-School Groups

In another type of grouping arrangement, designed to promote districtwide reform of immigrant education, California Tomorrow convened monthly meetings of all school staff who work with immigrant students in one school district's three high schools and the English Language Center for newcomers. In four full-day sessions each school year (called cross-site days), teachers of ESL, sheltered English, and bilingual classes at the schools grouped themselves by subject area—math and science teachers in one group, English language arts and social studies teachers in another. The teachers reviewed data on student progress; read research articles; interacted with speakers from outside the district; shared curricula, lessons, and instructional strategies; and visited the classes of teachers in other schools in the district and in neighboring districts.

Regularly scheduled discussions with educators from other schools who share similar concerns have helped these teachers to see structural problems in immigrant education at their own schools and to develop solutions. For example, as a result of examining data on student achievement, the teachers identified a group of students who were not progressing through the ESL sequence as expected (because their schooling had been interrupted and they had low literacy skills in their native language) and designed a program specifically for them. The teachers also created a districtwide, articulated sequence of ESL and core content courses, with placement criteria, a mastery test, and exit criteria for each level. As a result of this work, 14 new core content courses are now available to English learners that grant high school graduation credit and meet college application requirements.

Another important function of the cross-site meetings was professional development, some of it done formally by teachers and outsiders with expertise in facets of immigrant education, but much of it occurring informally as teachers shared concerns, instructional approaches, curriculum units, and materials with others in their field. In fact, all facets of the cross-site work contributed to participants' professional growth. For example, as social studies teachers reviewed an American history sheltered curriculum, tried out the materials in their classes, compared their experiences, and decided to purchase the curriculum, their expertise in sheltered content instruction expanded. Teachers in the high schools, who had had little contact with the English Language Center previously, also learned about resources that were available to them from the Center, including curricula and books for English learners and materials for parents, translated into a number of languages.

In another cross-site group structure designed for whole-district re-form, CSULB project staff brought together principals of reforming schools with project and district staff to discuss their priorities and ap-proaches for immigrant education. These quarterly meetings often in-cluded dinner at a respected local hotel, a location that served both prac-tical and symbolic functions. Removed from the familiar setting and press of daily responsibilities, administrators were encouraged to focus on broad priorities and refresh their commitments to project goals. The set-ting also reinforced their status as leaders: The onus for crafting, promot-ing, and protecting reform was on them, and the expectation was that they would describe substantial work and identify specific needs.

At a typical meeting during the project's second implementation year, principals reported on successful initiatives in their schools, but they also talked more personally about their deepening awareness of and concern for immigrant students' school success and their frustration with balanc-ing their schools' programs with the district's new, massive restructuring initiative. The principal of an alternative high school mentioned having talked individually with every immigrant student in his school about prospects for the future and how the school staff could be more helpful. A middle school vice principal worried about the lack of appropriate, high-quality elective courses that would suggest career options for stu-dents. Another principal outlined actions to defuse racial conflict involv-ing immigrant students. These principals also considered school-level im-plications of district-level initiatives to support English language learners, such as district curriculum frameworks designed specifically for them. They outlined the kinds of professional development needed to imple-ment those frameworks and ways to integrate that effort with other pro-fessional development they had planned.

These school-based teacher teams and cross-site teachers' and princi-pals' meetings have been crucial to reforming the schools involved in the Program in Immigrant Education. Because secondary schools have often had difficulty serving immigrant students appropriately, changing schools so that they do respond appropriately to these students requires that unique structures be created, rather than simply adding to traditional structures with traditional agendas and means of achieving them. Com-posed of members of the school community who share an understanding of their school's or district's culture and a deep concern with strengthen-ing immigrant education, these structures have succeeded at least in part because they present a venue for innovation within highly traditional or-ganizations and focus energy for designing changes within the complexi-ties of the local situation (Weiss, 1995).

BUILDING AN INFRASTRUCTURE FOR IMMIGRANT EDUCATION: PARTNERSHIPS BEYOND THE SCHOOL

Another aspect of building infrastructure that supports immigrant education involves establishing linkages beyond the school—with parents, other community members, and local organizations with a stake in education. Newman and Wehlage (1995) argue that "to build the organizational capacity required to promote student learning of high intellectual quality, schools need support from beyond their walls" (p. 41). In this section, we describe a number of linkages created by the local projects.

Partnerships with Parents

Current parent involvement arrangements generally do not attract immigrant parents to schools (Delgado-Gaitán, 1991), and tinkering with traditional models is not likely to work. Including parents of immigrant students in positive school change calls for structural innovations. The familiar strategies of holding large informational meetings (even when there is translation from English) or offering workshops and training sessions imply a hierarchical model in which schools have the knowledge and parents have the needs (Gándara, 1994). If these are the primary mechanisms for parents to relate to schools, and parents are cast as recipients of resources rather than as resources themselves for schools and students, their connection to schools can be expected to remain tenuous. Instead, structures and arrangements based on social relationships and activities that position parents as competent adults attract immigrant parents to become involved more powerfully than they have been in the past.

The CSULB project has successfully involved immigrant parents of secondary school students in several school and district structures. Key to their success is a parent involvement specialist, who is a parent herself and who shares the Mexican heritage and Spanish language with most of the parents with whom she works. This leader has galvanized relevant school staff, including assistant principals, to help establish or revitalize parent centers in the schools, where immigrant parents meet to plan activities and work with students. At a middle school, teachers partner with parents several afternoons a week after school to help students with homework assignments. This arrangement provides academic support for students as well as allowing immigrant parents to engage in their children's education and giving them tools to do so. As a result of this effort, three students who were in danger of failing their math classes passed, and all of the immigrant students involved improved their grades in math or another content area by at least one letter grade.

The CSULB parent involvement specialist also organized Immigrant Parent/School Leadership Teams whose purpose is to represent parents' concerns to schools and school districts. One project these teams undertook was to prepare an action plan for increasing immigrant parent involvement in the schools and present the plan to the district superintendent. The group succeeded in gaining district participation and funding for a kickoff event to recognize the contributions of immigrant parent school volunteers. Five hundred people attended this event, including the principal from each school in the district and two immigrant parent volunteers from each school, whose contributions were recognized. After that first event, the superintendent scheduled a similar one for the following year.

The Immigrant Parent/School Leadership Teams have also facilitated more equitable relationships among parents and district and school staff. For example, as a result of getting parents more involved in major school decisions, one immigrant parent with limited literacy in Spanish and English was appointed to a screening committee to hire new principals in the district. At first she hesitated to speak at committee meetings. However, during a year of participating in parent activities and serving on the committee, she became a vocal advocate for immigrant students, asking principal candidates how they had promoted immigrant students' school achievement and parents' involvement with schools. This parent also positioned herself as a broker to introduce other parents to the schools and facilitate parents' meetings with teachers and administrators about their children's education. Another immigrant parent reported that her protest concerning her son's placement in an alternative high school, informed by her work with the leadership teams, led to his reassignment to the comprehensive high school, where he is succeeding.

In another project, IDRA worked with a south Texas middle school to create opportunities for teachers, administrators, and parents to meet on an equal basis in social events grounded in the community. One such event was a *Posada* (Christmas celebration) organized by school staff, complete with *luminaria* (candles in white paper bags) stretching for two blocks, to celebrate the reconstitution of the school. Some 500 parents attended this function, far more than had attended traditional PTA activities before. Another community event, a "community walk" organized by school staff and leaders of a community-based organization, brought teachers from this school and the local high school into the *barrio* from which the schools draw their students. This walk upset the usual conditions under which parents and school staff meet by locating the school staff in the neighborhood and allowing parents and staff to assume parity as adults concerned about the same children. One parent, when asked what she thought the teachers might have gained from the community walk, said (in Spanish),

> Confidence. They gained confidence because when they went walking, people applauded them in some areas. They hung out the windows and cheered, "Bravo, there are the teachers!" In some areas, they didn't know who the teachers were, but in others they cheered. (IDRA, 1996, p. II-42)

Asked what she thought the parents had gained, this mother said,

> Now there's more understanding of the school on the part of the parents. There are many times when parents are afraid to speak to teachers. Maybe it's because of their English. But since the walk, I've seen a change. . . . The parents said how pretty the school was [when they stopped in during the walk], and how they are treated when they come here. (IDRA, 1996, p. II-43)

Partnerships with Other Institutions and Organizations

Other structural supports for immigrant education include new and altered relationships among schools and between schools and other educational institutions or organizations. These links strengthen and extend schools' capabilities and provide learning and service opportunities for the organizations. When they involve personal or institutional relationships that endure over time, new programs can evolve.

IDRA opened up possibilities for a middle school and a university's downtown campus to invent a partnership where no link had existed before. Out of exploratory conversations between the school's principal and a university dean, cooperative activities began to take shape. First, immigrant students took a field trip to visit the university facilities and talk with university students from backgrounds similar to their own. This trip was intended to introduce the notion that college could be an option for them. Next, university faculty carried out intensive professional development on sheltering instruction for English language learners at the middle school, and a student mentoring program pairing middle school and university students was introduced. This school/university relationship opened up the middle school as a learning laboratory for students in the university's new College of Education, which focuses on urban education and language-minority students. It also provided rich opportunities for intensive professional development of middle school staff by university professors, on topics selected by the teachers. Finally, middle school students could interact with university students, who could show the way to academic advancement.

Here again, structures focused on immigrant education were central to the success of specific initiatives. The middle school's Immigrant Education Implementation Team provided the venue for joint innovation, since the university dean attended their monthly meetings. Particularly in the early stages of the school/university connection, regular conversations among the university's leaders and middle school administrators and teachers, situated in the real functioning of the school, turned potential collaboration into active give-and-take.

California Tomorrow devised another structure for linking schools and other organizations in the culturally diverse school district where they have been working—a series of evening community forums for school leaders, guidance counselors, and teachers associated with immigrant education; the president of the teachers' union; a migrant education staff person; representatives from colleges and universities; an immigration lawyer; the school board president; immigrant high school students intending to go to college; and immigrant college students who had graduated from the district's high schools. One meeting focused on data regarding immigrant students' movement through school, credit accumulation, and college attendance. Project researchers compared the aspirations of English language learners with their grade point averages and their teachers' perceptions of their chances for college success. At another meeting, college representatives shared their views of what high schools could do to support immigrant students' college success. School staff members described school support programs, both for the benefit of current high school students and for comment by outsiders. Finally, the students themselves spoke. One college student talked about how Upward Bound had helped him, and another paid tribute to a particularly caring ESL teacher who had made him realize that he could go on to college.

These community forums have resulted in a strong network of organizations working to promote immigrant students' school success. Introducing the groups and their members to each other and guiding them to examine challenges and goals together has had the potential for enhancing the work of each one.

Connecting schools and outside organizations in more than superficial ways to improve the education of immigrant students remains an incompletely explored but attractive strategy. The Program in Immigrant Education, which involves linking local organizations and schools, illustrates some of the kinds of groups that have expertise to offer and some of the contributions they can make to schools. Although these relationships have been built carefully, they are still delicate. The role of "critical friend" (Sizer, 1992) that comes with outsiders' involvement, difficult to take on and difficult to accept, may be particularly problematic when the goal is immigrant education and society is experiencing anti-immigrant sentiments and actions. In an atmosphere that is often filled with rancor and distrust, schools and the organizations they collaborate with may need to work hard to develop trusting and productive relationships.

CONCLUSION

The various institutional structures created by the projects working in the Program in Immigrant Education, and the programs and products they have formulated, have made a difference in how the schools involved educate immigrant students and in the students' achievement. Among the implications of this work is that changing schools structurally to make them responsive to immigrants requires a range of players in addition to the ESL/bilingual teachers who have traditionally worked with and advocated for immigrants. Elmore (1996) warns of the threat of factionalization to school reform when the vanguard is isolated, as ESL and bilingual teachers have been and continue to be in many schools. Creating and protecting a place for immigrant students at the center of a school's operations requires the influence, the skills, and the political will of mainstream teachers, counselors, and administrators, as well as that of ESL and bilingual teachers. At the same time, school and district staff who are not directly responsible for these students and who are already juggling multiple demands and challenges may need to rely on ESL and bilingual teachers, who focus specifically on immigrant students' needs and progress, to lead the way.

In the schools and districts described here, some of the influential agents in developing the infrastructure to support immigrant students were new to this role, but were galvanized by confronting evidence of their schools' weaknesses in this regard and by realizing that improvement was both urgently needed and possible. For example, a newly appointed superintendent of a school district in California, facing the facts about immigrant education in the district, made student data available to project staff for professional development and project evaluation—a bold step, since schools typically guard data closely.

Building the infrastructure for reforming immigrant education at the secondary school level—the staff structures and the programs they build—requires time, resources, and leadership (Goldenberg & Sullivan, 1994; Newmann & Wehlage, 1995; Wagner, 1994). Creating teams and other groupings that make sense locally is crucial, but it is not enough: Time must be set aside for meetings during the school day and for regularly scheduled professional development, and resources must be made available for carrying out plans. Strong school leadership can push for the hiring of appropriate staff, protect professional development as a hallowed school function, and maintain the focus on immigrant students' achievement in the face of changing policy, personnel, and multiple demands on attention and resources.

No single solution or set of solutions—organizational, instructional, or curricular—will suffice as the proper approach to high-quality education for immigrant students if the infrastructure is not in place to allow a sustained, consistent focus on this goal. In a study of school restructuring, the Center on Organization and Restructuring of Schools found that

> When schools are unable to coordinate teachers' diverse aims for students into a curricular mission focused on high quality student learning, when teachers have few opportunities to work together to devise approaches suited to the school's student body, or when schools pursue multiple innovations without sustained, long-term consistency, it is difficult for even the most gifted teachers to make a positive difference for students. (Newmann & Wehlage, 1995, p. 29)

Immigrant education requires not only specialized curricula and classes to address the distinct needs of immigrant students, but also a coherent infrastructure grounded in collaboration across school departments, across schools within a district, and between schools and local organizations, and involving parents and other community members as equal and active stakeholders. Administrators must contribute timely, clear, accurate, and accessible data on students' achievement to guide decision-making and confront naysayers with evidence of the success of innovations. As we enter a time in this country in which immigrant students, long considered a minority and often forgotten, become the majority in many places (Orfield, 1996), the building of this infrastructure is no longer a luxury to be put off until we have more time to think about it, but rather a central focus in school reform, without which none of our students will succeed.

NOTE

1. The Program in Immigrant Education was established in 1993, with primary funding from the Andrew W. Mellon Foundation. We are grateful to Donna Christian (Center for Applied Linguistics), Jodi Crandall (UMBC), and Laurie

Olsen (California Tomorrow) for helpful comments on earlier versions of this chapter.

REFERENCES

Chasin, G., & Levin, H. (1995). Thomas Edison Accelerated Elementary School. In J. Oakes & K. H. Quartz (Eds.), *Creating new educational communities: Ninety-fourth yearbook of the National Society for the Study of Education* (pp. 130–146). Chicago: University of Chicago Press.

Chips, B. (1993). Using cooperative learning at the secondary level. In D. D. Holt (Ed.), *Cooperative learning: A response to linguistic and cultural diversity* (pp. 81–97). McHenry, IL, and Washington, D.C.: Delta Systems and Center for Applied Linguistics.

Crandall, J. A. (1994). Strategic integration: Preparing language and content teachers for linguistically and culturally diverse classrooms. In J. E. Alatis (Ed.), *Georgetown University Roundtable on Languages and Linguistics: Strategic interaction in language acquisition: Theory, practice, and research* (pp. 255–274). Washington, D.C.: Georgetown University Press.

Crandall, J. A. (1995). *Project We Teach: Annual report.* Unpublished manuscript, University of Maryland, Baltimore County.

Delgado-Gaitán, C. (1991). Involving parents in the schools: A process of empowerment. *American Journal of Education, 100,* 20–46.

Elmore, R. (1996). Getting to scale with good education practice. *Harvard Educational Review, 66*(1), 1–26.

Fullan, M. G. (1993). *Change forces: Probing the depths of educational reform.* Bristol, PA: Falmer.

Gándara, P. (1994). The impact of the education reform movement on limited English proficient students. In B. McLeod (Ed.), *Language and learning: Educating linguistically diverse students* (pp. 45–70). Albany, NY: SUNY Press.

Goldenberg, C., & Sullivan, J. (1994). *Making change happen in a language minority school: A search for coherence.* Santa Cruz, CA: National Center for Research on Cultural Diversity and Second Language Learning.

Goldstein, B. L. (1985). *The role of the public school in the maintenance and change of ethnic group affiliation.* Unpublished doctoral dissertation, Brown University.

House, E. R. (1996, October). A framework for appraising educational reforms. *Educational Researcher, 25*(7), 6–14.

Intercultural Development Research Association (IDRA). (1996). *Creative collaboratives: Empowering immigrant students and families through education.* Unpublished manuscript, Author.

Levin, H. (1987). Accelerated schools for disadvantaged students. *Educational Leadership, 44* (6), 19–21.

McNab, C. (1996). *Sheltered chemistry: A closer look.* Unpublished masters thesis, University of Maryland, Baltimore County.

Minicucci, C., & Olsen, L. (1992). *Programs for secondary limited English proficient students: A California study* (Occasional Papers in Bilingual Education, No. 5). Washington, D.C.: National Clearinghouse for Bilingual Education.

Newmann, F. M., & Wehlage, G. G. (1995). *Successful school restructuring: A report to the public and educators.* Madison, WI: University of Wisconsin–Madison, Center on Organization and Restructuring of Schools.

Olneck, M. (1995). Immigrants and education. In J. A. Banks & C. A. McGee Banks (Eds.), *Handbook of research on multicultural education* (pp. 310–327). New York: Macmillan.

Olsen, L., & Jaramillo, J. (in press). *When time is on our side: Redesigning schools to meet the needs of immigrant students.* In P. Gándara (Ed.), *The dimension of time and the challenge of school reform.* New York: State University of New York Press.

Orfield, G. (1996). *Dismantling desegregation: The quiet reversal of Brown v. Board of Education.* New York: W.W. Norton.

Ruddy, J. (1994). *Chemistry in the community: Curriculum modified for ESL students.* Unpublished manuscript, available from Project WE TEACH, Department of Education, UMBC, 1000 Hilltop Circle, Baltimore, MD 21050.

Sizer, T. (1992). *Horace's school: Redesigning the American high school.* Boston: Houghton Mifflin.

Wagner, T. (1994). *How schools change: Lessons from three communities.* Boston: Beacon.

Weiss, C. (1995). The four '*Is*' of school reform: How interests, ideology, information, and institution affect teachers and principals. *Harvard Education Review, 65,* 571–592.

CHAPTER 9

Preparing Secondary Teachers to Teach a Second Language: The Case of the United States with a Focus on California

Barbara J. Merino

University of California, Davis

Who are the teachers working to develop second-language skills at the secondary level? How are these teachers prepared? How do policymakers shape teacher preparation for second-language speakers in the U.S.? How do teacher educators/researchers describe how teachers are prepared? How do graduates of teacher preparation programs respond to teacher preparation? The purpose of this chapter is to describe the context and nature of teacher preparation for secondary teachers engaged in developing the proficiency of their students in a second language and to provide a synthesis and critical perspective of current research on the education of teachers of other second-language speakers in secondary schools. Emphasis will be given to teachers of language-minority students. This chapter draws from a search of ERIC abstracts tapping the past 10 years. In addition, all major teacher education journals in the U.S., as well as journals publishing on second-language education, were reviewed for the past 5 years. The descriptors used included *teacher education, teacher development and second language acquisition, bilingual education,* and *second and foreign language education.*

In discussing theoretical frameworks for research in teacher education, Yarger and Smith (1990) offer a simple model composed of the following domains: "antecedent conditions," which include student, teacher–educator, and institutional characteristics as well as contextual policy variables such as state and federal mandates and accreditation procedures; "processes," which deal with the way in which teacher education is delivered, the components of the structure, and the content of the curriculum; and "outcome variables," which include the ways in which students of teacher education, preservice, and inservice grow and respond to the experience of teacher education. Studies on teacher education may focus on any one of these elements in isolation, or explore linkages among them. Yarger and Smith identify five principal research methodologies in teacher education research: narrative studies, case studies, surveys, correlational studies, and causal/experimental studies. In their review of teacher education research, they found that research on the process of teacher education was the most scarce. Equally scarce were studies that linked process to outcome using an experimental methodology. Finally, they decry the failure of researchers to operationalize the terms used in teacher education research and to fully investigate the role of antecedent variables on teacher education processes and outcomes. These conclusions about the state of teacher education in general are echoed in most reviews of teacher education research on teachers of second language speakers.

Not all researchers of teacher education are such forceful advocates of experimental research or outcome studies. Doyle (1990) argues that it is more useful to look at teacher education research from the perspective of major themes. Quality control and teacher effectiveness research have guided a long tradition of research, investigating what kinds of teacher behaviors lead to student gains. Another major theme has been research on teachers' knowledge and beliefs (Shulman, 1986). The emphasis on teacher education research motivated by this paradigm has been to investigate those processes that lead to personal reflection and the evolution of teachers' knowledge and beliefs, for example, Carr and Kemmis, 1986. Research on teacher education for second-language teachers has also been driven by key themes. For many years, a key theme has been the search for an effective method of second-language teaching and effective ways to prepare teachers in the use of these methods (Stevick, 1980). More recently, second-language teacher–educators have shifted to a variety of themes: to the learner and individual differences in the learner and to the interplay of language and culture in acquiring a second language (Merino & Faltis, 1993; Richards & Nunan, 1990).

TEACHERS WORKING TO DEVELOP SECOND-LANGUAGE SKILLS IN SECONDARY STUDENTS

There are five major types of teachers engaged in the development of a second language in secondary students in the United States:

1. the regular classroom teacher involved in teaching language-minority students without any special training or authorization;
2. the regular classroom teacher, who has received some preparation to work with language-minority students as a part of inservice teacher education;
3. the teacher of English as a second language, who has received extensive training in ESL and holds a credential with this specialization;
4. the bilingual education certified teacher, who has received training in teaching the curriculum in English and another language, usually Spanish; and
5. the foreign language teacher, who usually serves native English-speaking students who are beginning to learn another language but may also serve students who are native speakers of the language, as in the teaching of Spanish to native Spanish speakers (Merino, Trueba, & Samaniego, 1993).

The first and by far the largest group is the regular classroom teacher engaged in teaching subject matter to students who are speakers of English as a second language. In the United States, the numbers of language-minority students have been increasing steadily since the 1960s. Although school districts use a variety of criteria for determining whether students are limited in their proficiency in English, based on 1988 national school enrollment information, of the 40 million schoolchildren in the nation's schools, almost 2 million, or 5%, are LEP (National Forum on Personnel Needs for Districts with Changing Populations, 1990, cited in Lasky, 1992). Between 1985 and 1990, the number of LEP students increased by 36.2% (Lasky, 1992). In California, the growth has been more dramatic—language-minority students have more than doubled in population over the past 10 years, from 613,224 in 1987 to 1,381,393 in 1997. At the secondary level, language-minority students were 12.4% of the total in 1987 and now represent 23.8% (Gold, 1997). Most of these receive instruction from regular classroom teachers for most of their instructional day. In most districts, English language development is provided as a complement but some LM (Language Minority) students (16%) do not receive any special services at all (California Department of Education, 1997).

According to Macias (1989), the United States will need at a minimum 97,000 bilingual teachers for language-minority students. The Task Force for Selected LEP Issues, in its report to the California State Department of Education, found that there were 8,000 teachers certified to work with bilingual students in 1990 and 4,000 teachers certified to work in English as a second language at a time when the LEP population was 861,551. Merino and Faltis (1993) reported that for California, for the Spanish-speaking this represents a shortage of 69%. More recent figures peg the shortfall at 58% (Gold, 1997), indicating that the state is making progress in meeting the need for bilingual teachers even as the population of Spanish-speaking students increases. No study of the shortfall for secondary teachers of language-minority students was available. Such a study would be complex, since the distribution of LM students by teacher, by credential, by course would be extremely cumbersome to establish.

Traditionally, the teaching of English as second language has been the concern of specially trained teachers, often with a very strong foundation in applied linguistics. These teachers often receive their training at the master's level and typically teach university-level students. Some of these, however, have gravitated to the secondary level, where they often assume leadership positions because of their extensive training. There are no reliable figures on the numbers of teachers with this level of preparation teaching in secondary schools in the United States. The numbers in California appear to be small (Walton, 1996), since the state requires a secondary credential and most students enrolled in graduate programs in linguistics do not hold such credentials. In California, teachers may teach language-minority students at the secondary level with as little as 45 hours of teacher preparation for credentialed teachers with 9 years of experience.

Another tradition of teachers are those trained in bilingual education to deliver instruction in English and another language. This type of teacher is most often seen at the elementary level. However, in states with large numbers of language-minority students from a few targeted language groups, a small but significant number of bilingual education–certified teachers work at the secondary level. Usually, teacher education programs in this area have much in common with ESL programs but give much greater emphasis to instruction in the primary language and knowledge about the structure of the primary language, as well as the literature written in the first language.

The most typical teacher with expertise in second-language development at the secondary level is the foreign language teacher. The most widely taught foreign language in the United States is Spanish. In a national survey of randomly selected elementary and secondary schools, Rhodes and Oxford (1988) reported that 87% of the nation's secondary schools reported teaching foreign languages. Spanish was taught at 86% of the high schools. After Spanish, the most widely taught languages were French, German, and Latin. However, enrollment in foreign language classes was substantially lower than the historical high of 36% attained in 1915. According to Rhodes and Oxford, only 23% of the secondary schools offering foreign-language programs reported that at least half of their students were enrolled in foreign-language study. Some of these Spanish teachers have been reassigned to teach language-minority students, particularly in high schools with large numbers of Spanish-speaking students.

TEACHER EDUCATION POLICY

National Issues

In the United States, the federal government plays a limited role in defining policy in teacher education. Much of its authority as regards the education of language-minority students comes through the Civil Rights Act of 1964. This law prohibits discrimination on the basis of national origin, among other categories, and was used in the ground-breaking *Lau v. Nichols* U.S. Supreme Court Decision (1974) to provide protection to children whose proficiency in English is limited. In lay terms, this decision, as interpreted by the U.S. Office of Civil Rights, requires that educators provide language-minority students with education that is especially designed to address their needs. Teachers must be trained to work with second-language speakers, but how teachers are prepared is left to individual states to decide. National policy as regards teachers of foreign language has usually been set through the provision of incentives. Special government programs that provide teacher preparation, such as the National Defense and Education Act (NDEA), are an example of this. Recently, however, calls for reform have come more as recommendations than as requirements. For example, LeBlanc (1990) discusses the role of the 1979 Report of the President's Commission on Foreign Languages and International Studies on the upgrading of entry-level requirements for foreign-language teachers and its effect on the state of Florida in developing assessment procedures for secondary teachers of French.

State Policy on Teacher Certification

Recently, states with high numbers of language-minority students have begun to institute additional requirements for teachers of these students at the secondary level. In the case of California, teachers must add an authorization to their base credential, entitled Cross Cultural Language and Academic Development (CLAD). This new authorization, put in place in 1992 by the California Commission for Teacher Credentialing (CTC), is now offered at almost all of the universities offering credentials in California for preservice teachers (Walton, 1996). The CLAD certification is designed to address the minimal knowledge and skills that teachers will need to teach the English language to second-language speakers and to provide Specially Designed Academic Instruction in English (SDAIE) to language-minority students. For teachers already credentialed, CLAD may be added through a 12-unit course of study. Alternatively, teachers may take a battery of tests to receive the authorization, or, under recent legislation, experienced teachers may take as little as 45 hours of instruction if they have 9 years of teaching experience. In California, teachers teaching language-minority students may also have credentials in bilingual education (available since 1972) or hold a Language Development Specialist Certificate (available since 1980). Each one of these routes to certification has its own history and varies in the degree and depth to which teachers are prepared to serve language-minority students.

Calls for National Reform

The decade of the 1980s produced an educational reform movement that began with a focus on the schools and gradually shifted to teacher education. One of the most influential reports focused on teachers was a study entitled *A Nation Prepared: Teachers for the 21st Century* (Carnegie Forum on Education and the Economy's Task Force on Teaching as a Profession, 1986). The impetus for this report came from a recognition that to maintain the economic competitiveness of the United States, all American students need to achieve at the high levels usually demanded only of "the privileged few." This report called for a major restructuring of schools and teacher education programs. It envisioned highly qualified, well-paid teachers who would be given greater autonomy in their work and who would in turn agree to higher standards for themselves and greater accountability for their students' performance. Regarding teacher education, this report called for a more substantive period of training that would require some graduate work for all teachers and, most importantly, the creation of a National Board for Professional Teaching Standards designed to establish higher standards for teacher knowledge and skills and to certify teachers who meet these standards. *Tomorrow's Teachers* (The Holmes Group, 1986) was another influential report focused on the reform of teacher education. The Holmes Group, a consortium of deans at schools and colleges of education in major research universities in the United States, sought to improve teacher education by upgrading standards for entry into credential programs, making programs more intellectually challenging, restructuring curriculum to address the needs of culturally and linguistically diverse students, and launching aggressive campaigns to recruit minorities into teaching. Finally, the Holmes Group reform agenda called for closer collaboration with the schools through joint partnerships and greater articulation with arts and sciences faculty.

Reform's Effect on Language Secondary Teacher Education

To the degree that these reforms ask society to reinvest in teaching and the preparation of teachers, the reaction of teachers and teacher educators has been extremely positive. Research universities have participated actively in implementing some of these reforms, as have many major teacher education centers in the country. Many of these reforms have met with some controversy, however. For example, the call for a national assessment center is perceived by some as possibly less responsive to local conditions and needs, particularly as regards the needs of culturally and linguistically diverse students. For many, however, the increased accountability and the potential for rewarding those teachers who have advanced in their training make a national teacher certification alternative attractive.

In more recent discussions, researchers in teacher education have begun to look beyond the surface implications of the proposals for reform (Lanier & Little, 1986). For some, these reforms reflect a tradition of reform in American history. Thus, Liston and Zeichner (1990) identify four traditions of reform in U.S. teacher education: academic, social efficiency, developmentalist, and social reconstructionist. In their view, these currents of reform continue to ebb and flow, sometimes in complementary fashion but sometimes not. Academic reforms place a focus on improving the academic rigor of schooling. Within foreign-language education, the crisis of Sputnik challenged Americans to upgrade how foreign-language teachers were taught and resulted in the NDEA institutes, designed to train foreign language teachers in audiolingual methodology. More recently, social reconstructionist reforms have created a major influence in the education of language-minority students, resulting in the creation of programs that seek to redress the social inequities that exist in American schooling, particularly for students of color. These reforms, however, are more frequently found at the elementary level (McCaleb, 1994).

Description and analysis of the implementation of reforms is beginning to appear in the literature, although at this point, most reforms have focused on structural reorganization, particularly in engineering the relationship between schools and teacher education programs. This restructuring does not always lead to substantive change, particularly in the context of American high schools, where traditions of accountability and a standard curriculum are more difficult to challenge (Carbone, 1990). Hawley (1990), analyzing the effects of simplistic tinkering on teacher education policy, concludes that many of the reforms implemented have had little influence in upgrading teacher effectiveness because many of these reforms have been applied too broadly. For example, simply adding a fifth year to a credential program makes little difference. However, requiring advanced subject-matter coursework for secondary teachers does make a difference in improving pupil achievement. Some, however, do provide information on specific approaches to restructuring. Galluzzo and Craig (1990) discuss the results of a survey of 90 institutions offering teacher education programs. The focus of this survey was on structural changes such as the lengthening of credential programs, the development of formal partnerships with schools, and the implementation of a recruitment program. Very few have actually tried to manipulate some of the features of the reform. Moreover, not all reactions to calls for reform have been thoughtful. Indeed, some of the reform initiatives have been simplistically implemented. For example, the state of Texas passed a bill that limits education courses to 18 credit hours.

With a few exceptions, the literature on second-language teacher education does not connect with the calls for reform directed to teacher education in general in any systematic way. One rare exception is Bernhardt and Hammadou (1987), who provide a focused response to the Holmes Group reforms through a systematic review of the literature on foreign-language teacher education. One other noteworthy effort is the development of standards by the National Board for Professional Teaching Standards for English as a New Language (1996).

How Teacher Education Reforms Address Cultural and Linguistic Diversity

One of the areas that has received most attention in the reform movement of teacher education is the preparation of teachers to work in culturally and linguistically diverse settings. Syntheses of this literature reveal the following issues: (1) a predominance of position papers and a competency approach to the definition of what teachers should know and be able to do when working with culturally and linguistically diverse students; (2) a scarcity of rich descriptions of what teacher preparation programs actually do to address cultural and linguistic diversity; (3) a widespread failure to describe or evaluate the impact of coursework and experience on student teachers and their practice (Grant & Secada, 1990; Merino & Faltis, 1993).

John Goodlad's book *Teachers for Our Nation's Schools* (1990) is considered by many to be one of the most influential recent publications on schooling and teacher preparation in the United States. The book draws on a study of teacher preparation programs in 29 colleges and universities in 8 states and presents a candid but thoughtful analysis of teacher education. Goodlad also proposes the conditions or postulates necessary for effective teacher education programs. Little mention is made of teachers of language-minority students or of second-language speakers, however.

There are elements in Goodlad's proposals that imply a support for greater attention to the needs of language-minority students. In terms of institutional commitment, he sees the need for strong leadership that views the program as a major responsibility to society and that provides the program and faculty adequate support, programmatic security, unit identity, budget constancy, and personnel stability. In discussing programmatic conditions for effective teacher education programs, Goodlad (1990) describes the ideal graduate as, among other things, an educated person who is a critical thinker; a reflective inquirer into discipline, teaching, and schooling; a professional practitioner committed to equity and excellence in schooling; a change agent who produces modifications in the curriculum, the organization, and instruction; and a thoughtful student of practice, theory, and research. The vision of the teacher as a thinking, independent professional that Goodlad espouses is affirmed as well in second-language teacher education (Gebhard, Gaitan, & Oprandy, 1990). Calling for programs that respond to the needs of society endorses the notion that states like California with high LM populations cannot ignore these students.

DEFINING THE CONTENT OF TEACHER EDUCATION

In recent years, researchers have labored to articulate the range of competencies that teachers of language-minority students should develop. Some have based their recommendations on the basis of research on effective teaching practices as identified by empirical research, both quantitative and qualitative (Garcia, 1990). Others have reflected on their own experiences in education and research and drawn up qualities, skills, and knowledge teachers of language-minority students should have (Thonis, 1991). Others have focused on the kind of work teachers of language-minority students must do and have sought to identify systemic changes in the contexts in which teachers work. In this tradition, Milk, Mercado, and Sapiens (1992) call for moving away from an "emphasis of a limited set of discrete skills to programs that develop teachers who reflect on what they do in the classroom and [investigate] how this affects language minority students and second language learners" (p.11). They outline three principal frameworks that have been used to drive teacher education for language-minority students: (1) the effective practices framework, which focuses on identifying the effective practices of teachers either through nomination procedures or through the link of teacher practices to student achievement; (2) the coaching framework, which gives greater emphasis to the implementation of effective practices through structured coaching, typically by trained peers; and (3) the collaborative research framework, in which teachers and teacher educators work together within schools to provide and investigate effective practices for language-minority students.

A significant challenge for teacher–educators of language-minority students has been the scarcity of research on teacher education. Merino and Faltis (1993) call for the use of multiple traditions of research to identify effective practices for teacher–educators and underscore the need for research about teacher education practices themselves. Reviewing research on teacher education for language-minority students, Merino and Faltis found few examples of direct research on how teachers are prepared to work with language-minority children. Indeed, to capture how teachers are prepared to teach language-minority students to read, they had to rely on reviews of textbooks used in teacher education programs or on a few accounts by teacher–educators of how they organized their courses.

A major challenge to researchers and practitioners of teacher education for language teachers has been the need to articulate a theoretical framework that is cohesive and productive. Language teachers are prepared in many diverse contexts. ESL teachers are often prepared in graduate programs driven largely by perspectives drawn from applied linguistics research. Foreign-language teachers usually enroll in teacher education programs that integrate foreign language departments with the perspectives of schools of education. Teachers of language-minority students typically enroll in programs within schools of education that draw from anthropology, linguistics, and psychology to conceptualize the curriculum. Freeman (1989), in his critique of ESL teacher education, decries the failure to define terms and articulate a model of language teacher education that captures the complexities of the product and process of language teaching and language teacher development.

Research Traditions in Language Teacher Education

In this section, we focus briefly on four traditions of research on teacher education for second/foreign language teachers at the secondary level: the foreign language teacher, the ESL teacher, the bilingual teacher, and the subject-matter teacher. We begin with the tradition of research on the preparation of foreign-language teachers. Despite periodic calls for more research on teacher education for the foreign-language teacher (Freeman, 1989; Jorstad,1980; Bernhardt & Hammadou, 1987), very little research on how to prepare teachers of a foreign language exists today. In the 1960s, a great deal of attention was given to the teachers' proficiency in the foreign language. Carroll (1967), for example, assessed the proficiency of 2,782 seniors majoring in French, German, Italian, Russian, and Spanish in the four language skills (listening, speaking, reading, and writing). He found that a majority of these students failed to attain minimal levels of proficiency in the foreign language, particularly in speaking. He also found that those students who had studied abroad performed significantly better than those who had not. This finding led many to recommend that travel abroad be instituted as a requirement for future foreign-language teachers (Jorstad, 1980). While scarcity of funds has prevented any systematic implementation of such a requirement, universities have begun to give greater focus to the development of functional proficiency in the foreign language and moved away from simply accepting the completion of a requisite number of courses as testimony of reaching adequate levels of proficiency. Nonetheless, in many teacher education programs for secondary teachers, the completion of the major in the foreign language is taken as evidence of having satisfied command of the subject matter (Walton, 1996).

Bernhardt and Hammadou (1987) reviewed the literature between 1977 and 1986, examining both foreign language and ESL teacher preparation research. Of the 78 articles written on this topic during this period, they found that only 8 were based on empirical data. Most were position papers on what competencies teachers should have or descriptions of methods courses, teaching assistant, MA, or inservice programs. These descriptions were usually done as anedoctes by teacher–educators, with little emphasis given to the impact of these programs on student teacher growth.

Position papers usually result from collaborative efforts by professional organizations or state agencies designed to articulate competencies for teachers. The American Council on the Teaching of Foreign Languages has periodically developed such guidelines for teacher education (1987), for example, as has TESOL (Teachers of English for Speakers of Other Languages). As reviewed by Merino and Faltis (1993), most of these efforts have been the result of experts meeting together and defining critical domains to consider in teacher preparation. The link between these efforts and systematic research is largely through allusions to the research literature on how students learn/acquire the second language and to some degree on how teachers teach, but very seldom is reference made to research on how teachers are prepared. In some instances, individual researchers or teacher–educators have articulated competencies for teachers or defined the curriculum for teacher education, either in a hypothetical approach focusing on what teachers should know (Thonis, 1991) or through the illustration of a particular program (Lange, 1990). These efforts are useful in setting parameters for defining the domain of teacher education and can offer practical scenarios from which to develop other programs. Often, these are personal journeys of teacher–educators in a dialogue with colleagues and their students.

One example from the ESL perspective is Larsen-Freeman (1983), who argues for a distinction between teacher training and teacher education in her description of what ESL teachers need to know, affirming that the emphasis in teacher education prepares the teacher to work in any situation, whereas teacher training focuses more on particular settings and students. In her view, teacher education is about learning how to make informed choices and to make these choices intelligently. The teacher needs to have an awareness of the choices to be made, a positive attitude toward learning and taking risks as a teacher, the knowledge necessary for a language teacher, and the skills to create learning contexts for students. Six content domains are defined in developing a teacher education program for Language 2 (L2) teachers: language teaching, language learning, language, culture, interpersonal communication, and professional development. Examples are given from the MA program at the School for International Training in Vermont, to illustrate the matrix.

A review of other researcher attempts at defining what teachers of language-minority students should know reveals the influence of the history of the researchers' training and experience. Garza (1991), with experience with bilingual students and multicultural education in the United States, gives greater importance to developing teachers expertise in linking L1 to L2 acquisition as well as in understanding the cultural context in which language-minority students function. Thonis (1991) presents a more balanced approach, including competencies that focus on knowledge of the structure of the language, language acquisition theory, and research, as well as developing pedagogical knowledge of teaching culturally and linguistically diverse learners. Thonis also differentiates between competencies for elementary and secondary teachers, pointing out that elementary teachers are generally considered specialists in children but generalists in subject matter, whereas secondary teachers are specialists in subject matter but generally turn to other support staff to deal with personal student issues. She calls for greater emphasis in preparing secondary teachers to address the emotional and social needs of the students, as well as better preparation addressing the literacy development of language-minority students within the subject area.

Teacher–educators of teachers of language-minority students must also respond to the licensing agencies that stipulate the content of teacher education. Each state in the United States issues guidelines for institutions to follow in the development of their own teacher education programs, either through the state's department of education or through a specially dedicated agency that focuses on the certification of teachers. In California, the Commission for Teacher Credentialing (CTC) is charged with the development of standards for institutions to follow as well as with the monitoring of the implementation of these standards through periodic reviews. In addition, the agency also develops and administers the examinations that the state requires of its teachers. In the state of California, over the past 20 years the CTC has developed and administered several tests for secondary teachers of language-minority students. These include the Certificate of Competence in Bilingual Education, the Language Development Specialist Certificate Examination, and most recently the CLAD and BCLAD examinations. These tests can have tremendous influence on the content of teacher education programs, particularly at the inservice level, depending on how requirements for entry into teaching are set. For example, the Language Development Specialist Certificate Examination was required of all candidates seeking this authorization whether they had been enrolled in a full-length university program or not. Most teachers chose to enroll in a series of short-term workshops, often designed to simply enable them to pass the test. The Bilingual Education certificate as well as the CLAD/BCLAD examinations, on the other hand, are offered as alternative routes to formal university programs. While these examinations are usually considered by university faculty developing their own programs, they have had less influence on the content and structure of the programs.

Most efforts to define the teacher education curriculum for future teachers of language-minority students rely on experts' or policymakers' informed opinion on what teachers should know. Efforts to define this knowledge empirically are very rare. A description of one of these studies will illustrate one avenue of inquiry used in defining the necessary knowledge for teachers through empirical means. The empirical trajectory for this approach would involve establishing first what effective teachers know by testing teachers' knowledge and determining if there is any relationship between what teachers know and their students' achievement gains. The next step in this line of inquiry is to prepare teachers in the knowledge that has been connected with student achievement, verifying if this knowledge develops in teachers, and seeing if this change in teacher knowledge results in greater achievement gains. In practice, this full line of inquiry has not been carried out in the education of teachers of L2 speakers. The beginning of this loop was explored by Politzer and his students in the late 1970s and early 1980s. Merino, Politzer, and Ramirez (1979), for example, found that teachers in bilingual education programs who had achieved a high degree of proficiency in Spanish, particularly in the curriculum areas of the elementary school, had students with high adjusted gains. A similar relationship was also found for teachers with knowledge of the structure of the English language and L2 acquisition (Ramirez & Stromquist, 1979). This line of research is extremely expensive and time-consuming and, perhaps for those reasons, has seldom been pursued. Moreover, Politzer and his associates studied this relationship in combination with observation of teacher and student performance in the classroom and found that classroom behaviors generally contributed to the prediction of gains to a higher degree. Finally, in recent years researchers in teacher education have focused their attention on the individual journeys that teachers take as they progress from preservice to novice and into expert, giving less emphasis to effects investigated in groups.

EMPIRICAL INVESTIGATIONS OF APPROACHES TO THE DELIVERY OF LANGUAGE TEACHER EDUCATION CONTENT

Narratives and Reflections

The literature on language teacher education is perhaps richest in narratives and reflections of a particular approach or technique implemented in teacher education programs. Bailey (1990), for example, describes how diaries have been used with language teachers in training. She describes the uses of diaries in language learning in general and outlines how diaries can and have been used to prepare teachers of a second language. Reviewing published diaries of teachers in training, she cites what benefits diarists have found in the development of their practice. She also cautions against the overuse of diaries, noting that some students may not be comfortable with such intense self-examination and introspection.

Porter, Goldstein, Leatherman, and Conrad (1990) present learning logs as a useful technique to help teacher–educators see the impact of their practice through a social experience that gives student teachers an opportunity to influence their own experience. Based on their cumulative experience in their use of learning logs, they present strategies for implementing learning logs, outlining how logs can function in different kinds of classes, theory, methods, and practica and summarizing the benefits of learning logs through the entries of students in their classes. Among the benefits cited are the opportunities for teacher–educators to understand what creates difficulties for students and the increased willingness of reticent students to participate in a dialogue with the teacher–educator, as well as the opportunity for students to improve on their reflective and writing skills.

There are many narrative pieces of language teacher education in the literature. The central value of these pieces is their contribution to the development of teacher–educators' arsenal of ways in which to work with novices. If these are rich descriptions that include some limited data on student impact, they can serve as a catalyst for other teacher–educators to emulate in practice. A danger of these pieces, however, is that the focus tends to be on the positive, on the students for whom the technique or approach worked. Moreover, many times these accounts do not delve deeply enough into the difficulties of implementation, in part because the authors are quite committed to the techniques or approaches implemented.

Surveys of Graduates of Language Teacher Education Programs

One traditional approach to research on teacher education has been the use of a survey. In the state of California, state-approved credential programs for public school teachers (K–12) are required to periodically survey their graduates to determine their perceptions of the credential program's effectiveness. Usually these surveys also solicit data from the graduates' supervisors. Often these surveys are conducted 1 year after graduation, presumably after experience in the field has made teachers more aware of their needs. Most of these surveys are never published but are submitted as part of the external assessment conducted by the Commission for Teacher Credentialing. Some surveys have been conducted of all graduates in the system. Thus, in 1990, the California State University (CSU) system conducted a survey of its graduates on their perceptions of their competence. In general, graduates reported a moderate to high satisfaction with the competencies surveyed, with the exception of expertise in dealing with culturally and linguistically diverse learners. Abramson, Pritchard, and Garcia (1993) report that they surveyed 511 students, 142 of whom had completed the secondary program single subject credential, on their satisfaction and experience in areas related to the instruction of language-minority students. Respondents represented 26.8% of the total surveyed and had been enrolled in seven CSU campuses. A five-point Likert scale was used to rate six statements. One indicated a high agreement with the statement; five, disagreement. Students in general were very satisfied with their program, giving an average rating of 2.4 for 66.3% of those surveyed. However, they were less satisfied with aspects of the program dealing with instructional strategies for teaching LEP students. For example, "Courses in my teacher preparation program covered how to modify instruction in content areas (reading, math, science) to meet the needs of LEP students" received a low level of agreement, with rating 3.41 indicating a trend toward disagreement and only 26.4% agreement, as did a related statement asking about methods courses for developing English language skills. Students had more positive feelings about the impact of courses on their familiarity with the wide variety of cultures and ethnic backgrounds represented in California. A difficulty with surveys of satisfaction is that students with strong negative feelings about the program may be more likely to respond.

In the ESL context, Richards and Hino (1983) surveyed non-Japanese members of the Japan Association of Language Teachers (JALT) through the mail and through distribution at their annual conference to identify the type of training teachers received and how relevant teachers rated that training. Two hundred surveys were sent, and an additional 60 were distributed at a JALT conference. A total of 116 responded, for a response rate of 45%. Most of the respondents were American, had been teaching English as a second/foreign language for 8 years, and were teaching in a college or university at the time of the survey. Eighteen percent were teaching in junior or senior high school. Most used a combination of methods in teaching and were principally involved in teaching speaking and listening, teaching reading and writing only some of the time. Respondents reported that much of their own teacher preparation coursework focused on the structure of the English language and linguistics, with 97% reporting a course on phonology/phonetics. While three-fourths of the respondents reported taking courses on the teaching of speaking, listening, reading, and writing, fewer had taken courses with a pedagogical focus, curriculum/syllabus design (58%), or classroom management (47%). Only 72% reported having had practice teaching. This degree of emphasis reflects the source of training of ESL teachers in the United States, where most receive their training from linguistics or ESL departments. Respondents expressed dissatisfaction with this lack of practical classroom focus in their training. Indeed, of the top five most useful courses rated by the teachers, four focused on classroom pedagogy, with practice teaching listed as the most useful.

Studies of Implementation

The use of case studies of individuals going through programs or of programs themselves has become one of the richest sources for descriptions of the teacher education experience in the United States.

Cases of Individual Teacher Socialization. Recently, researchers in teacher education in the United States have focused their attention on teacher growth. Kagan (1992), for example, reviewed 40 studies of preservice teacher growth focusing on five key areas: image of self as a teacher, amount and level of self-reflection, growth in planning, knowledge of classrooms, and the use of problem-solving strategies. All but one of these studies was done in mainstream monolingual settings, but one researcher, Bullough (1990), studied a high school English/Spanish teacher in the first year of teaching and focused on the teacher's changes in beliefs and perceptions of the classroom. In this case study, as well as in a larger study of 15 secondary students, Bullough concluded that preservice teachers needed to have a clear image of themselves as teachers before growth could occur, otherwise the student teachers tended to blindly imitate their cooperating teacher. Kagan (1992) tends to hold to a linear model of development of teacher growth, positing, for example, that without command of procedures and knowledge of pupils, teachers' growth tends to remain static. Grossman (1992) attacks this view, pointing to a competing literature that focuses on the role of knowledge of subject matter and the interaction of this knowledge with pedagogical knowledge. In her view, growth in these areas occurs simultaneously and seems to be an individual journey for each teacher, given her history, experience, range of knowledge, and communication skills.

Group Studies. In their review of the literature between 1973 and 1988, Grant and Secada (1990) found 16 studies that investigated the impact of multicultural education on preservice teachers, and 7 on inservice teachers. The ways teacher–educators sought to create change in these studies varied and included instructional modules on sex-role typing, the historical contributions of specific groups, and analysis of textbook and classroom discrimination, as well as experiences with ethnic minority students or research on effective approaches for teaching in culturally diverse settings. Typically, impact was studied via attitude scales or growth in knowledge, rarely on changes in student teachers' instructional practice. Usually, results were mixed. For example, Contreras (1988) studied beginning secondary student teachers' knowledge of the historical experiences of minority students and of their attitude toward these students at the end of a multicultural education course. The measurement of knowledge about the cultural history of minority groups focused on narrow facts and was mixed. Only 65% knew that the first to die in the Revolutionary War was a black man. Moreover, some expressed negative attitudes toward teaching minority students, stating they would do so only if no other job was available. In another, more recent study that measured attitude, Deering and Stanutz (1995) investigated whether a course in multicultural education, combined with a field experience, changed 16 secondary student teachers' sensitivity to diversity as measured by a Likert Attitude Scale, the Cultural Diversity Awareness Inventory. They found that there was no significant change in attitude in these students. An inherent danger with this approach to measuring change is respondents' ability to discern what is being measured. Most subjects are savvy and unwilling to disclose attitudes that may be labeled racist, and may favor more neutral responses as a way of avoiding the disclosure of their true attitudes.

Cabello and Burstein (1995) sought to address the limitations of attitude scales by using a parallel case study design and doing a qualitative review of student teachers' portfolios over the course of their participation in a teacher education program. Data were collected from 2 groups of 10 teachers. The first group was culturally diverse and the second was not. They found greater growth in the culturally diverse group.

These sample studies illustrate the complexities of teacher development in programs whose focus is usually not linguistically diverse students. Perhaps a program that stresses both language and culture may be more effective in developing student teacher competence and advocacy for language-minority students. Language is sometimes more easily apparent as a possible obstacle to educational equity. Moreover, it may be easier to place student teachers in the role of learner of another language than in the role of learner of another culture.

Case Studies of Programs: The Experience of California. To better illustrate how individual universities deliver a program to prepare prospective teachers of language-minority students at the secondary level, data will be drawn from several institutions throughout the state of California. Institutions will be referred to by code and identified only by their source of funding (private or public). This review is based on the review of program summaries presented to the Commission for Teacher Credentialing (CTC) while the author served as UC representative to the CTC from August 1993 to January 1996, oral presentations by the faculty from these programs at official CTC meetings, review of the written documents for a subsample of programs, and systematic review and visitation to four programs as a member of a CTC-sponsored review team, as well as periodic interviews with CTC professional staff.

The Design of Course Content

One of the major vehicles for influencing the content of teacher education programs is the licensing agency's definition of standards. In the state of California, the typical approach is for legislation to mandate either a new need or a new population to be served, as is the case with the language-minority population, or for the agency itself to begin restructuring within existing legislation in response to concerns from the field.

In the case of CLAD, this restructuring began within existing authority of the agency. Through a task force of experts, the agency produced a new set of standards for the certification. Once these were approved by the agency, institutions began to respond to the market and within a 3-year period, over 75 institutions had received approval for the new certification. This task force identified six domains of knowledge and skill. Three are common to both CLAD and BCLAD and three are reserved for BCLAD. The common areas are:

1. language structure and first and second language development,
2. methodology of bilingual English language development and content instruction, and
3. culture and cultural diversity.

The last three are relevant to BCLAD only:

4. methodology for primary-language instruction,
5. the culture of emphasis, and
6. the language of emphasis.

Although the process was swift, it was not always smooth. Depending on the history of the institution, faculty varied in their level of expertise and attitude toward the new CLAD component. Some institutions opted for the development of additional courses to cover almost all of the new competencies required. Others chose to largely infuse the new competencies within existing coursework. Some chose to propose the new certification within a very limited range, the English Single Subject (secondary) credential, for example. CLAD programs were developed by almost every institution in the state at the elementary level. However, in the yearly report of existing approved programs, the CTC reported in July 1996 that there were 9 secondary CLAD programs in the California State University system, 5 in the University of California system and 21 in the private university system. See Appendix A for a detailed list.

To give a more detailed view of how institutions actually shaped coursework, a brief discussion of three cases will be presented to illustrate contrasting patterns. One private research university, (A), relied on the model of additional coursework. Students were asked to take three courses (nine quarter units) focused specifically on CLAD issues. Two courses were basically theoretical courses: one focusing on second language acquisition, the other on a choice between one course related to African American English issues and one on bilingual education. The third course focused on methods and was geared for all secondary program students addressing both English language development and content instruction in the second language. Issues of culture were infused throughout much of the coursework in the program. Assignments in the theoretical courses were largely term papers or a take-home exam. The methods course principally targeted foreign language methodology and resources. Assignments focused on preparing materials and activities for teaching a second language.

Two public universities offer an interesting contrast to this approach. One, (B), gave greater emphasis to coursework on the role of culture. Students learned how to conduct mini-ethnographies to study the community of the school. The methods course emphasized the infusion of culturally relevant pedagogy and strategies for improving teachers' understanding of students' home and school discontinuities, but gave less emphasis to issues of language and specific techniques for teaching a second language. The other institution, (C), divided its secondary students into two areas of emphasis. In one area, Single Subject, English, and Foreign Language students were given extensive coursework in English language development through ESL methods courses in the Linguistics Department, while in the other area, the content area students, such as science, math, and so on, were given a single course on English language development and sheltering academic content for English language learners. Students also studied cultural issues but focused more on culturally relevant pedagogy and on classroom strategies for investigating students' backgrounds, with some limited exposure to the study of the community. This variance in emphasis could play a key role in the efficacy of teachers in the schools. Future research must seek to follow up and investigate the practice of teachers who come from programs with different orientations. Furthermore, it may well be that depending on the needs of the students and their communities, different orientations may be more effective. For example, students who have recently arrived at a secondary school who speak a primary language very different from English may be in greater need of a teacher who has greater preparation in the structure of English phonology and techniques for facilitating the development of comprehensible English. It is also possible to imagine an alternative scenario where students coming from a cultural group that is experiencing a fundamental alienation from the school may be in greater need of teachers who are better prepared to access the local community and its cultural capital to design a more inclusive context for students.

The Faculty

The faculty teaching the CLAD components of these programs vary considerably by institution. In the private institutions, frequently part-time faculty are recruited to provide these special courses. In the University of California system, several campuses rely on faculty in Linguistics TESOL programs (C) or in foreign language programs (D), combined with education faculty and school personnel recruited from the schools. The CSU system embarked on a systemwide faculty professional development program to prepare any faculty willing to participate. Within the CSU system, bilingual faculty were frequently the leaders in spearheading the CLAD programs (Program Descriptions, CTC, Institutions E and F). There is greater variation in faculty within private universities, depending on their resources and their institutional history. At one extreme, some may rely on part-time rotating faculty (G). At the other, a university may have prominent faculty combined with doctoral students or part-time expert teachers from the schools (A). The preparation of the faculty often comes from bilingual education, linguistics, or foreign language education. In some cases, anthropology and culture may be the driving force of a particular unit. In others, it may be psychology. Some institutions systematically seek to integrate all disciplines. During the quick period of program design in CLAD, a concern was raised that at some institutions, some faculty simply declared themselves as expert based on limited experiences in workshops or a brief research experience (E and H). Institutions are asked to submit the curriculum vitae of their proposed faculty. These vitae are reviewed to ensure that faculty do have the requisite expertise for the course proposed (P. Walton, personal communication, February 3, 1995). When programs are reviewed at the site, the qualifications of the faculty are reviewed once again. A question for future research is to explore the impact of differing orientations in CLAD programs. Do teachers prepared in a program that gives greater emphasis to the role of culture function differently than those in programs giving more importance to language issues? Are programs driven by the perspectives of a targeted discipline producing teachers with a different type of expertise (e.g., culture versus language)?

The Role of the Field Experience

By regulation, the CTC requires collaboration with local educators in designing the placement for practice teaching, a field experience prior to entering teaching and a structured advancement to daily teaching responsibilities, as well as careful selection of supervising teachers and effective guidance, assistance, and feedback in the field in a placement appropriate to CLAD (Standards 17–22). In practice, institutions face a difficult challenge in finding secondary teachers working in certain areas such as science and math who have also received training in the instruction of language-minority students. In this period of transition, the CTC has urged institutions to provide training for cooperating teachers and to provide more intensive support for student teachers developing these skills (P. Walton, personal communication, June 2, 1995). A related issue has been finding placements in schools and classrooms in which language-minority students are enrolled. For some institutions, in Southern California, for example, such placements are easier to find. However, for some institutions in some areas of California, the placement may be more of a challenge.

One private university, (A), addressed this dilemma by stipulating that students would be placed in an assignment that involved either an ESL placement or a sheltered content course in the subject matter of authorization with a minimum of 25% students who are classified as Limited English Proficient (LEP). Others have specified a goal of 25% but a minimum that is lower: 10% for content courses (C and E). There are several practical difficulties that institutions face in developing appropriate placements. Secondary student teachers in science and mathematics need experience in several subject areas. Some of these may be more advanced college preparatory classes, in which language-minority students are not permitted to enroll. Supervising teachers may have expertise in working with language-minority students in ESL but not in teaching subject matter to these students. Finally, university supervisors may also have limited abilities in working with language-minority students. Kato (1993), in a survey of 284 university-based supervisors in California, found that only 50% felt capable of providing feedback or consultation that addressed the needs of linguistically and culturally diverse student teachers and that only 48% rated themselves competent to teach and model instructional techniques that address the needs of culturally and linguistically diverse public school students. Forty-four percent of these supervisors worked in secondary credential programs. Data were not reported by level, but Kato reports (personal communication, May 8, 1997) that the tendency was for secondary supervisors to report less competence in this area than elementary supervisors.

A major dilemma in defining competence in the field for the supervising teacher has been created by changes in policy on teacher certification for teachers of language-minority students. In California, there are five different ways in which teachers can be said to be certified to teach second language speakers at the secondary level. The first two are the Language Development Specialist Certificate, which was a 36-unit program designed for ESL students, or a "comparable" examination and no longer exists. The second two are CLAD, again through coursework (9 semester units or 12 quarter units) or a CLAD examination developed by

National Evaluation Systems. Finally, in 1995, the CTC approved a more limited inservice program of 45 to 90 hours of inservice, depending on the teachers' years of experience. Some institutions provide certificate programs for teachers. All the UC schools do so through extended learning programs. Some collaborate with districts in providing training. Increasingly, more and more teachers are being certified, although unfortunately their level of expertise varies greatly. Exit interviews of student teachers at UC Davis have shown that student teachers with limited opportunities to work with linguistically diverse students and adequately qualified teachers feel less competent to work with these students than student teachers with extended opportunities.

The approaches institutions use in evaluating student teaching performance in providing instruction for LM students vary a great deal. Assessing teaching performance is probably one of the most complex constructs to assess, since it involves such a complex array of knowledge and behaviors. With the renewed focus on teacher accountability, many states have been actively engaged in refining instrumentation and approaches through complex systems (Andrews & Barnes, 1990). However, less attention has been given to assessing teachers' performance in working with LM students, even by states that have large LM populations. For example, the Florida Performance Measurement System Screening/Summatiave Observation Instrument (Office of Teacher Education, 1983), based on teacher effectiveness literature, makes no mention of any behaviors linked to increased achievement in LM populations. More recently, researchers have begun to focus on the distinction between novice and expert performance (Reynolds, 1992) and on addressing the needs of LM students through broad categories, usually focusing on equity or teaching "cross-culturally." In California, for example, the Far West Lab in collaboration with the CTC and the Department of Education have moved to systematize how teaching competence is assessed by defining six major domains:

1. demonstrating knowlege of one's content area;
2. planning and designing instruction;
3. organizing and managing the classroom to create a positive learning environment;
4. delivering instruction to all students;
5. diagnosing and evaluating student learning; and
6. participating in or creating a learning community.

Most institutions have adapted these domains to design their own instrument (A). Some rely on the work of the Far West Lab in this area.

Others have designed instruments that include these domains but add additional parameters. For example, the K.A.R.E. (knowledgeability, authenticity, reflectivity, and engagement) scale used at St. Mary's College in Moraga (Unrau & McCallum, 1996) emphasizes one domain that does not figure very overtly in the CTC system, authenticity, and places greater emphasis on reflection. Authenticity, although problematic to quantify, targets behaviors of genuine commitment to the learning environment and to the empathy a caring teacher should show to all learners. For example, "Demonstrates interest in helping people work through problems in learning" is one item on the five-point Likert scale. This type of behavior is particularly important in culturally and linguistically diverse contexts, where learners may not respond to "traditional" strategies. Assessment of teaching performance is perhaps one of the most complex challenges facing teacher–educators. The challenges are magnified when the needs of LM students have to be considered. Likert scales are useful in targeting key behaviors but are problematic to implement reliably. Many institutions combine rating scales with portfolios, using an integrated approach to candidate assessment.

Program Evaluation

California has been going through a radical restructuring of its accreditation process over the past few years. Through the late 1970s, 1980s, and early 1990s, institutions were periodically reviewed by teams of experts who would come to visit the institution, review its program document, and interview faculty students, supervising teachers, and other participants in the program from the school and the local community. Initially, these reviews were largely focused on holding the institution accountable for its approved program. In the mid-1980s, this review process shifted in emphasis toward a quality review. The reports from these reviews were then forwarded to the CTC for their endorsement.

The CTC is composed largely of appointed commissioners, selected by the governor to represent various constituencies. The Superintendent of Public Instruction appoints one voting member. In addition, the three major systems of institutions of higher education also appoint non-voting members, one for each system, and the California Post Secondary Education Commission appoints another. In an effort to make the review more representative, more rigorous, and more like other professional groups, a new body, the Committee on Accreditation, was established and members were appointed in 1994. The members of this body were, by design, to include educational leaders from four distinct groups: university professors and administrators from education units from the school of education, as well as teachers and administrators from the public schools.

A new system of review has been developed that gives greater emphasis to the outcomes of teacher education: How competent are teachers exiting from a program? Rather than: Was the process of program implementation in adherence with the approved program? Several models for review are available and in use for institutions in California: one is standard-driven and directed by CTC staff, one follows the National Council for Accreditation of Teacher Education model (NCATE, 1987), and one gives greater latitude to the institution to define the parameters of the program, the Experimental Model. Each one of these is an onerous process, and usually institutions must be reviewed every 5 to 8 years.

Recently, the UC system and several CSU branches, as well as some private institutions have submitted CLAD programs that are using the Experimental Model. The promise of an Experimental Model is that it offers greater opportunities and latitude to experiment within an authorized research agenda. Currently, there are two experimental CLAD secondary programs, both at the University of California. UCLA has a two-year credential/master's program, and UC Davis has a one-year credential program. The UC Davis program is exploring the development of teachers' pedagogical and subject matter knowledge as they are prepared to fulfill four key roles: the role of a reflective practitioner, the role of teacher researcher, the role of an active, collaborative member in a linguistically and culturally diverse community of learners, and the role of an advocate for educational equity. Both programs were recently approved and are in the process of data collection and analysis.

The UCD program is implementing its research agenda in two phases. In the first phase, teacher–educator, student teacher and collaborating educator perspectives on the process of implementation and the extent of student teacher growth are the focus. In this phase, teacher–educators and student teachers develop rich descriptions and reflections of their experiences through the vehicle of portfolios. In the second phase of the research, student teacher growth over time will be the primary focus. In the first phase, key elements in the program have been identified and developed to facilitate student teacher growth. For example, to develop the role of teacher researcher, student teachers conduct teacher research about an issue in their practice or create an intervention to address the needs of an individual case. To develop the role of reflective practitioner, student teachers design lessons in their subject area to address the needs of language-minority students. Periodically, students are asked to reflect on their change over time through collaborative dialogues with their university supervisor and other students. Students maintain journals on their experiences in school and are asked periodically to react to their work with LM students. Preliminary analyses have revealed that student teacher growth is influenced by the context and degree of linguistic diversity in the practicum placement, by the degree to which they are asked to reflect about their accommodation to LM students in lesson design, and by their study of the context and support given LM students at their site.

As in previous calls for further research on teacher education and development, the growth of empirical research continues to be problematic even as the numbers of LM students escalates rapidly. There are, however, several new initiatives in policy and research practice that may finally change the research landscape in this area, at least in California. More institutions have become aware of the Experimental Model option for accreditation and are starting to use it. The sharp growth in the number of institutions offering CLAD at the elementary level, from zero in 1992 to 58 in 1996, offers many opportunities to design and investigate innovative practices. Many of these may also be used for secondary programs. The increased focus on teacher assessment both at the state and the national level offers the possibility of better tools for assessment of growth. The increasing representation of language-minority students in states like California will make ignoring these students more difficult.

APPENDIX A

Roster of California Institutions with Single Subject Secondary Programs with a Cross-Cultural Language and Academic Development Emphasis, July 1996

California State University

Chico, Dominguez Hills, Hayward, Northridge, Pomona, San Bernardino, San Diego State University, San Francisco State University, San Marcos.

University of California

Berkeley, Davis, Irvine, Los Angeles,* Riverside, Santa Barbara,* Santa Cruz, San Diego.

Private Universities

Bethany Bible, California Baptist, California Lutheran, Claremont Graduate, College of Notre Dame, Concordia University, Dominican College,

Fresno Pacific, Holy Names College, Loyola Marymount, Mills College, Mount St. Mary's, National University, Pepperdine Los Angeles, Pt. Loma Nazarene, Santa Clara University, Southern California College, Stanford University, University of La Verne, University of San Francisco, University of Southern California.

Note: Since June 1996, institutions with an asterisk have added CLAD programs.

REFERENCES

Abramson, S., Pritchard, R., & Garcia, R. (1993). Teacher education and limited-English-proficient students: Are we meeting the challenge? *Teacher Education Quarterly, 20,* 53–65.

Andrews, T. E., & Barnes, S. (1990). Assessment of teaching. In W. R. Houston, M. Haberman, & J. Sikula (Eds.), *Handbook of research on teacher education* (pp. 569–598). New York: Macmillan.

Bailey, K. M. (1990). The use of diary studies in teacher education programs. In J. C. Richards & D. Nunan (Eds.), *Second language teacher education* (pp. 215–226). New York: Cambridge University Press.

Bernhardt, E. B., & Hammadou, J. (1987). A decade of research in foreign language teacher education. *Modern Language Journal, 71,* 289–299.

Bullough, R. V. Jr. (1990). Supervision, mentoring and self-discovery: A case study of a first year teacher. *Journal of Curriculum and Supervision, 5,* 338–360.

Cabello, B., & Burslein, N. D. (1995). Examining teachers' beliefs about teaching in culturally diverse classrooms. *Journal of Teacher Education, 46,* 285–293.

California Department of Education. (1997). *Annual Language Census.* Sacramento, CA: Author.

Carbone, M. (1990). A critical-ecological perspective on conservative education reform. *Teacher Education Quarterly, 17,* 81–95.

Carnegie Forum on Education and the Economy. (1986). *A nation prepared: Teachers for the 21st century.* New York: Carnegie Education Foundation.

Carr, W., & Kemmis, S. (1986). *Becoming critical: Education. knowledge and action research.* London: Falmer.

Carroll, J. (1967). Foreign language proficiency levels attained by language majors near graduation from college. *Foreign Language Annals, 1,* 131–151.

Contreras, A. R. (1988, April). *Multicultural attitudes and knowledge of education students at Indiana University.* Paper presented at annual meeting of the American Educational Research Association, New Orleans.

Deering, T., & Stanutz, A (1995). Preservice field experience as a multicultural component of a teacher education program. *Journal of Teacher Education, 46,* 390–394.

Doyle, W. (1990). Themes in teacher education research. In W. R. Houston, M.

Habermna, & J. Sikula (Eds.), *Handbook of research on teacher education* (pp. 3–24). New York: Macmillan.

Freeman, D. (1989). Teacher training, development, and decision making: A model of teaching and related strategies for language teacher education. *TESOL Quarterly, 23,* 27–45.

Galluzzo, G. R., & Craig, J. R. (1990). Evaluation of preservice teacher education programs. In W. R. Houston, M. Haberman, & J. Sikula (Eds.), *Handbook of research on teacher education* (pp. 599–616). New York: Macmillan.

Garcia, E. (1990). Educating teachers for language minority students. In W. R. Houston, M. Haberman, & J. Sikula (Eds.), *Handbook of research on teacher education* (pp. 717–729). New York: Macmillan.

Garza, A. (1991). Teaching language minority students: An overview of competencies for teachers. *Teacher Education Quarterly, 18* (2), 23–36.

Gebhard, J. G., Gaitan, S., & Oprandy, R. (1990). Beyond prescription: The student teacher as investigator. In J. C. Richards & D. Nunan (Eds.), *Second language teacher education* (pp. 16–25). New York: Cambridge University Press.

Gold, N. (1997). *Teachers for LEP students: Demand, supply and shortage.* Sacramento, CA: State Department of Education.

Goodlad, J. (1990). *Teachers for our nation's schools.* San Francisco, CA: Jossey Bass.

Grant, C., & Secada, W. (1990). Preparing teachers for diversity. In W. R. Houston, M. Haberman, & J. Sikula (Eds.), *Handbook of research on teacher education* (pp. 403–422). New York: Macmillan.

Grossman, P. (1992). Why models matter: An alternative view on professional growth in teaching. *Review of Educational Research, 62,* 171–179.

Hawley, W. (1990). Systematic analysis, public policy-making, and teacher education. In W. R. Houston, M. Haberman, & J. Sikula (Eds.), *Handbook of research on teacher education* (pp. 136–156). New York: Macmillan.

The Holmes Group. (1986). *Tomorrow's teachers.* East Lansing, MI: Author.

Izu, J. A., Long, C., Stansbury, K., & Tierney, D. (1992). *Assessment component of the California new teacher project: Evaluation of existing teacher assessment practices.* San Francisco, CA: Far West Laboratory for Educational Research and Development.

Jorstad, H. (1980). The education and reeducation of teachers. In F. Grittner (Ed.), *Learning a second language: Seventy-ninth Yearbook of the National Society for the Study of Education* (pp. 168–185). Chicago: University of Chicago Press.

Kagan, D. M. (1992). Professional growth among preservice and beginning teachers. *Review of Educational Research, 62,* 129–170.

Kato, A. (1993). *Perceptions of self-efficacy and roles among university supervisors of student teachers.* Unpublished doctoral dissertation, University of San Francisco.

Lange, D. (1990). A blueprint for a teacher development program. In J. C. Richards & D. Nunan (Eds.), *Second language teacher education* (pp. 245–268). New York: Cambridge University Press.

Lanier, J., & Little, J. (1986). Research on teacher education. In M. Wittrock (Ed.), *Handbook of research on teaching* (pp. 527–569). New York: Macmillan.

Larsen-Freeman, D. (1983). Training teachers or educating a teacher. In J. E.

Alatis, H. H. Stern, & P. Strevens (Eds.), *GURT '83: Applied Linguistics and the Preparation of Teachers*. Washington, D.C.: Georgetown University Press.

Lasky, B. (1992). How long will they have to wait? The demand for teachers to instruct the LEP student. *Teacher Education Quarterly, 19,* 49–55.

Lau v. Nichols, 414, U.S. 563 (1974).

LeBlanc, L. (1990). Raising the entrance requirements: The foreign language educator's role in implementing Florida's new model for teacher certification. *Foreign Language Annals, 23,* 511–515.

Liston, D. P., & Zeichner, K. M. (1990). *Teacher education and the social conditions of schooling* New York: Routledge.

Macias, R. (1989). *Bilingual teacher supply and demand in the United States.* Los Angeles, CA: USC Center for Multilingual, Multicultural Research and the Tomas Rivers Center.

McCaleb, S. P. (1994). *Building communities of learners.* New York: St. Martin's Press.

Merino, B., & Faltis, C. (1993). Language and culture in the preparation of bilingual teachers. In B. Arias & U. Casanova (Eds.), *Bilingual education: Politics, research and practice.* Chicago, IL: National Society for the Study of Education.

Merino, B. J., Politzer, R., & Ramirez, A. (1979). The relationship of teachers' Spanish proficiency to pupils' achievement. *NABE Journal, 3,* 21–37.

Merino, B. J., Trueba, H. T., & Samaniego, F. (1993). *Language and culture in learning: Teaching Spanish to native speakers of Spanish.* London: Falmer Press.

Milk, R., Mercado, C., & Sapiens, A. (1992). *Re-thinking the education of teachers of language minority children: Developing reflective teachers for changing schools* (FOCUS: Occasional Papers in Bilingual Education No. 6.). Washington, D.C.: National Clearinghouse for Bilingual Education.

National Board for Professional Teaching Standards. (1996). *English as a new language: Draft standards for national board certification.* Washington, D.C.: Author.

National Council for Accreditation of Teacher Education. (1987). *NCATE standards, procedures, and policies for the accreditation of professional education units: The accreditation of professional education units for the preparation of professional school personnel at basic and advanced levels.* Washington, D.C.: Author.

Porter, P. A., Goldstein, L. M., Leatherman, J., & Conrad, S. (1990). In J. C. Richards & D. Nunan (Eds.), *Second language teacher education* (pp. 227–240). New York: Cambridge University Press.

President's Commission on Foreign Languages and International Studies. (1979). *Strength through wisdom: A critique of U.S. capability.* Washington, D.C.: U.S. Government Printing Office.

Ramirez, A. G., & Stromquist, N. P. (1979). ESL methodology and student language learning in bilingual elementary schools. *TESOL Quarterly, 13,* 145–158.

Reynolds, A. (1992). What is competent in beginning teaching? A review of the literature. *Review of Educational Research, 62,* 1–35.

Rhodes, N. C., & Oxford, R. L. (1988). *A national profile of foreign language instruction at the elementary and secondary school level.* Los Angeles, CA: Center for Language Education and Research.

Richards, J. C., & Hino, N. (1983). Training ESL teachers: The need for needs assessment. In J. E. Alatis, H. H. Stern, & P. Strevens (Eds.), *Applied linguistics and the preparation of second language teachers: Georgetown University Roundtable on Languages and Linguistics, 1983.* Washington, D.C.: Georgetown University Press.

Richards, J. C., & Nunan, D. (1990). *Second language teacher education.* New York: Cambridge University Press.

Shulman, L. (1986). Paradigms and research programs in the study of teaching: A contemporary perspective. In M. C. Wittrock (Ed.), *Handbook of research on teaching* (pp. 3–36). New York: Macmillan.

Stevick, E. (1980). *Teaching language: A way and ways.* Rowley, MA: Newbury House.

Thonis, E. (1991). Competencies for teachers of language minority students. In M. McGroarty & C. Faltis (Eds.), *Languages in school and society: Policy and pedagogy* (pp. 281–292). Berlin: Mouton de Gruyter.

Unrau, N. J., & McCallum, R. D. (1996). Evaluating with K.A.R.E.: The assessment of student teacher performance. *Teacher Education Quarterly, 23,* 53–76.

Walton, P. (1996). *The cross-cultural academic development credential: Inventory of programs.* Sacramento, CA: Commission on Teacher Credentialing.

Yarger, S., & Smith, P. (1990). Issues in research on teacher education. In W. R. Houston, M. Haberman, & J. Sikula (Eds.), *Handbook of research on teacher education* (pp. 25–41). New York: Macmillan.

CHAPTER 10

CHANGING METAPHORS FOR SECONDARY
ESL AND BILINGUAL EDUCATION

Paula M. Wolfe

ARIZONA STATE UNIVERSITY

On seeing the title of this chapter, many readers may associate metaphor with Freshman English and understand it in this light as a figurative anomaly that needs explanation to uncover some hidden meaning. However, there is a different tradition, rooted in philosophy, anthropology, and linguistics, which conceptualizes metaphor as central to the task of accounting for our perspectives on the world: how we make sense of things, how we understand our relations to the physical world, and how we select for attention a few salient features from an otherwise overwhelmingly complex reality. Metaphor in this sense forms an essential basis of human thinking (Lakoff & Johnson, 1980).

Often metaphors are so basic to our way of thinking that we do not realize we are using them at all. Consider a classic example from two of the foremost figures in metaphor research, George Lakoff and Mark Johnson. Lakoff and Johnson (1980) argue that adults in Western Anglo society associate good with up and bad with down (e.g., "Stocks went up," "I feel down today," "The level of commitment from the team is falling," "I need a little pick-me-up," etc.). This metaphor, which Schon (1980) defines as deep-level, is so basic to how these adults view the world that they are largely unconscious of it.

It is important to understand that metaphor is different from description. Within metaphor, one domain (good and bad, for instance) is cross-mapped with another, already familiar domain (up and down). Metaphor allows people to map a more abstract domain onto a more concrete

one, and therefore gives them a way of conceptualizing the abstract domain in terms of something they have already "named" (Schon, 1980). In
this way the metaphor forms a story (good is like up), and each story
selects and names different features and relations that become the
"things" of the story, what the story is about. Once people have determined what the story is about, they can set about framing the purposes
to be achieved (we want stocks to go up, not down). So how people set
problems and determine solutions to those problems has a great deal to
do with how they metaphorically divide up reality.

The answer to the question of why metaphor is important to our
understanding of second language acquisition is this: as educators in
secondary schools, we must be able to see the metaphors underlying our
understanding of L2 participation. This will help us see how the problem
of teaching English to non-native speakers is framed and therefore
which solutions will be offered in the form of secondary ESL and bilingual programs. Bringing metaphors to light involves critical inquiry and
often involves the difficult process of reevaluating our largely unconscious assumptions about how we divide up reality. Once we look below
solutions to how we name problems, "The glide from facts to recommendations no longer seems graceful or obvious" (Schon, 1980, p. 268). The
question becomes, then, not what is real and what is not, but what purposes and values we seek to realize, and the directions in which we seek
solutions.

By reflecting on the metaphors and the problem-setting processes
that are ordinarily kept tacit, we can avoid the human tendency to notice
only what fits our ready-made categories, and we can begin to explore
how metaphorical frames shape responses. With this in mind, it is argued
that the metaphors that shape second language participation in secondary school are being used without thoughtful analysis, trapping educators
into ways of talking and thinking about secondary ESL and bilingual students that require critical examination.

Another point is necessary here. If metaphors are indeed the main
tool people use to divide up reality, then it is important to remember that
people use metaphors unconsciously and that they are deeply embedded
in and constitutive of the structure of language. To not use these deep-
level metaphors is to make oneself nearly incomprehensible. Rather than
a critique of the use of these metaphors, then, this chapter is intended as
an initial investigation into the often unconscious metaphors people in
Western Anglo society use to think and talk about ESL and bilingual education and to explore the wider implications these metaphors hold for
students, teachers, and society.

METAPHORS AND EDUCATION

Until recently, little attention has been paid to the metaphors that underlie ESL and bilingual education. Authors have explored metaphors underlying other educational issues, such as teacher beliefs (Munby, 1987),
classrooms as communities (Winkelman, 1991), and school funding (Cole,
1990). Before dealing with the metaphors used in ESL and bilingual education, I want to offer a cursory look at the deep-level metaphors that
underlie education and language acquisition in U.S. academic circles.
One of the most profoundly shaping metaphors for learning in U.S. culture is *learning as acquisition* (e.g., "Second language acquisition," "He finally got it," "She lost her mother tongue," "I can't take all of that in").
This acquisition metaphor also shows up as knowledge being taken into
the self like food ("He devoured that book," "That's a tasty tidbit of news,"
"I can't wait to sink my teeth into that report," "I'm starved for information," "He just sucked up all of that knowledge"). This acquisition metaphor stems from cognitive psychology, where human understanding is
presented in terms of a deeper-level "container" metaphor: the human
brain is a container into which information can be added. This conception of learning as owning or acquiring is so basic to the conception of
learning, and especially language learning, that it has influenced the entire American education system.

One group of educators who have argued for a different metaphor
have been whole language educators. Researchers such as Graves (1983),
Atwell (1987), and Goodman (1987) base their understanding of language acquisition on a metaphor first articulated by Frank Smith. Smith
(1982) argued that the process of literacy development was not an individual acquiring knowledge, but was more like a young person joining a
"literacy club." Similarly, anthropologists have envisioned learning as a
by-product of participating in a community of practice (Lave & Wenger,
1991). While there is not space in this chapter to fully explore these writers' arguments, there is a clear difference of implications for educational
programs based on these differing metaphors. By conceptualizing students as needing knowledge that teachers can put into them, students are
seen as somehow lacking, as empty, as deficient. Researchers from a holistic tradition argue that we need to see students as active neophytes seeking membership to a club to which most adults already belong. Students
are then viewed as resources, as a way to keep the club interesting and
vital. Teachers look for the strengths learners bring with them rather
than deficits in their prior knowledge.

While these metaphorical differences may not seem on the surface to be vitally important to language education, it is important to remember that metaphor is inherently evaluative. In other words, any situation being described (in this case language learners) is seen as good or bad based on the domain to which it is cross-mapped. Accordingly, we judge language learners as basically bad (deficient, limited) when we understand them to be lacking English, or as basically good (active, resourceful, becoming) when we see them as neophyte members of a community. While this is certainly simplistic, it is an attempt to encourage readers to see descriptions of language learners as descriptions, not as reality. Metaphor analysis is a way to demonstrate how education in Western culture gives the story of "language learning" a specific (and often deficit) reading.

METAPHORS FOR ESL/BILINGUAL STUDENTS

Once deep-level metaphors have been established and largely accepted (learning as acquisition or learning as joining the community of practice), people begin to generate problems and solutions based on these metaphors. How people think about practice is based on surface-level metaphors, which in turn represent the deep-level metaphors already held (Schon, 1980). A deep-level metaphor such as MIND is a CONTAINER will give rise to mid-range metaphors such as LEARNING is ACQUISITION and KNOWLEDGE is an OBJECT (to be acquired), which in turn generate the actual surface-level metaphors people use in everyday speech. For example, people often judge challenging material to be heavy—"Physics is a heavy subject"—while knowledge easy to acquire is light—"She picked up French easily." How educators talk about learning, then, is inherently evaluative (i.e., a full container is better than an empty container) and reflects how they have "divided up reality," how they understand the "things of the story" of education. Both the deep- and surface-level metaphors teachers use to shape their understandings of secondary immigrant and bilingual students and of curricular and programmatic designs carry social and political implications based on metaphorical cross-mappings that are largely unexplored.

Because the container metaphor is so profoundly important to how Western society understands the learning process, it is not surprising that this metaphor has shaped much of secondary ESL/bilingual language participation research. One of the most common mid-level metaphors growing out of the container metaphor is that students are often written about as if they are computers. The terms "input" and "output" are commonplace in research literature, and this implies that the human mind is a container that processes information in complex ways. While the input/output model is still used in research literature, there is a more powerful model, also based on the container metaphor, that has shaped, and is shaping, much of the current understanding of ESL and bilingual education.

Much of our understanding of secondary ESL and bilingual education is based on sophisticated, cognitive-psychological theories generated from the container metaphor (e.g., language as iceberg, balloon). These mid-level metaphors of icebergs and balloons are familiar to ESL and bilingual educators who have long been part of the debate over whether exposure to a student's L1 will in fact develop the iceberg (or, in Cummins's [1981] term, Common Underlying Proficiency—CUP) underlying the students performance or whether it will inflate the L1 balloon, but do nothing to inflate the L2 balloon (Separate Underlying Proficiency—SUP). While one (the CUP model) is clearly more supportive of bilingual education, both conceptualize learning as the student *acquiring* language and therefore proficiency.

A well-known example of this container metaphor, Cummins's theory of the differences between basic interpersonal communication skills (BICS) and cognitive academic language proficiency (CALP), has been profoundly important in determining the direction of research in secondary ESL and bilingual instruction. Though Cummins later refined this theory to include contextual and situational considerations, the metaphor underlying BICS and CALP has so influenced research in ESL and bilingual education that I will focus on the earlier version of the work simply to illustrate the point.

The Container Metaphor

Once people have accepted the notion that the human mind is a container, it is a very comfortable extension to understand language differences as subcontainers. Educators see the "BICS" container as sufficiently full to allow children to do the BICS tasks they need to do, but argue that the "CALP" container needs to be filled up with "academic language" in order to allow students to do more decontextualized tasks. If we accept that learning is adding to a container, then it seems to make sense that there are subcontainers for different kinds of language, and it also makes sense that the solution is adding language to the more "desirable" container. In order to show more clearly how the deep- and surface-level metaphors are connected, I have created the following chart of the cross-mapping and have included some examples taken from various ESL/Bilingual research and professional documents:

MIND is a CONTAINER
LEARNING is ACQUISITION (KNOWING is OWNING) ("there are dif-
ferent rates of *acquisition*," "students *have* a native language")
TEACHERS give students LANGUAGE ("special instruction in English must
be *given* to ESOL learners")
BICS CONTAINER holds INTERPERSONAL COMMUNICATION SKILLS
CALP CONTAINER holds COGNITIVE ACADEMIC LANGUAGE SKILLS
CONTAINERS can be filled to different LEVELS ("it can take six to nine
years for ESOL students to achieve the same *levels* of proficiency in
English")

Because the container metaphor is so powerful in second language
acquisition literature and curricula, it is nearly impossible to question
why Cummins draws a dichotomous distinction between BICS tasks and
CALP tasks. Likewise, it is difficult to question the assumption that academic and basic interpersonal communication tasks are in fact different
when we are caught in a container metaphor. If we assume that there are
rigid containers for language in the brain, then it is difficult to question
whether or not academic language actually is more decontextualized or
whether there is, in fact, any difference at all in the nature of BICS and
CALP language.

This container metaphor has generated numerous curricular designs
and (perhaps more importantly) evaluation procedures. Since educators
have largely accepted that there is a CALP container that either does or
does not contain academic language, they have, from this assumption,
generated tests that evaluate the amount or "level" of this language that
the student CALP container has acquired. Much effort has been generated in testing the amount of CALP without even questioning whether
there is such a thing. These tests in fact measure the ability to do the
types of decontextualized tasks (word decoding, synonym matching,
sounding out flashcards, etc.) that educators assume are evidence of the
presence of a full CALP container (Edelsky, 1991). These solutions are
products of a deep-level container metaphor that influences educators
and researchers to confuse task and text. Rather than questioning
whether or not the ability to do decontextualized tasks is actually evidence of proficiency with language (and, therefore, whether or not language proficiency can be taught with decontextualized tasks), educators
are trapped by our container metaphor to constantly debate how it is
best to fill the "decontextualized" CALP container so that students can be
proficient with traditional school-like tasks.

The metaphors that underlie ESL and bilingual education and descriptions of immigrant and bilingual students have, of course, had a

hand in shaping secondary ESL and bilingual curricula and programs. Through the process of defining problems (adolescents' containers lack English) and setting solutions (give them more English), the container/acquisition metaphor gets institutionalized. Programs are built up around our vision of how adolescents acquire (or are acquired by) a language. These metaphors trap educators into generating a fixed number and type of solutions to the already named "problem" of ESL/bilingual instruction. In other words, the student containers must be housed in other containers (schools). It is the site of the metaphorical representation of the nature of these school containers where the differences between educators' visions of "regular" education and ESL/bilingual education become starkly visible.

The Water/Earth Metaphor

While the container/acquisition metaphor shapes almost all education in Western society, there is a set of surface-level metaphors that is used only in ESL/bilingual instruction. Almost all types of secondary programs (pullout, transitional bilingual, self-contained ESL, high-intensity language training) have been influenced by the metaphors of WATER and EARTH that underlay the differences between "mainstream" education and ESL/bilingual instruction at the secondary level:

> SCHOOL is a STREAM/CHANNEL ("ESL students have been left out of *mainstream* schooling")
> ANGLO NATIVE ENGLISH SPEAKERS are in the WATER ("students *in mainstream* classes")
> ESL/BILINGUAL students are not in the WATER ("Bilingual students are *placed in sheltered* classes")
> NATURE OF THE STREAM is DANGEROUS/VIOLENT so CURRICULA DESIGNS differ based on LEVEL OF THREAT TO ESL/BILINGUAL STUDENTS (listed in pairs of more to less dangerous options):
>> SUBMERSION–IMMERSION
>> PUSH IN–PULL OUT
>> BRIDGE PROGRAM–SHELTERED INSTRUCTION

I contend that almost all of the ESL/bilingual programs designed for secondary students over the last 20 years have WATER as an underlying metaphor. Starting with the earliest programs (submersion and immersion), this powerful metaphor has continued to shape program considerations until the present day. As mentioned earlier, it is important to explore the nature of the domain (WATER) that is cross-mapped with secondary

ESL/bilingual instruction so as to understand how we have defined the problem and how this metaphorical cross-mapping has trapped us into a certain set of solutions.

In my search of a vast body of research literature and professional documents for ESL/bilingual teachers, the most common label applied to Anglo, native English speakers was "mainstream." By defining native English speakers as "mainstream," regular school is seen as a stream moving toward a goal like streams move toward their ultimate goal, the ocean. Those students who are not part of the stream are left on the banks of the stream and are part of the earth rather than part of the water. These students are not moving toward a goal, but are stagnant. The most well-known ESL/bilingual program designs are based on the metaphorical problem of moving ESL/bilingual students from the EARTH into the WATER. There is also an implication about the violence of the water into which ESL/bilingual students are pushed. For example, immersion is more peaceful, while submersion is more violent, in fact deadly. Submersion programs were criticized for being "sink-or-swim" programs that did not offer students the support they needed to "keep their heads above water."

In a search of up-to-date research literature, I found that many of the newest secondary programs being developed are called bridge programs—again the water metaphor is in evidence. We must consider, however, that bridges move people over water and not into water, and so not into the mainstream. Another label for programs designed to move students from the earth into the water is *transitional programs*. Transitional programs also move people from one place to another or from one state (earth—outside of stream) into another (water—in the stream).

Other programs are "pullout" or "push-in" programs. These programs are clearly designed around the idea of how and when educators move ESL/bilingual students into the "mainstream" and when they pull them out. Clearly, to push someone into a stream is much more violent and dangerous than to rescue someone by pulling him or her out. Often, when these students are "pulled out" of the stream they are housed in shelters on the banks in "sheltered content" classes.

Shelter Metaphor

Over the last 10 years, the most exciting innovation in secondary ESL teaching has been the development of sheltered content programs (see Adger & Peyton and Short, both in this volume). Sheltered content is based on the idea that students acquire language not through learning *about* it but by learning *through* it. Sheltered content teachers teach content in a way that is understandable to ESL/bilingual students, but do not teach English directly. While I fully support this move toward a focus on authentic learning through content, I also would like to explore the metaphor that shapes this curriculum design.

The metaphor of sheltering has some unexplored implications for secondary ESL and bilingual education. To shelter, of course, implies to protect. When we envision a curriculum's main goal as protecting ESL students, we, as educators, make the statement that the school that these students attend is dangerous and unwelcoming. There is no doubt that this is, to a large extent, accurate. In the high school where Faltis and I conducted the research for Chapter 4 of this volume for example, even though the majority of students were native Spanish speakers, no notes, posters, or club announcements were written in Spanish. Dances were advertised in English, as were sports tryouts. None of the business of schooling (poetry contests, notes home, announcements, counseling sessions, etc.) was done in Spanish. In fact, the only Spanish we saw in the school was in a bilingual classroom (and not on the walls, mind you, in the textbooks). At the elementary level, Escamilla (1994) found very little support for Spanish outside the bilingual classroom in a school touted as a *good* bilingual school.

As well as implying that the school itself is an unwelcoming place for language-minority students who are becoming bilingual, the sheltering metaphor also implies that there is something fragile and deficient about them. They must be protected from the content that "mainstream" students are given. All too often we have seen that sheltered content means watered-down content. ESL students are seen as lacking and as in need of protection. School becomes a place where these adolescents can be protected and *given* the things they need to assimilate into the world beyond school. Clearly, these students are not seen as resources or as members of the larger school community. ESL students must be *protected from* rather than *become a part of* the academic community of practice.

Social and Political Implications of the Water/Earth Metaphor. As we continue to explore the unconscious (and perhaps unintended) implications of the WATER versus EARTH metaphor, we must also look at the political and social situation for ESL/bilingual students implied by the metaphor. If native English-speaking students are seen as a stream moving toward a goal while ESL/bilingual students are left on the banks, it is true that streams erode their banks and these banks become silt carried by water. The silt is never really part of the stream, it simply "muddies" the water. Similarly, it can be argued that nonwhite students can never really fit into culture of schooling, that they muddy the waters while their political and cultural heritage is washed away by the violent stream of conformity to the "main." Eventually, as the river reaches its goal, the silt drops away and is deposited on the bottom of the ocean (Edelsky, 1996). Unfortunately, this is all too often the case for ESL/bilingual students also. By considering schooling as a moving stream into which ESL students are pushed or are not, it is difficult to conceive of the school changing in order to see that all students are equal members. It would be nearly as difficult for the school to change as it would be for a roaring, dangerous river to change its nature or its path.

METAPHORS AND THE FUTURE OF
SECONDARY ESL AND BILINGUAL EDUCATION

What would a different metaphorical base imply for bilingual and ESL school program designs? It is almost impossible to say. Because there has been so little research into secondary classrooms based on this more holistic and integrative metaphor, conceptualizing them proves difficult. The only solution to this dilemma would be a wide-ranging exploration of high school ESL programs that are based on a more holistic metaphor. As a first step, I would like to more fully explore the "generative metaphor" (Schon, 1980), which offers new perspectives and explanations, allowing us to see things in new ways. It tells the "story" of reality in a new way and generates new problems and new solutions. The "generative" metaphor I would like to offer ESL/bilingual educators is the metaphor used by Gee (1992) of learning as acquisition by a community and by Lave and Wenger (1991) of learning as legitimate participation in a community of practice. It is necessary to look at the implications of this metaphor, both positive and negative.

This metaphor conceptualizes students as active, as resources, as becoming rather than gaining, and in this sense is clearly in line with how holistic educators believe students come to be part of "the club" of language users. Students are not expected to acquire and reproduce knowledge but, through meaningful activity (doing the things that club members really do and doing them with the club members), they are expected to move toward talking and acting more like the people already in the club. The club also changes as new members offer challenges to the established order and bring resources that change the nature and design of the club (Lave & Wenger, 1991). The club, then, is not in pursuit of simply initiating new members but is designed for a larger purpose. New members are needed to keep the club vital. It is not the new members who must change to be accepted in the club, but the club that must make a place for all new members.

However, the metaphor of being *acquired* by a community of practice also implies being "taken in" (Edelsky, 1996). There is an insidious implication to the "being acquired" or "taken in" metaphor that cannot be easily answered. "Taken in" often means, in Western society, to be deluded. As the critical theorist Allen Luke (1994) argues, as educators we believe that if students "have" academic discourse, if they are highly literate when they leave school, then they have the opportunity to become successful in our society. Many educators believe that acquiring ESL kids into the academic community will allow them opportunities—and that these opportunities will help to reduce racist employment practices, promote social justice, or equalize economic resources. Luke argues that this is a naive belief. Convincing ESL/bilingual students that success in school will ensure them success in society may possibly be fulfilling the more negative meaning of taking ESL students "in."

Even with these problems, the metaphor of being invited into a community of practice may prove a valuable one for secondary ESL and bilingual education. This metaphor seems to more accurately capture the relational nature of adolescent language learning as having a great deal more to do with forming or resisting relationships than with personal or cognitive development. Rather than growing through and with language, L2 development in adolescents involves adding to an already well-defined identity through membership in a club while changing that club through the resources one brings.

CONCLUSION

This paper has been an attempt to offer an initial critical inquiry into the nature of the metaphors that shape secondary L2 instruction. Because the field of secondary ESL and bilingualism has long been ignored in research, it is difficult to get a clear picture of the underlying assumptions and understandings that shape instruction in the high school. However, it is essential that we come to understand what frames we as educators hold so that we can formulate new problems and generate new solutions.

REFERENCES

Atwell, N. (1987). *In the middle: Writing, reading and learning with adolescents.* Upper Montclair, NJ: Boynton/Cook.

Cole, B. (1990). The "Third Sector" and education reform: Some metaphors. *Phi Delta Kappa, 71,* 797–799.

Cummins, J. (1981). The role of primary language development in promoting educational success for language minority students. In C. F. Leyba (Ed.), *Schooling and language minority students: A theoretical framework* (pp. 3–50). Los Angeles: California State University, School of Education.

Edelsky, C. (1991). The effect of "Theory" on several versions of a popular THEORY: Plus ça change, plus c'est la même chose. In C. Edelsky (Ed.), *With literacy and justice for all* (pp. 58–72). London: Falmer Press.

Escamilla, K. (1994). The sociolinguistic environment of a bilingual school: A case study. *Bilingual Research Journal, 18*, 21–48.

Gee, J. (1992). *The social mind: Language, ideology, and social practice.* New York: Bergin & Garvey.

Goodman, K. (1987). *What's whole in whole language?* Portsmouth, NH: Heinemann.

Graves, D. (1983). *Writing: Teachers and children at work.* Exeter, NH: Heinemann.

Lakoff, G., & Johnson, M. (1980). *Metaphors we live by.* Chicago: University of Chicago Press.

Lave, J., & Wenger, E. (1991). *Situated learning: Legitimate peripheral participation.* Cambridge, UK: Cambridge University Press.

Luke, A. (1994). From psychology to linguistics in the production of the literate: Metanarrative and the politics of schooling. In F. Christie (Ed.), *Literacy in social processes* (pp. 18–43). Woodangag, New South Wales: Literary Technologies.

Munby, H. (1987). Metaphor and teachers' knowledge. *Research in the Teaching of English, 21*, 377–397.

Schon, D. A. (1980). Generative metaphor: A perspective on problem-setting in social policy. In A. Ortony (Ed.), *Metaphor and thought, 2nd edition* (pp. 254–283). Cambridge, UK: Cambridge University Press.

Smith, F. (1982). *Writing and the writer.* New York: Holt, Rinehart and Winston.

Winkelman, C. (1991). Social acts and social systems: Community as metaphor. *Linguistics and Education, 3*, 1–30.

Conclusion

Christian Faltis and Paula Wolfe

Arizona State University

A major theme threaded throughout all of the chapters in this book is that providing quality education for immigrant and bilingual secondary students is possible, but not without change in the status quo of secondary education and bilingual education as we know it. The researchers in this book make it clear that questions that may be appropriate for secondary education and elementary bilingual education need to be refocused for secondary bilingual education. These are, however, difficult times for educational change in America.

TRADITIONAL SECONDARY EDUCATION: NO HELP

Secondary education has a long history in the United States, and its history will show it to be virtually unaffected with respect to meeting the needs of ethnic and language-minority students. Secondary teachers are, after all, primarily teachers of subject matter. The majority of their preparation for teaching in the secondary school is done in departments of social science, mathematics, English, science, physical education, music, foreign language, and health, not in the college of education. Significant numbers of secondary teachers are members of the dominant culture, monolingual English speakers, and men. With the exception of foreign language teachers, precious few have ever taken high school or college-level coursework related to their subject matter in a language other than English. Secondary teachers teach out of a homeroom and work with up to 150 different students each day. As Merino (this volume) points out, few secondary teachers nationwide are prepared during their formal education on ways to work effectively with immigrant and bilingual students. Those who do must all too often sit through coursework designed for students who intend to teach in the elementary grades.

When bilingual programs are available in secondary schools, they are more often than not fragmented, isolated, and administered from the top down (Lucas, 1993; Minicucci & Olsen, 1992). This means that teachers in these programs are less likely to talk with one another, plan curricula together, and provide input about their students to teachers outside of their areas. Students in these programs are also more likely to take classes that do not lead to graduation, that are segregated from the rest of the student body, and that have limited sequential offerings geared to their special needs.

TRADITIONAL BILINGUAL EDUCATION: LITTLE HELP

These scenarios leave little to be desired. Nonetheless, while much of what goes on in secondary schools has failed to meet the needs of immigrant and bilingual students, bilingual education, as a field of study and as the primary agent responsible for preparing bilingual teachers and conducting research, compares well with secondary education in its lack of attention to immigrant and bilingual students at the secondary level. For every one research article that focuses on topics related to secondary bilingual/ESL education, there are hundreds that deal with topics concerned with elementary bilingual/ESL education. For every secondary school bilingual or sheltered content class, there are hundreds of elementary school classrooms. For every bilingual/ESL teacher at the secondary level, there are hundreds of elementary bilingual/ESL teachers. Yet, as Waggoner (this volume) shows dramatically, the number of secondary school–age immigrant and bilingual students is immense and growing steadily.

What works well with young children who are becoming bilingual does not transfer well into the fragmented academic and social life of secondary school communities. As the chapters in this book show, the questions that motivate research in the secondary school are basic, and inextricably tied to the particular needs of adolescents and their teachers. While students at the secondary level mostly come from the same countries of origin as elementary students, the fact that they may be newcomers to U.S. schools as young adults means that they are fully socialized into ways of being, thinking, and acting according to their cultural backgrounds. Some are highly literate, others have little previous schooling

(García, this volume). Boys and girls may have different interactional styles and expectations for interacting in class, depending on the theoretical orientation of the classroom (Wolfe & Faltis, this volume). Some have been struggling with academic English as a second language for years, while others are true beginners (Valdés, this volume). Likewise, most secondary teachers working with adolescents are left to their own devices to figure out what works best with students who are becoming bilingual.

In secondary school, no two bilingual/ESL programs are alike, and most that do offer some kind of special instruction offer it sparsely and base availability on which teachers have the time and ability to teach which class (Minicucci & Olsen, 1992). The issues in assessment at the secondary level, where content knowledge, academic language, and language proficiency intersect, are far more complex than at the elementary level (Gottlieb, this volume). Most secondary immigrant and bilingual students are faced with standardized testing that requires not only testwiseness, but also the ability to make sense in English of topics and problems that may be well outside their cultural experiences.

THE NEED FOR NEW RESEARCH FOCI

Clearly there is a need for a new set of questions about secondary education involving immigrant and bilingual students. The authors in this volume provide a clear direction for continued research in a vein based upon different assumptions about what immigrant and bilingual students need. One of the most immediate directions for research and change is teacher preparation. Secondary teachers working in multilingual school communities need new ways of teaching content so that students who are becoming bilingual can participate and benefit from classroom activities (Short, this volume). Teachers need to be retooled in the area of assessment in order to account for student learning in ways that minimize English proficiency and maximize learning potential. There needs to be a specialization within secondary education for those teachers who plan to teach immigrant students with little previous schooling, as these students require a different kind of pedagogy. There is precious little research on good teacher practices and what beginning and practicing secondary teachers need to know and be able to do to work with these students. What do secondary teachers with no previous preparation in working with immigrant and bilingual students need to know and be able to do in order to be effective? A related area for action is the need for continued research on academic language, particularly as it relates to gender, cultural background, and subject-matter discipline. Are there different discourses that students need to be invited into for each of the disciplines, or is there a genre of academic language that cuts across disciplines? How does the teacher's theoretical commitment to language, gender, and literacy interact with academic language across disciplines? There are myriad questions that await reflection and further study.

SOCIAL AND POLITICAL OBSTACLES TO CHANGE

All of the changes needed and questions to be addressed, unfortunately, will have to occur in one of the most anti-immigrant, anti-bilingual education, and anti-pluralism eras in postmodern history. Affirmative action programs are being dismantled. The number of language-minority students entering college is dropping, while the number of the same students who leave high school before graduation is increasing. Anti-immigration movements are growing nationwide, but especially in the border states of California, Arizona, and Texas. In the U.S., there are now more Immigration and Naturalization Service (INS) border patrol officers than there are FBI agents (Border patrol officers, 1998). Round-ups of suspected illegal immigrants are happening across the nation. Anti-immigration stems from the historical and present-day appeal to assimilation, which is directly tied to notions of patriotism, progress, and national unity. For many Americans, the perception is that too many of America's recent immigrants, most of whom are brown-skinned and poor, are not assimilating, not learning English at all or fast enough, and remain loyal to their countries of origin. The federal response to this national concern is to close up the nation's borders and to send illegal immigrants back to their countries. We see this response as deeply rooted in the politics of cultural and racial supremacy, and in opposition to the politics of cultural pluralism in a democratic state. Accordingly, prevailing attitudes against immigrants make change in secondary schools a more difficult task.

Another obstacle to improving conditions for immigrant and bilingual secondary students is the ferocious move on the part of English-only advocates to eliminate instruction in any language other than English for subject-matter content and literacy development. In California, Ron Unz, a successful businessman, is spearheading a state initiative called "English for Children" supported by U.S. ENGLISH (a lobby group) to make sheltered English immersion classes the method of choice for immigrant and bilingual children in school. Under his initiative, schools will no longer be able to provide native-language instruction for immigrants who are non-English-speaking unless parents request them, and the sheltered English immersion classes will be available for no more than 1 year. Unz's initiative is part of a nationwide push by U.S. ENGLISH advocates to make English the official language of the U.S. and to keep non-English languages out of public schools and government agencies. Again, the forces of assimilationist politics are at work to dismantle any efforts to support bilingualism or the use of languages other than English for instruction in schools. These policies may be especially harmful to secondary students, who need highly prepared bilingual teachers and extended time to develop literacy in English (Valdés, this volume).

Charter schools and voucher systems also threaten public education. Though not as widespread at the secondary as at the elementary level, charter schools in general tend to be traditionally oriented, with teachers and administrators unprepared and at times unwilling to take on the challenge of meeting the needs of immigrant and bilingual students. Voucher systems for allowing parents to choose a particular school are least likely to work well for immigrant and bilingual students, many of whom are unfamiliar with secondary schools in the U.S.

In these times of xenophobia, anti-bilingualism, and assimilationism, secondary school communities need our attention more than ever. Although these are difficult times for change in secondary schools, especially in schools where there are large numbers of immigrant and bilingual students, now may be the most fertile time to launch an offensive. Democracy gains strength when it is under attack. Educators ban together for social justice when the need becomes so blatant. This book is surely the first of many in the coming years that will take a stand in favor of improving education for immigrant and bilingual secondary students through research and action.

REFERENCES

Border patrol officers increase in 1997. (1998, January 26). *Tempe Tribune*, p. A9.

Lucas, T. (1993). Secondary schooling for students becoming bilingual: Issues and practices. In M. B. Arias & U. Casanova (Eds.), *Bilingual education: Politics, research and practice* (pp. 113–143). Chicago: National Society for the Study of Education.

Minicucci, C., & Olsen, L. (1992). *Programs for secondary limited English proficient students: A California study* (Educational Practice Report: 17). Santa Cruz, CA: National Center for Research on Cultural Diversity and Second Language Learning.

GLOSSARY

Note. This glossary is not intended as a criticism of researchers' and educators' uses of the terms included herein. Rather, we believe that labels and terms are often used uncritically and without exploring the assumptions about language and schooling in the United States that underlie these words. These assumptions are all too often left unexamined and are unconsciously reflected and supported by the language of the field.

Academic Language: A set of discourse practices within the various content areas classes that students need to acquire in order to participate successfully in mainstream schooling. In the literature on secondary bilingual and ESL education, *academic language* commonly refers to the specialized language used in learning subject-matter content in formal schooling contexts. This meaning of academic language stems from Jim Cummins's (1981) theoretical distinction between everyday and school-based language. Cummins presented academic language as CALP, cognitive academic language proficiency. He likened CALP to language and cognitive activities underlying the development of high-level literacy skills in any language. Cummins claimed that students who achieve the ability to complete cognitively demanding tasks without the help of contextual clues have CALP. Moreover, he and others who support this claim argue that it takes anywhere from 4 to 7 years to develop CALP in a second language, namely, English.

Cummins's notion of academic language has been criticized on many grounds. The distinction between everyday language and CALP is difficult to sustain in real classroom settings. The concept of CALP is tautological: Students have CALP if they perform well on standardized language and literacy tests. If this is the sole criterion for determining who has and doesn't have CALP, the concept is meaningless in the context of classrooms and schools, where social interaction and literacy have a profound impact on teaching and learning.

Academic language has also been defined more recently as discipline-specific language. This approach to academic language sees it as a register, special vocabulary, and/or language style that students must learn in order to demonstrate their proficiency in the subject matter.

Others define academic language as a set of discourse practices that enable students to succeed in school. This perspective argues that academic language is much more than a register. It is a way of thinking, using language, and acting like an insider in the community (Gee, 1992), namely, the subject matter discourse. From this perspective, students must want to, and be invited to, participate in the academic discourse of the class. Achieving academic discourse is not primarily a cognitive feat, but rather a social one that may be indirectly supported by students' willingness to construct a new identity as a member of the academic discourse community.

English Language Learners: A label applied to students who enter school proficient in a language other than English. The focus of the term is on learning English to succeed in school.

This label disregards the broad spectrum of knowledge and experiences students who are proficient in a language other than English bring to school. Moreover, by focusing only on the need to learn English, many other essential areas students need to learn are left unmentioned (for example, history learners or mathematics learners).

ESL or English as a Second Language: A term that applies to students who are native speakers of languages other than English and who are learning English within a setting where English is used by a majority of the speakers in the nation. ESL differs from English as a Foreign Language (EFL) in that in EFL settings, English is not the language of wider communication in the nation where students are learning.

ESL may be inaccurate for many students. For example, many students learning English speak more than one language, making English an additional, but not second, language. Moreover, even though students live in the U.S., a supposed ESL setting, they may have no contact whatsoever with English in their particular community.

There are other issues as well. Bialystok and Hakuta (1995) have shown that many immigrants to the U.S. acquire the varieties of English necessary to participate in their communities, which are often bililngual. Pedrasa, Attinasi, and Hoffman (1980) point out that adolescents in particular acquire multiple styles and dialects of English and their first language. For example, in their work in New York's Puerto Rican community, young teens acquired code-switching abilities, Ebonics, and local varieties of Spanish and English. ESL instruction in the secondary school rarely touches upon this kind of variation, except to extirpate from the students' repertoire. The focus of most ESL programs is on the acquisition of only one variety of English; namely, standard or academic English.

The focus on standard English has political and cultural overtones. Standard English is the dialect of convention, and the one believed to be spoken and written by mainstream middle-class English speakers. Standard English is the dialect of choice for use in school, government, and business. It is not, however, the only variety of English. Teachers who choose to place this dialect of English above all others without acknowledging the diversity within dialects, as well as within languages, are diminishing all other (and often non-White) varieties of language.

Also, by referring to students as ESL, teachers may inadvertently be reinforcing the idea of "changing" these students into mainstream ways of being. There is no space in this label for an expectation on the part of the school or the society to change in order to include linguistically diverse students. Also, there is no reference to the language(s) that students bring with them to school as a resource. The same problem rests in the acronym TESOL, or Teachers of English to Speakers of Other Languages. While the acronym does refer to the people involved ("Speakers"), they are again reduced to their task as recipients of English rather than as resource-bringers or active critics.

One new title or label that has been used in high school contexts is "students who are becoming bilingual" (see Lucas, 1992; Faltis & Hudelson, 1997). This label focuses on the adolescents involved rather than their task and allows educators to see the students as active participants in the schooling process rather than as passive recipients of knowledge. Plus, there is also the implied expectation that students will maintain their home language.

ESL Lifer: A term used mainly by administrators and high school teachers in the U.S. to apply to those students who enter high school from an elementary or junior high bilingual/ESL program and who are likely to remain in ESL or sheltered content classes throughout high school.

Students designated as ESL lifers are never "mainstreamed." In most cases, this means that they will not complete the core course requirements needed for graduation. Some students may graduate with a provisional certificate saying that they completed a certain number of core courses. Nearly all students who fit the profile of an ESL lifer do not attain native-like or advanced proficiency in academic English.

Students may become ESL lifers because they did not receive any kind of instructional support in their native language, or because the instructional support they received was of very low quality. In either case, they are woefully unprepared for the academic demands of high school and post-secondary education.

Finally, the term "ESL lifer" may reveal how some mainstream teachers view ESL programs. For them, ESL programs are holding cells where students can be placed and never released into "mainstream" education.

Immigrant: A catch-all term to label secondary students who are foreign-born and who have immigrated to the United States within the past 3 to 5 years. Immigrant students who are recent arrivals are often referred to as newcomers. There are several problems with the label. For example, if a child immigrates to the U.S. as an infant, is she still an immigrant by the time she reaches high school? Many children of Mexican-origin migrate to and from Mexico. If a child is born in the U.S. of immigrant parents and travels frequently to Mexico, is he an immigrant? Are Puerto Rican children who come directly from the island to attend high school immigrants? Technically, they are not, but in many aspects they resemble other immigrant groups. At what point do newcomers cease being newcomers?

Language Minority: A general term applied to ethnic minority students living in the United States who may or may not speak a conventional variety of English.

The term does not reflect the diversity within languages, and it also obscures an insidious message. The term *language minority* reflects the power issues involved in the teaching of English in the United States. Because of social movements such as civil rights and feminism, *minority* is a term that has come to mean not only numerical differences (i.e., fewer people speak Hmong in the U.S. than English), but also and perhaps more importantly, power differentials between groups. English is the majority language not because more people speak it, but because more people who are powerful speak it. Often the inability to speak English proficiently (or at least the standard dialect of English) is used as a justification for unjust employment, educational, and social practices. *Language minority*, then, is perhaps an accurate reflection of the treatment of non-Anglo, non-native speakers of English. However, it is unclear whether educators who use this term intend to invoke issues of power and discrimination. Rather, the point is that this term is often used uncritically, without conscious awareness of the political and social implications it carries.

Another term often used in place of or along with language minority is *linguistically diverse*. This term has the opposite problem. While educators may use the term "minority" without being aware of the important issues of power it reflects, we believe that educators and researchers often argue for diversity in order to mask issues of power tied up in language as the medium of learning. While "linguistically diverse" does move away from the belief that all people are the same and that they must leave behind differences to join the mainstream, there seems to be an implication that nurturing diversity is enough without exploring the differential power attached to the language students speak. This term also implies that students who are becoming bilingual differ only in the language they speak, thus ignoring the social complexities involved in learning English in the United States.

LEP or Limited English Proficient: A label applied to students who are judged (based on a series of sentence-based and story-retelling tests) to be unable to participate in mainstream high school classrooms due to insufficient proficiency in English. The term LEP is an official designation of the U.S. federal government.

Underlying the LEP label is the view that students who speak languages and dialects other than standard English and who have limited ability to use English are probably unable to carry out the higher levels of thinking associated with standard English speakers. There is a basic flaw with this argument: Teachers would not judge an English monolingual learning Spanish, with limited abilities, as lacking or incapable of higher-level thinking.

Once a label such as *limited* has been applied to students, it is difficult for teachers to see the strengths the students bring to the class or the school. Once the focus is on a perceived deficit or limitation of a student in terms of linguistic ability, it is all too easy to extend the perception to the person. In other words, the person is perceived as limited, rather than her proficiency with a language. As Wink (1993) argues, labels that highlight deficiency are part of a cycle that eventually serves to generate practices that focus solely on that aspect of the students' learning, thereby intensifying and regenerating the deficit label. Once the label cycle is instituted, it is very difficult to stop.

Sheltered Content Teaching: An instructional approach designed primarily for secondary contexts. The approach, first introduced by Stephen Krashen as "subject matter teaching," relies on three main tenets: (1) input to students must be comprehensible; (2) the focus is on academic content, not language per se; and (3) only students who are becoming bilingual, and with at least intermediate ESL proficiency, should be in the classes (Faltis, 1993). All of the teaching and teacher-initiated interaction in sheltered-content classes are expected to be in English. Teachers modify their input using visual, physical, nonverbal, and paraverbal support to facilitate understanding and participation. In this way, students learn about academic subjects such as English literature, history, math, and science without having to compete with native English speakers; hence, the notion of being sheltered.

In practice, however, students are often placed in sheltered content classes that are not equivalent to regular credit-bearing courses for native English speaking-students. Few texts and materials are available for sheltered content classes. Moreover, many sheltered content teachers have little preparation in working with students who are becoming bilingual. Finally, the fact that students who are becoming bilingual are separated from native English-speaking peers for more coursework while in high school may serve to alienate them even more. Separation for sheltered content learning helps students transition into regular classes, but when the separation means that students are linguistically and socially isolated from English-speaking peers, the students will not benefit because they are not participating in regular classroom settings.

Subject Matter/Content Area: Two terms used to describe the concepts and ideas that high school students read, write, and talk about in formal classroom settings. Subject matter refers to the day-to-day topics (e.g., the American Revolution), while content area refers to the larger field or discipline of study (history). Students need to have taken and passed a specified number of core subject matter courses across several disciplines in order to graduate from high school.

Subject matter and *content area* are used by second language educators to refer to what happens in classrooms. Referring to what happens in classrooms as *matter* or *area* reinforces a transmission-oriented approach to teaching. School subjects are "matter," an object given to students, and content is an "area" that the teacher must cover. These terms imply a set amount (matter) of the object that students must acquire at a set rate (area to be covered). This perspective leaves few options for incorporating students' experiences or community knowledge. Also, it implies that students acquire the matter of the classroom without reflection, critique, or action.

From this perspective, students are taught details and facts from history or mathematics or science, but are not invited to explore their world or think about issues (through the lens of history or math or science). Again, these terms reflect and support a theoretical and ideological approach to education that rarely is examined critically. How the ideology of "transmission" education gets enacted is not only through classroom practice, but also through the seemingly neutral terms teachers and researchers use to conceptualize and describe the educational process.

These understandings are especially important for teachers of students who are becoming bilingual. Teachers who work in this field should be aware of how misconceptions and unexamined assumptions about language become institutionalized and severely impact students who are becoming bilingual. For this reason, it is essential that members of the second language acquisition (SLA) community be especially vigilant about the wholesale adoption of terms from "mainstream" educational research that often carry unwanted implications for and about teaching and learning for students who are or are becoming bilingual.

Transitional or Bridge Programs: Programs designed to move students from bilingual and sheltered content classes into mainstream content classes taught only in English, and with no special modifications for students from such programs. Sheltered content classes are specifically set up to serve as "bridge" classes to move students from primary language instruction and sheltered learning into mainstream English classrooms. Students may continue to enroll in bilingual and/or sheltered content classes as they take mainstream English content classes. Apart from the metaphorical implications (see Wolfe, this volume), there are several considerations.

Bridge or transitional programs may be an effective way of moving ESL students into mainstream programs, but few, if any, change the ways in which students participate in learning. Most remain transmission-oriented, where the teacher deposits knowledge that students must recall upon demand in order to be considered knowledgeable. In transmission-oriented classrooms, the participation structure favors the teacher as knower, and students may rarely, if ever, be encouraged or allowed to use their native language or to exchange ideas with peers in small groups. Also, experiences from the students' community are typically not drawn upon for comparison or contrast. Diversity is likely not to be viewed as a resource, but rather as a problem. While students are moved out of their social and linguistic isolation, because no changes are made to the new classroom learning environment, the new class may continue to be alienating or isolating. Regular mainstream teachers are not prepared or expected to modify their classrooms for students who are becoming bilingual. Rather, it is the students who are expected to change if they are to succeed in regular classrooms.

REFERENCES

Bialystok, E., & Hakuta, K. (1995). *In other words*. New York: Basic Books.
Cummins, J. (1981). The role of primary language development in promoting

educational success for language minority students. In California State Department of Education Office of Bilingual Education (Ed.), *Schooling and language-minority students: A theoretical framework* (pp. 3–48). EDAC, California State University: Los Angeles.

Faltis, C. (Ed.) (1993). Trends in bilingual education at the secondary school level. *Peabody Journal of Education, 69,* 136–151.

Faltis, C., & Hudelson, S. (1997). *Bilingual education in elementary and secondary school communities: Toward understanding and caring.* Needham Heights, MA: Allyn & Bacon.

Gee, J. (1992). *The social mind: Language, ideology, and social practice.* New York: Bergin & Garvey.

Lucas, T. (1992). Secondary schooling for students becoming bilingual. In M. B. Arias & U. Casanova (Eds.), *Bilingual education: Politics, practice, research* (pp. 113–143). Chicago: National Society for the Study of Education.

Pedrasa, P., Attinasi, J., & Hoffman, G. (1980). Rethinking Diglossia. In R. Padilla (Ed.). *Theory in Bilingual Education* (pp. 75–97). Ypsilanti, MI: Eastern Michigan University.

Wink, J. (Sept., 1993). Labels often reflect educators' beliefs and practices. *BE Outreach,* 28–29.

About the Editors and Contributors

Carolyn Temple Adger is a Research Associate at the Center for Applied Linguistics (CAL) in Washington, D.C., where she directs several projects that focus on enhancing the academic achievement of language-minority students. She is currently conducting applied research on implementing content standards in culturally diverse middle schools. She has also addressed issues of dialect differences in schools.

Christian J. Faltis (Ph.D., Stanford University) is professor of bilingual education at Arizona State University. He has written and edited 9 books, edited 2 major research journal volumes, and written over 40 articles on language education. His most recent books are *Bilingual Education in Elementary and Secondary School Communities* (Allyn & Bacon) and *Joinfostering: Adapting Teaching for Multilingual Classrooms* (Merrill). Professor Faltis is also the editor of *TESOL Journal,* a refereed journal for informed ESL and bilingual practitioners with a circulation of over 12,000.

Ofelia García is presently Dean of the School of Education at Long Island University, Brooklyn Campus. For many years she was a professor of bilingual education at City College of New York. García has been a Fulbright Scholar, a Spencer Fellow of the National Academy of Education, and a Fellow of the Inter-University Consortium for Political and Social Science Research. She has published extensively in the areas of bilingualism, bilingual education, and sociology of language. Her most recent book, *The Multilingual Apple: Languages in New York City,* was co-edited by Joshua A. Fishman (Mouton de Gruyter).

Margo Gottlieb (Ph.D., Public Policy Analysis, Evaluation Research ad Program Design) is Director, Assessment and Evaluation, for the Illinois Research Center. Throughout her career as an ESL/bilingual teacher, coordinator, evaluator, and consultant, she has developed comprehensive assessment instruments and systems for school districts, the state of Illinois, and a national evaluation project. She serves on national- and state-level assessment committees and has been invited to speak at international, national, and local conferences. Her areas of interest include performance assessment, assessment planning and implementation, and portfolio design for linguistically and culturally diverse students.

Linda Harklau is assistant professor in TESOL and foreign language education at the University of Georgia. Her research explores second language learning and academic contexts encountered by language-minority students in adolescence and young adulthood. Her most recent work compares academic reading and writing experiences of immigrant students in the transition from high school to college. She is co-editor of a forthcoming book, *Language Minority Students, ESL, and College Composition* (Lawrence Erlbaum Associates).

Barbara J. Merino is Professor of Education and Linguistics at the University of California, Davis. She works in teacher education, bilingual education, and Spanish for native speakers. She served as Director of BICOMP, a bilingual interdisciplinary computer-assisted curriculum singled out as an exemplary approach to bilingual education. She has written numerous articles on bilingualism, second language acquisition, and teacher education. She recently co-edited *Language and Culture in Learning: Teaching Spanish to Native Speakers of Spanish* (Falmer Press).

Joy Kreeft Peyton is Vice President at the Center for Applied Linguistics (CAL) in Washington, D.C., and Director of the ERIC Clearinghouse on Languages and Linguistics. She was Associate Director of the Program in Immigrant Education, coordinating the work of the four projects described in her chapter with Adger. She has worked extensively with teachers to implement and document innovative approaches to working with English language learners. She is also co-editor (with Donna Christian) of the Topics in Immigrant Education book series, published by the Center for Applied Linguistics and Delta Systems.

Deborah J. Short is a Director of the English Language and Multicultural Division at the Center for Applied Linguistics in Washington, D.C. Her research interests and publications are in the areas of sheltered and content-based language instruction, program design, and professional development. She recently directed the ESL Standards and Assessment Project for TESOL and develops curricula and other materials for integrated language and content classes.

Guadalupe Valdés is Professor of Education and Professor of Spanish at Stanford University. She works in sociolinguistics and applied linguistics.

Her research has focused on the English–Spanish bilingualism of Latinos in the United States. Recent publications include *Con respeto: Bridging the distance between culturally diverse families and schools* (Teachers College Press); "Dual language immersion programs: A cautionary note concerning the education of language minority students" (*Harvard Educational Review,* 1997); and "Bilinguals and bilingualism: Language policy in an anti-immigrant age" (*International Journal of the Sociology of Language,* 1997).

Dorothy Waggoner was one of the original program officers for the program implemented under the federal Bilingual Education Act beginning in 1969. She helped develop the first national counts of limited-English-proficient children and adults and was chair of the Subcommittee on Race and Ethnicity for the 1980 census, which devised the questions about language usage that were used in 1980 and 1990. She is the author of *Undereducation in America: The Demography of High School Dropouts* and numerous articles on language minorities and education in the United States. Dr. Waggoner is editor and publisher of *Numbers and Needs,* a monthly newsletter on ethnic and linguistic minorities.

Paula M. Wolfe is a Ph.D. candidate in Language and Literacy at Arizona State University. She also serves as Senior Editorial Assistant on the *TESOL Journal.* She was selected as the G. Richard Tucker Fellow to conduct research during the summer of 1996 at the Center for Applied Linguistics in Washington, D.C. Prior to starting her doctoral studies, she was a high school teacher of language-minority students as well as a lecturer at the University of Regina in Canada. She has also taught at Arizona State University.

INDEX